THE NATURAL CALAMITIES IN ORISSA IN THE 19TH CENTURY

THE NATURAL CALAMITIES IN ORISSA IN THE 19TH CENTURY

Braja Bandhu Bhatta

COMMONWEALTH PUBLISHERS
NEW DELHI (INDIA)

The Cost of the Publication is Partly supported by The University Grants Commission, New Delhi.

FIRST EDITION, 1997

ISBN 81-7169-452-7

Published by : Ajay Verma for Commonwealth Publishers, 4378/4-B, Gali Murari Lal, Ansari Road, Darya Ganj, New Delhi-110 002 Ph.: 3272541

Typesetted by : S.P. PRINTECH, G-19, Vijay Chowk, Laxmi Nagar, Delhi-110 092, Ph.: 2214076

Printed by : Efficient Offset Printers, 215, Shahzada Bagh, Industrial Complex, Phase II, Delhi-110 035

Dedicated to

My Parents

(Late) PRAVAKAR BHATTA

and

HENA DEVI

Preface

Frequest occurrence of natural calamities have told upon the economic progress of the state of Orissa in all the ages. Much of our planned efforts therefore have been directed towards rehabilitation of the affected people. As far as the impact of natural calamities on the economy is concerned, it is incumbent to carry on intensive research on the subject. In this context a historical study on the gravity and frequency of the natural calamities and related policy measures of British Government has greater relevance to the formulation of prospective policies. The present study, a Ph.D. work of years of research, is an attempt in this direction.

A work of this magnitude could not be carried out without the help, cooperation and guidance of others. I am very much grateful and greatly indebted to my esteemed teacher and guide Dr. K.S. Behera, Professor, Post Graduate Department of Ancient Indian History, Culture and Archaeology, Utkal University, whose active, valuable and timely guidance has enabled me to give a concrete and visible shape to my ideas at every stage of preparation of this monograph. I also wish to acknowledge the valuable suggestions given by Dr. K.K. Sharma, Professor, Department of History, Meerut University, Meerut and Dr. B.S. Das, Retired Professor, Department of Humanities and Social Sciences, I.I.T., Khargapur.

I am very much thankful to the authorities of the Orissa State Archives, Bhubaneswar, Parija Library, Utkal University, Bhubaneswar, Kanika Library, Ravenshaw College, Cuttack, Orissa State Library (H.K. Mahtab State Library,), Bhubaneswar, Orissa State Museum Library, Bhubaneswar, Board of Revenue, Orissa Cuttack's Records Room and Library, National Archives, New Delhi, National Library, Calcutta for giving me access to various source-materials and documents.

I am also grateful to my esteemed teachers, Dr. H.S. Patnaik, Reader, Post-Graduate Department of History, Utkal University and Dr. N.R. Patnaik, Reader, Government Women's College, Puri for their constant help and advice as and when required.

My special thanks go to the authorities of Indian Council of Historical Research, New Delhi, which has financed the whole venture by awarding me a fellowship.

I am also thankful to the authorities of Utkal University for providing me partial financial assistance from the University Grants Commission, New Delhi for the publication of this work.

Words fall short to express my indebtedness to my elder brother, Dr. Dinabandhu Bhatta, Head, Post-Graduate Department of Chemistry, Utkal University and every distinguished members of my family whose constant encouragement, blessings and cooperation have enables me to complete this work. I am grateful to my friend Dr. N.K. Sahoo, younger brother Shri P.K. Das, Lecturer in History, Mahima Mahavidyalaya, Joranda, Dhenkanal, Shri Suresh Chandra Jena, Utkal University and Shri Sarat Chandra Jena, Orissa State Archives for their help in preparation of this monograph. I am very much obliged to Mrs. S. Behera, who has inspired me time and again for the early completion of this work. Indeed I owe a deep sense of special indebtedness to my wife Mrs. Rekharani Khuntia, whose constant encouragement and help made this work complete. I would be failing in my duties if I do not express my sincere gratitude to all those well-wishers of mine to whom I owe the successful completion of this work.

Finally, I want to express my gratitude to Mr. B.R. Verma, Commonwealth Publishers, New Delhi for undertaking its publication.

Braja Bandhu Bhatta

Contents

List of Tables

List of Figures

Abbreviations

Bd. Doc	...	Board Document
BDG	...	Bengal District Gazetteers
BdRP	...	Board of Revenue Proceedings
BID	...	Bengal Irrigation Department
BJP	...	Bengal Judicial Proceedings
BPP	...	Bengal Public Works Proceedings
BRLP	...	Board of Revenue Land Proceedings
BRP	...	Bengal Revenue Proceedings
Commr.	...	Commissioner
CPC	...	Calendar of Persian Correspondence
CRR	...	Cuttack Revenue Records (Volume)
EIRF	...	East India Report of Famine Commission, Present to both houses of Parliament
EPW	...	Economic and Political Weekly
GAROD	...	General Administration Report of Orissa Division (Annual)
IGI	...	Imperial Gazetteer of India
LP	...	Lower Province
LR	...	Land Revenue
Lt.		Lieutenant
Maddox Report	...	Final Report on the Survey and Settlement of the Province of Orissa, 1890-1900 by S.L. Maddox
OC	...	Orissa Circle
Offg.	...	Officiating

OHRJ	...	Orissa Historical Research Journal
Orissa Records	...	Guide to Orissan Records
OSA	...	Orissa State Archives, Bhubaneswar
Pr.	...	Para
RAB	...	Report on the Administration of Bengal
RAC	...	Report of the Administration of Customs Department, Bengal Presidency.
RBR	...	Records of the Board of Revenue.
RCC	...	Report of the Commissioners appointed to enquiry into certain matters, 1884.
RCF	...	Report of the Commissioners appointed to enquire into famine in Bengal and Orissa, 1866.
RIC	...	Report on the Indian Irrigation Commission
RIF	...	Report on the Indian Famine Commission
ROC	...	Records of Orissa Canal Project
SE	...	Superintending Engineer
Secy	...	Secretary
UD	...	Utkal Dipika

Introduction

Historical Background

After the death of Mukunda Deva in 1568, the medieval Orissa lost her independence to the Afghan power. Yet the latter could not succeed in consolidating its hold over this province for a longer period due to the rapid growth of the Mughal empire. Orissa fell a prey to the expansionist zeal of Akbar and his general Mansingh conquered it in 1592. Then it was apportioned into five Sarkars and included into the Subah of Bengal. The Sarkars were Jaleswar, Bhadrak, Cuttack, Kalinga Dandapat and Rajmahendri. Passing under the Mughal rule for more than one and a half centuries, Orissa went to the hands of the powerful Marathas in 1751, following the decline of the Mughal empire after the death of Aurangzeb in 1707. The Marathas too could not prolong their supremacy over this land in the teeth of an imperialist British East India Company, which conquered the province on the 14th of October 1803. And since then it remained under the control of Bengal Presidency, governed by a Commissioner. The then Orissa consisted of three coastal districts of Cuttack, Puri and Balasore known as the *mughalbandi* areas and seventeen tributary states or the *garjat* areas, each ruled by its own *raja* under the general supervision of the Commissioner, who was also entitled as Superintendent of the tributary states. With an area of 24,307 square miles Orissa then stretched from Medinapur in the north to Ganjam in the south. The geographical tract stretching along the sea coast over a surface of 8000 square miles was called as *mughalbandi* with a population of about 11,25,000. The hilly regions stretching towards central India formed the Tributary mahals covering an area of 16,307 miles and it contained a population of about 3,37,500.

After the British occupation of Orissa, Lt. Col. George Harcourt and John Melville, a civil officer, were entrusted with the charge of settling the newly conquered territories. In 1805, Bengal laws and regulations were introduced in Orissa, Puri was its capital till 1816 when it was transferred to Cuttack. In 1814, the Commissioner of Orissa was appointed as the Suprintendent of tributary mahals. In 1829 Orissa was divided into three districts of Cuttack, Puri and Balasore and it remained under the regulation of Bengal Presidency up to 1912.

In 1912 Bihar-Orissa province was created and in 1936 Orissa became a separate province under British India and included 6 districts and 24 tributary states. After independence and merger, Orissa had 13 district.

Perspective

Orissa is endowed with aboundant natural resources. It has rich mineral, forest and marine resources. Yet the irony of fate is that it is one of the poorest states of India with more than half of its population living below the poverty line. The ambitious plans and programmes of the State Government for ameliorating the poor economic condition of the people of Orissa have failed to achieve the desired objective. The nature has become the potent enemy in the economic development of the state. The geography peculiarities of Orissa has made her a continuous victim of natural calamities. The flood, famine and cyclone are the recurring features in the history of Orissa. There is hardly a year which is not affected by a natural calamity.

Every year the vast stretches of land in delta and fertile area of coastal districts of Cuttack, Puri, Balasore and Ganjam are severely affected either by flood, cyclone or famine with colossal loss of life and property. Agriculture, the economic backbone of the state is heavily affected by the natural calamities. The figures of loss and damage are staggering to be believed. Hence, a substantial part of the Government revenue is spent on the physical and economic rehabilitation of the affected people. Since Independence, a major portion of time, efforts and money has been devoted towards meeting scarctiy caused by natural calamities leaving scanty resources for the economic development of the state. In view of the high frequency of occurrence and magnitude of loss, the Government has directed its efforts to find a solution to the problem.

Against this backdrop, there is a high correlation between the frequency and magnitude of natural calamities and the economic progress of the state. A historical enquiry into the occurrence of major natural calamities will, no doubt, provide an insight into the impact of various natural hazards on the economic development of the state. Besides, a historical study of the Government policies will highlight major policy lapses in confronting these natural challenges. In fact, it is the faulty policy of the Government which creates an environment in which the effective implementation of future economic measures is weakened. It creates a vicious circle in which further economic progress becomes regressive rather than progressive.

Review of Literature

Though much of the research endeavour has been directed towards the socio-political and religious history of Orissa during 19th century, a little attempt has so far been made by the scholars to study the intensity of natural calamities and its impact on the economic condition of the people of Orissa. Hence an attempt has been made in this dissertation to provide an indepth study of various aspects of natural calamities in the State of Orissa during 19th century.

The British historians were the first to write the history of Orissa. Andrew Stirling, an administrator, was the first to make an attempt in this direction. His work, "An account (geographical, Statistical and Historical) of Orissa proper or Cuttack" published in 1825, gives a brief general outline of Orissa from ancient times to modern period. But it contains scanty information on natural calamities in Orissa.

Sir William Hunter was the first person who made a systematic effort to write the "History of Orissa" in two volumes published in 1872. His book provides an extensive coverage on natural calamities like flood, famine and the consequent socio-economic problems. In his view, improved irrigation and drainage system, developed road and railway network could protect, to some extent, the life and property of the people.

Similarly George Toynbee's book on "A Sketch of History of Orissa", published in 1873, highlights the administrative aspects of British East India Company in Orissa from 1803 to 1828. He has described in brief the scarcity of food grains during the period 1806 to 1809.

N.N. Banerjee's, "Report on the Agriculture of the districts of Cuttack" (1898), provides some insight into the history of natural calamities in the district of Cuttack. However, two other coastal districts namely Balasore and Puri identified as most cyclone prone zones have been ignored. Hence, the study is considered to be partial in its approach.

S.L. Maddox's, "The Final Report on the survey and Settlements of the Province of Orissa, 1890-1900", (1900) provides a brief outline of natural calamities in Orissa. But the major concern of the study is the problem of settlement and not the recurrent natural calamities.

The autobiography of "Fakir Mohan Senapati" (1917) in Oriya gives a vivid picture of 1866 famine in Orissa. He was an eyewitness of the terrible famine of 1866. He has not however, touched the other famines, floods and cyclones during 19th century.

R.D. Banerjee's "History of Orissa" Vol. II (1939) has made a brief mention of the various natural calamities in Orissa in different years. But he has not dealt with the intensity of the natural calamities and their impact on the society. Similarly nothing has been said about the then British policies.

H.K. Mahtab in his "History of Orissa Vol. II (1960) has analysed causes and consequences of the great famine of 1866, besides highlighting the failure of famine code (1883) in Orissa.

B.M. Bhatia's, "Famines in India" (1963) has mainly dealt with great famines of the country as a whole and the famine policy of British Government. However, its implication to Orissa has been ignored by the author.

P. Mukherjee's, "History of Orissa" Vol. VI (1964) has provided an outline on natural calamities in Orissa and the great famine of 1866.

H.S. Srivastav's "The History of Indian Famines" (1968) has highlighted the major famines in India and the British policies. But if we consider the study from a regional perspective it fails to provide a complete picture of the incidence of famine in Orissa.

B.S. Das's, "Studies in Economic History of Orissa from Ancient Times to 1833" (1970) has described cyclone as the main hindrance to economic progress of Orissa. However, the study throws more light on the socio-economic aspect than on the incidence of natural calamities.

J.K. Samal in his, "Orissa under the British Crown" (1978) has emphasized the causes and consequence of the great famine of Orissa in 1866. However, many important aspects of the famine have not been given due weightage in this study.

G.C. Patnaik's, "The Famine and Some Aspects of the British Economic Policy in Orissa 1866-1905" (1980) has reviewed the socio-economic condition of Orissa before and after the great famine of Orissa (1866). He has also studied the remedial measures undertaken by the British Government for rehabilitating the people affected by the great famine. But the study excludes all other famines which occurred in the latter part of 19th century.

P.C. Das's, "Economic History of Orissa in the 19th Century" (1989) has highlighted natural calamities as major hindrances to the economic development of the state. However, the study seems to be inadequate if the whole of the 19th century is taken into consideration.

H.K. Mishra, in his "Famines and Poverty in India' (1991) has highlighted on the great famine of 1866 and other famines and scarcities after it and also the British Policies towards these one. But regarding the occurrence of natural calamities in the state in the first half of the 19th century, the book deals little.

From the review of above works of scholars, it is clear that no single study has dealt with all the aspects of natural calamities. Even though they are not comprehensive, both the terms of time and coverage, they provide some insight for making further intensive studies on the topic. The present study includes within its ambit many new areas not explored previously by scholars.

Objectives

The primary objectives of the study are to assess the various dimensions of the natural calamities in Orissa and the consequent British policies towards these ones in the 19th century. More specifically the study has the following objectives:

(*i*) To examine how recurrent natural calamities and the deterioration of the standard of living of the people in its wake, led to the growth of the poverty and to what extent the British Government took measures for the protection of the people from the perilous impact of natural calamities.

(*ii*) To analyse the causes and economic effects of recurring natural calamities.

(*iii*) To examine the magnitude of the remedial policies of the British administration and the response of the people of Orissa to it.

Significance of the Study

Occurrence of flood, famine and cyclone is common on the soil of Orissa. The economic condition of Orissa is purely dependent on the vagaries of monsoon and devastating effect of natural calamities. The vast coastal belt of the state has made her prone to the different calamities like flood, famine and cyclone. The socio-economic condition of the people of Orissa is significantly guided by the interplay of various natural forces. There is a high degree of correlation between the economic progress of the state and the natural calamities.

All the factors contributing to the economic progress of the state such as agriculture, manufacturing, trade, mining and other allied activities are completely dependent on the mercy of the nature. That is why a study dealing mainly with the major natural hazards of the state is considered to be significant. No doubt the past has significant bearing on the future. It is necessary to relate the current economic condition of the state to the foul play of natural forces in the past. Besides, the future economic policy of the state can be formulated keeping in eye the occurrence of the various natural calamities in the past. The trend of natural calamities in the past will, no doubt, act as a sign of caution in future.

The present work will be an important contribution towards economic history not only of Orissa but also of India and also for regional development and economic growth of the region. Studies made so far provide a limited knowledge on the topic. The present study is considered to be an intensive one both in dimension and coverage. It will significantly add to the existing store of knowledge and the future research on the topic.

Research Methodology

The methodological framework of the study is primarily based on the following:

(*i*) A detailed survey of contemporary literary works on the economic history of Orissa and the natural calamities.

(*ii*) Collection of archival materials such as manuscript, printed Government reports, Census reports and Gazetteers. The archival sources have been collected from (*a*) State Archives of Orissa, Bhubaneswar, (*b*) Board of Revenue, Orissa, Cuttack, (*c*) Kanika Library, Cuttack, (*d*) State Library, Orissa, Bhubaneswar, (*e*) West Bengal State Archives, Calcutta, (*f*) National Library, Calcutta, (*g*) National Archives of India, New Delhi.

(*iii*) Collection of contemporary Vernacular newspapers and periodicals like "Utkal Dipika", "Sambalpur Hitaisini" and "Utkal Putra" and "Balasore Sambada Bahika" etc.

(*iv*) Analysis of collected materials with the help of suitable statistical tables, charts, graphs maps along with the data application of ratio, percentage etc., for the purpose of better interpretation.

Scope of the Study

The main aim of the work is to study various aspects of natural calamities in Orissa in the 19th century and the consequent British policies towards that but the task is so broad that it is not possible to cover every minute details of the topic. Besides, there is constraint on the availability of related materials and records. Hence, the scope of the study has been made limited to certain major aspects of natural calamities such as flood, cyclone and famine.

Broadly the "Natural Calamities", in the study covers the floods and cyclones in the 19th century, the famines in the first half of the 19th century, the great famine of 1866 and other famines during the 2nd half of the century and their causes, courses and consequences.

The period of the study is 1803 A.D. to 1900 A.D., *i.e.*, the whole of the 19th century. Even though the study is on the whole of Orissa province, the area of the study is limited to the so called British Orissa covering Cuttack, Puri and Balasore districts and some parts of the tributary states. It also attempts to cover the Ganjam district which was under the jurisdiction of the then Madras Presidency.

Limitations of the Study

The present study is constrained by a number of limited factors. Though attempts have been made to overcome some of the minor limitations, the major constraints affecting findings of the study have been brought to light. The major limitations of the study are as follows:

1. The concept of "Natural Calamities" is so broad that it includes

within its ambit the interplay of a number of natural forces. Since it is not possible to give a detailed description of all such forces because of paucity of materials, only three natural hazards namely flood, cyclone and famine have constituted the main theme of the topic.

2. The period of the study is limited to nineteenth century only *i.e.*, from 1803 to 1900. This period has been selected keeping in view the main objectives of the study.
3. The probability of occurrence of floods, cyclones and famines in Orissa is so uncertain that it is not possible to fix a deadline or demarcate a period after which the intensity of natural calamities has been increased or decreased.
4. The study covers only those areas and districts which constituted the so called British Orissa. Besides, those areas where the intensity of natural calamities was not significant, have been ignored for the sake of convenience.
5. It was not possible to provide a quantitative approach to the impact of natural calamities on the socio-economic condition of the people and remedial policy measures of the British Government. So the study has been made descriptive.

Thesis Organization

Keeping in view the objectives of the study, the thesis is organized in a manner to focus on major aspects of natural calamities in Orissa and the contemporary British policies. The thesis is divided into eight chapters. Each chapter is divided into suitable sections and subsections so as to study the minute details about the main topic.

Chapter I, highlights the occurrence of "Floods and Inundations in the 19th Century". It studies the basic causes of flood in the reported period and the consequent losses to the people and economy of Orissa. It also examines various aspects of the remedial measures pursued by the British Government to withstand the devastating effect of flood.

Chapter II, deals with the "Cyclones in the 19th Century" in a similar fashion as in the Chapter I.

Chapter III on "British Policy towards Floods and Cyclones" examines the specific control measures adopted by the British Government in tackling the problem. It evaluates the effectiveness of such measures with due consideration of the requirement of the people.

Chapter IV yields a vivid picture of "Famines in Orissa from 1803 to 1964". It highlights the various causes and consequences of the major famines. It also studies the extent to which the developmental activities were undertaken by the British Government to mitigate the economic loss caused to the people and also analyses other causes which were responsible for the economic hardship of the people.

"The Great Orissa Famine of 1866" is contained in Chapter V. It studies the various dimensions of the devastating famine, such as causes, courses and consequences. It also examines response of the British Government in terms of extent, adequacy and effectiveness of the British relief measures.

Chapter VI on "Famines and Scarcities after 1866" describes the frequency of occurrence of famine after the Great Famine of Orissa in 1866 and the consequent economic scarcities. It brings to light certain measures undertaken by the British Government to check the devastating effects of famines.

Chapter VII yields an overall analysis of the "British Policy towards Famines and Scarcities" in the 19th century. It analyses the major findings and recommendations of the Famine Commission set up for the purpose.

Chapter VIII, is the final chapter dealing with conclusions. It summarises the major aspects of the study followed by major findings.

1

Floods and Inundations in the Nineteenth Century

Frequent occurrence of floods, considered as a curse for Orissa, leads the province to the State of devastation almost all the years. And the drought following the flood causes a wide-scale loss in some or many parts of the State every year. Mahatma Gandhi has rightly said thus "Flood is a permanent disease in Orissa".[1] The 19th century Orissa witnessed a series of floods almost every year. It deteriorated the economic condition of the agriculturists and brokedown the morale of the people of Orissa.

After the British conquest of Orissa in 1803, the problems which the British Government had to reckon with here was not of any internal turmoil or the apprehension of any foreign onset, but how to control the floods in the State and the supply of water in the rivers.[2]

Flood hazard is a global phenomenon. From the year 1874 to 1979 nearly 10,700 people died due to floods in the world.[3]

Orissa also suffered from floods every year. Orissa in the first half of the 19th century witnessed a series of floods which broke down the economic conditions of the people of Orissa. The table shows the floods in Orissa from 1803 to 1858.

TABLE 1.1
FLOODS AND INUNDATIONS IN ORISSA (1803-1858)

1804, 1806, 1807, 1809, 1812, 1814, 1817, 1820, 1823, 1826, 1831, 1834, 1835, 1837, 1838, 1840, 1841, 1842, 1844, 1845, 1846, 1847, 1848, 1851, 1852, 1853, 1854, 1855, 1856, 1857, 1858.

Sources : Bihar and Orissa Document; File No. NF-21/1929; Government of Bihar and Orissa Deposit; Revenue Department, March 1930; No. 9 L.S.S.O.' Malley, Bihar and Orissa District, Gazetteer, Cuttack, p. 127.

1. S.N. Das, *Unabimsa Satabdir Orissa*, Cuttack 1979, p. 50.
2. W.W. Hunter, *Orissa*, Vol. II, London, 1872, p. 174.
3. K.S. Valdiya, *Environmental Geology*, Indian Context, New Delhi, 1987, p. 331.

The important rivers which caused frequent floods in Orissa were the Mahanadi, the Kathjori, the Brahmani, the Baitarani and the Subarnarekha.

Why Floods Occur?

Basic Causes : Whenever the magnitude of flow of water exceeds the carrying capacity of the channel within its banks the excess water overflows on to the floods plains and causes floods. Thus, two factors are mostly responsible for the occurrence of floods (*i*) the flow of excess water resulting from increased run off in the catchment area, and (*ii*) reduction in the carrying capacity of the channels as a consequence of accumulation of sediments or the obstructions built on floods ways.[4]

The floods of Orissa generally occur on the following grounds.[5]

(1) Cyclones also bring heavy downpours for prolonged periods.
(2) Tidal waves and hurricane in the Bay of Bengal and the Chilka lake bring about devastating floods.
(3) Depression in the Bay of Bengal causing widespread and continuous rainfall..
(4) The bursting of embankments causes catastrophic floods.
(5) The deterioration of the shape of river channels.
(6) The inter-connection of rivers.
(7) Deforestation or excessive jungle clearance in the upper reaches of important rivers.
(8) Configuration of the catchment basins.

Flood Frequencies (1803-1858)

According to Hunter, "flood is the scourge of the Orissa Province".[6] Generally in July, August and September, when the rice plants were in the last ebb of their growth or in flower, the highest floods occurred by which embankments got breached, the rice fields inundated and the crops materially damaged.[7] The people of Orissa were accustomed to such calamities due to the frequent occurrence and they took shelter for time being in comparatively high lands with their property and cattle.

---

4. K.S. Valdiya, *op.cit.*, p. 331.
5. P. Mukherjee, *Irrigation, Inland Navigation and Flood Problems in North Orissa during the British Rule*, Bhubaneswar, 1967, p. 41.
K.S. Valdiya, *op.cit.*, pp. 531-535.
S.N. Dàs, *op.cit.*, p. 51.
B.N. *Sinha, Geography of Orissa*, New Delhi, 1971, pp. 67-69.
6. N.N. Banerjee, *Report on the Agriculture of the District of Cuttack*, Calcutta, 1898, p. 176.
7. *Ibid*.

Sometimes, the floods were so heavy and so prolonged that some parts of the country remained under water for weeks together and the crops were seriously damage.[8] By frequent floods, the economic background of the people naturally got crippled or ruined.

In 1805, the Zamindaries of Kotrahang in Puri district suffered from inundation. They required a deduction for inundation of *kahans* 15,851,13 P. But the Tahasildar who was deputed to inspect the loss, fixed the loss at only K. 5,769,5.[9] Cuttack district also suffered from flood of 1807.

The people of Cuttack town suffered from scarcity of food due to temporary cut off of the communications between Cuttack town and the interior parts in the months of July, August and September on account of flood.[10] The province suffered from a severe flood and the crops of 1809-10 were destroyed to a large extent. Many petitions were then made to Charles Buller, the Special Commissioner, for remission of revenue. But he declined to make enquiries on the plea that he had concluded a permanent settlement of the province.[11] There often the distress of the Zamindars was great, collections fell to 84% and 271 estates with annual Jama of Rs. 2,04,842 were sold in three years.[12] In 1818, some portions of northern Orissa suffered severely from the most violent and sudden inundation ever to be remembered.[13]

Some parganas of Central Cuttack suffered on account of the loss of crops sustained from the flood in October 1834 of the Mahandi and Kathjori river and other smaller streams.[14] The Government sanctioned remission of a large sum of revenue because of the damage to crops by the above flood.[15]

In October 1835, Cuttack was affected by a dreadful and destruction inundation. The Mahanadi overflew with flood water and topped the baks which guard the city. Thousands of poor people were rendered houseless and destitute by this sad calamity. Beasts of various kinds, as

---

8. L.S.S.O'Malley, *BDG*, *Balasore*, Calcutta, 1907, p. 96.
9. C. Grome, acting Collector, Jagannath to Thomas Fortescue, Secretary to the Commissions for the affairs of Cuttack, Revenue Department, 12 September 1805.
10. G. Toynbee, *A Sketch of the History of Orissa*, 1803-1828, p. 87.
11. *BRP*, No. 22, of 13 May 1819, Trower to Stirling, 26 November 1818.
12. *Maddox Report*, Vol. I, p. 162.
13. Magistrate Cuttack to the Secretary to Government, 26 March 1818.
14. F.I. Halliday, Secretary Sudder Board of Revenue Fort-William; 4 June 1836 to R.D. Mangles, Secretary to the Government of Bengal, Revenue Department, Fort-William, No. 221.
15. Bihar and Orissa Document; File No. IVF-21/1929, Government of Bihar and Orissa Deposit, Revenue Department, March 1930, No. 9.

elephants, cows, sheep, together with men, women and trees washed from the hills were seen floating down the torrent.[16] About 4 lives were lost in 1835-36 in pargana Khurda in inundation.[17]

In 1840, Crops were destroyed in some parts of Southern and central districts of Cuttack by the high inundation in September and a partial failure of the stable crop viz., the *sarada* rice in consequence of the early cessation of the rains throughout three districts.[18] The injury done to the crops both from inundation and drought was no doubt in some parts severe.[19] In Central Cuttack alone 255476-3-7 has been remitted during the last ten years, on account of losses from inundations.[20] The Commissioner also informed the Collector of Puri about the low lands where the crops might be destroyed due to heavy fall of rain. There the ryots should be given the privileges to understand, before cultivating their lands that they had understood all risks. The remission for such losses should not be given to the ryots.[21]

In the year 1845 Puri district suffered from inundation. In pargana Koterahang, the rice crops had been entirely destroyed by the overflowing of the Kushabhadra river. In Rahang pargana Chabiskud, the damage done to the rice crops due to the overflowing of the Chilka lake was greater than the former. It was quite distressing and painful to view the total failure of every prospect of a harvest, in the ravages made by the inundation. The Collector himself witnessed the injury that had been sustained in the estates of Bulpur, Rahang and Kokloo and estimated that not less than half the assets had been swept away. In other estates like Paschimduai, Purbaduai, Untrood, Koterahang etc., the inundation had been very destructive but it had not been so general in its effects.[22]

In 1846 the Zamindars of estates in pargana Ayas, Katiah and Dolegram of Balasore district sustained greater loss from the torrents of water from the Kharswan river which had done considerable damages.

---

16. Orissa, its Geography, Statistics, History etc., pp. 233-234.
17. K.C. Ghose, Deputy Collector, Embankment Committee (O.S.A., No. 33, 194 Bd. Doc.)
18. *BRP*, A.J.M. Mills, Commissioner to the Suder Board of Revenue, No. 4925, 25 November 1840.
19. *BRP*, A.J.M. Mills, Commissioner to the Acting Collector of Cuttack, No. 4886, 21 November 1840.
20. *BRP*, A.J.M. Mills, Commissioner to the Secretary, Suder Board of Revenue, Fort William, No. 4409, 13 October 1840.
21. *BRP*, A.J.M. Mills, Commissioner to the Collector of Puri, No. 2420, 12 June 1840.
22. *BRP*, Collector, Subdivision of Zilla., Cuttack Collector's Office, Camp-Kaanas to A.J.M. Mills, Commissioner, for 19 Division Cuttack, L.No. 7J, 3 January 1846.

The report of W.Brown, the Deputy Collector noted below, gives a comprehensive statement about the casuality in the parganas Ayas, Katiah and Dolegram.[23]

Phs.	*Mahals*	*Villages*	*Mahal injured*	*Village injured*	*Remarks*
Ayas	67	78	5	16	Loss from 2 annas to 16 annas
Katiah	56	67	11	25	Loss from 3 annas to 14 annas
Dolegram	60	84	26	60	Loss from 2 annas to 16 annas

The crops of Kanika and Aul as well as some other of the ward's estates, suffered extensively from inundation in the year 1845-46.[24]

In Puri district, the Jagir mahals suffered severely from inundation in the year 1854. The statement noted below gives the loss of crops by inundation in the subdivision of Cuttack for 1261 Umlee.[25]

No.	*Name of Pargana*	*Name of Mahal*	*Mufassil Jama*	*Loss of crops*	*Balance*
1.	Malud	Malud	1442-2-4	781-1-6/$_4$	66-11-9¾
2.	Bajrakot	Bajrakot	2128-7-$^3/_2$	741-7-9	1386-15-6½
3.	Gurjit Undharee	Undharee	1789-15-9¾	241-13-7	1548-2-2¾
Total			5360-9-5¼	1764-6-10¼	3596-2-7

Some of the pargana of Balasore district suffered severely from the inundation which had in many places completely swept away the crops. The great loos occurred in the Dokhynpat and in pargana at Bhograi, due to the breaches in the Punchopolee bund and Bhograi bund respectively. The ryots also suffered considerably from the inundation by loss of cattle and the destruction of the houses. Now the Collector sought permission from the Commissioner to grant remission on account of

23. *BRP*, The Collector of Balasore to the Commissioner of Revenue for the Division of Cuttack No. 158, 30 December 1846.
24. Selections from the records of the Government of Bengal, No. III, Papers on the settlement of Cuttack and on the state of the Tributary Mahals, Calcutta, 1867, p. 35.
25. E. Dimond, Collector of the Southern Division of Zilla Cuttack to Commissioner for the 19 Division, Cuttack, 15 May 1854.

these losses.[26] The Commissioner, however informed that the remission would be granted to the ryots whose loss would exceed above 20 percent of their aggregate crop. But is would be only after an enquiry was made to calculate the damage.[27]

In July 1855 there was a very high flood in Cuttack district. The Mahanadi rose to an enormous height and the maximum reading (127.13) on the Lalbagh gauge was recorded.[28] About 1365 embankments were breached by this flood[29] and 52 square miles were reported to be permanently left waste for fear of inundation. However the flood fell as quickly as it rose and did less damage compared to other protracted floods.[30] This flood directed more attention to the critical state of the revetment which protects the town of Cuttack from the flood of Kathjori. Lieutenant Harris was placed on special duty by the Superintendent of Embankments to survey the Mahanadi and generally to investigate the question of the disposal of the flood waters. His first report of 9th June 1856, dealt chiefly with flood situation as it affected the town cantonment of Cutack.

It was certain that for a considerable period prior to 1855 the volume of flood had been increasing in the Kathjori branch and lessening in the Mahanadi main channel. The result was that the town was liable to be severely flooded from the Kathjori while it was fairely secure on the Mahanadi side. Lieutenant Harris described the Kathjori on the following words:

> "The Katjuri (Kathjori) has doubtless sprung from nothing originally, risen from insignificance within the speace of a few centuries".[31]

On the 8th of August the Bhargabi riven began to rise and by the 11th instant the flood water was topping all the embankments. This flood was caused by the spring tides in the Bay of Bengal and Chilka Lake, stopping the progress of the rain drainage. And before this rise subsided, the rain water in the Mahanadi (which at Cuttack, was above 27', nearly equal to that of 1855) came down heavily and made high floods in the lower parts of the Bhargabi, Nuna and Daya rivers. The Sauparra Bungalow was built at a level higher than that of adjacent villages and was never known to be approached by previous floods; but by the August flood the villages had been washed away and the flood rose above

26. From Offg. Collector of Balasore to the Commissioner of Revenue for the division of Cuttack, No. 198, 13 December 1854.
27. Commissioner's Office, Cuttack Division to the Offg. Collector of Balasore, No. 228, 16 December 1854.
28. L.S.S. O'Malley, *BDG, Cuttack*, Calcutta, 1907, p.127.
29. W.A. Inglis, *The Canals and Flood Banks of Bengal*, Calcutta, 1909, p. 205.
30. L.S.S.O' Malley, *op.cit.*, p. 127.
31. W.A. Inglis, *op.cit.*, p. 205.

2 feet of the plinth of the Bungalow.

Other portions of the division also suffered substantially. The Kuakhai embankments breached in about 8 places. This floods in the Daya river had been destructive and the embankments of nearly 15 feet high had been topped. At Neepur there were three breaches; one of which was about 2000 ft. long. The main portion of this flood appeared to have come from the Mahanadi.

The severity of the flood also affected Puri district to a great extent, which occurred due to the closing of the head of the Mahanadi.[32] The Board was good enough to instruct the local officers to institute a searching enquiry into this matter and communicate the result for the information of His Honour.[33]

On the 15th August 1857, the Cuttack revetment almost gave way. The services of the prisoners of the Cuttack Jail were requisitioned to save the revetment.[34] The government estate of Nuanund also suffered from inundation in August 1857 and they also demanded for remission.[35]

Afterall there was not any specific policy regarding the control of flood or any relief measures were adopted by British during the period of flood in Orissa besides granting some remissions and suspensions on the subject of loss from calamity of season. Ewer pointed out that the refusal to grant any remission to the Zamindars for the failure of crops had been constantly urged upon by them as a very serious hardship. Petitions were numerous to that effect.[36] The number of parganas and estates in different years were as flollows:

	Estates	*Parganas*
1849	335	51
1852	885	72
1853	235	32

But it was found that relief was granted only to 65 estates in 7 parganas and other were improperly put forward. The commissioner believed that in many parganas losses had occurred more than the revenue assessed on them and though the revenue had been paid up, the ryots

32. G. Rajner, Offg. Executive Officer, Puri Embankment Division to Captain W.O. Short, Superintendent of Embankments, C, 26 August 1857.
33. From Junior Secretary to the Government of Bengal to the Secretary to the Board of Revenue, No. 2233, Fort William 24 October 1857.
34. T.N. Armstrong, Executive Engineer to R.N. Shore, Magistrate No. 257, Quoted in P. Mukherjee, *History of Orissa*, Vol. VI, Cuttack, 1964, p. 357.
35. From Offg. Collector of Balasore to the Commissioner of Revenue for the Division of Cuttack, 22 February 1858.
36. K.M. Patra, *Orissa Under the East India Company*, New Delhi, 1971, p.73.

were starving and the Zamindars were in a deplorable condition.[37] Under the Maratha administration, the continuous deductions from the rent roll in proportion to the damage sustained in seasonal calamities were made. But the British Government did not follow the practice of the Marathas towards the peasants and Zamindars of Orissa.[38]

Orissa under the East India Company suffered a lot due to the lack of any relief policy to protect the people of Orissa from the peril of floods. According to W.W. Hunter, the British Government during their first twenty seven years in Orissa *i.e.*, 1803 to 1830 remitted £ 65,094 due to flood alone. But such remissions proved wholly indequate to meet the evil. The calamities of the province forced the British officials to remit £ 91,889 during the period 1830-31 to 1851-52 for the losses which occurred due to floods. During the next fifteen year (1852 to 1867) the Government remitted no less than £ 105,536 for the above cause alone.[39] Though the Government remitted from time to time, yet it was inadequate to meet the frequent occurrence of calamities in the province. Inundations were more common and in general more destructive than any other calamities. The frequent occurrence of floods and inundations destroyed the economic background of the Orissa people and they became poorer day by day.

The Second Phase (1859 to 1900)

The second phase of 19th century also witnessed a series of floods which did considerable damage to the state economy. The following table speaks of the flood years in Orissa.

TABLE 1.2
FLOODS AND INUNDATIONS IN ORISSA FROM 1859-1900

1859, 1862, 1863, 1864, 1866, 1868, 1870, 1871, 1872, 1874, 1875, 1877, 1879, 1880, 1881, 1882, 1883, 1884, 1885, 1886, 1888, 1889, 1891, 1892, 1893, 1894, 1895, 1896, 1900.

Source : Bihar and Orissa Document; File No. NF-21/1929, Government of Bihar and Orissa Deposit, Revenue Department, March 1930, No.9.

The Floods of 1859 and 1862

Puri district suffered most from the flood occured in September 1859 and it had been more destructive than the previous floods and continued at full height for eight or ten days. The embankment on the Bhargabi

37. *BRP*, No. 535, G.F. Cockburn, Commissioner to the Collector of Cuttack, 26 January 1857.
38. *BRP*, No. 15 of July 17, 1818, Ewer to Government May 18, 1818.
39. W.W. Hunter, *Orissa*, Vol. II, p. 181.

river suffered most. At Surdaipur, the flood line was three feet two inches above the river bank. About a mile westward on the right bank of the river at Allanpur, the embankment was topped by the flood and a breach was formed of about one hundred and fifty feet in length. No damage had been done to crops for the water having passed off through the Mattia river. At Biddapur, on the left bank, the embankment had been breached in two places measuring together one hundred and forty feet. At Nursingpur, on the right bank, about a mile west of the Puri Road, there was a breach of about eighty feet long.

On the Sunamukhi and Nuna South, there was one large breach of about two hundred feet and there were five small ones, all under fifty feet each and were all cuts to discharge the flood. The Sunamukhi was also exposed to the strong sea winds, and the waves thus caused, eroded the embankement and made the breach on the whole of the Sunamukhi embankments.

On the Daya river, at Tottaparra, about six hundred feet of the embankment fell into the river. At Nuagaon by the same river more than half the embankment had been eroded for four hundred feet in length. Some portions of "Khasmahal" and "Lakharaj" suffered from flood.[40] The province was visited by a very unexpected disaster in the sudden floods caused by heavy rainfall which occurred on 20th October 1862. The rabi or spring crops had been totally destroyed by it and the low lands, which produced the heaviest crops of the year were damaged to a greater extent. In injured tracts, a large numbers of cattle had perished. In the flood a considerable loss of life also occurred. The principal loss happened in the central district along with the low lands lying between the rivers Brahmani and Kharswan. The large estate of Pattamunadai paying about 27,000 sadar *jama* suffered from flood parganas like Hatimunda, Kaima and higher up the river. Choudakulat and Barruwa where remissions were necessary had been swept away. On the other hand the Mahanadi had done little damage.

To amount of remissions necessary in injured tracts did not exceed Rs. 10,000/- to Rs. 15,000/- representing a loss of rents to the extent of about Rs. 50,000/-

The damage in Puri district was principally confined to the lands adjacent to Chilka lake especially two Zamindaries like Kokale and Rorang which had lost half of their crops and they probably required Rs. 5000/- as remissions.[41]

---

40. From Executive Engineer, Puri Division to G.F. Cockburn Commissioner Cuttack, Camp-Kunttee, 21 September 1859.
41. From Commissioner of Orissa to the Secretary, Government of Bengal, Fort William No. 598, 21 November 1862.

The inundation affected chiefly the portions of the district adjacent to the rivers Kharswan, Baitarani and its tributaries, the Salandi and Matai, and the villages on the banks of the Burabalang and Subarnarekha had been injured but to a less extent.[42] So Balasore suffered more than any other district of the province.

The Flood of 1866

Floods have disastrous effects upon human habitations and take away heavy tolls of human life and cattle, property etc.[43] The flood of 1866 was more disastrous in character than that of 1865. Of course compared to 1855 it was not so high but it continued for longer time. It came at a critical time when the people of Orissa suffered from a terrible famine.[44] It desolated the homesteads of $1^1/_3$ million of husbandmen. At that time in six fiscal divisions of Puri district only 92,017 acres could be cultivated, while 50,475 or 78 square miles were left waste for fear of floods.[45]

The Mahanadi stood at 125.50 feet on the Bellevue gauge, as above mean sea level, carrying away the regulating embankments extending from Naraja at the junction of the Kathjori and Mahanadi rivers to the heads of the Cuttack delta. It spread over the whole low lands of the delta extending from Puri and the southern extremity of the Chilka to the Dhamra and Baitarani rivers between Cuttack and Balasore.[46]

In Puri district the damage caused by this flood was enhanced by the mouth of the Chilka Lake. The Kathjori and its tributaries devastated the Puri district. In Puri district alone 2,300,000 maunds of paddy were lost due to inundation.[47] According to inundation committee, in Cuttack alone 78,11,247 maunds of paddy; valued at Rs. 2,17,35,644 was destroyed by flood.[48] The Brahmani and Baitarani rivers also submerged their country land, not so high as the Mahanadi. In Balasore district, the Bhadrak subdivision suffered partially by flood water from the Baitarani and to the north of Balasore by Subarnarekha floods.[49] The loss of crops in Balasore was comparatively small to other districts.

---

42. W. Cornell, Officiating Collector of Balasore to the Commissioner of Revenue, Cuttack No. 240, 29 November 1862.
43. B.N. Sinha, *Geography of Orissa*, p. 71.
44. L.S.S.O'Malley, *BDG*, *Cuttack*, p. 127.
45. W.W. Hunter, *Orissa*, Vol. II, pp. 183-184.
46. From T.E. Ravenshaw, Offg. Commissioner of the Cuttack Division to the Secretary to the Board of Revenue, Lower Provinces, No. 958, 1 November 1866.
47. P. Mukherjee, *Irrigation, Inland Navigation and Flood Problems in North Orissa during the British Rule*, p. 46.
48. N.N. Benarjee, *op.cit.*, p. 176.
49. From T.E. Ravenshaw, Offg. Commissioner of the Cuttack Division, to the Secretary to the Board of Revenue, L.P. No. 958, 1 November 1866.

The country side was dislocated and cultivable lands fell barren. At that time Orissa famine of 1865-66 was very terrible and the flood water created hindrance in relief operation. It is difficult to assess the total damage done by the floods but the type of damage may be categorized on the following heads.[50]

(*a*) To crops, houses, livestock, personal property and land.

(*b*) To flood embankments and protection works.

(*c*) To roads and bridges etc.

This flood caused damage to crops and to human habitations extensively than any other previous floods. The Government setup a committee in the same year to investigate the inundations which occurred in the province.

The Flood of 1868

The lower Bengal comprising the districts of Cuttack, Burdwan and the presidency suffered from disastrous inundations in the year 1868. The inundation occurred due to an unusual heavy rain off the south-west monsoon. It appeared to the highest everywhere between the 16th and 17th June. The rainfall shown in the month of June 1868 was measured at the following stations of Cuttack district.[51]

		1st to 7th	*8th to 14th*	*Total*	*15th to 30th*	*Total per month*
1.	Puri	5.50	1.90	7.40	3.60	11.00
2.	Cuttack	4.65	8.50	13.15	3.98	17.13
3.	Akhuapada	5.63	9.10	14.73	4.68	19.41
4.	Balasore	11.10	18.70	29.80	6.40	36.20

So 1868 was marked as a year of devastating floods in Orissa division. In Puri division, the Kathjori and its branches did not rise higher than ordinary floods, reading only 121.80 on the Bellevue gauge. The total number of breaches in embankments in the Puri division was nine. Among them six on the Bhargabi, aggregating 1,585 feet in length, two on the Kusabhadra of 340 feet long and one on the Daya 7,000 feet in length. Some damage was done to the standing crops.

Some considerable injury was done by the breaches in the Kusabhadra to the local road between Phoolmora and Madhub. Trifling injury also

50. B.N. Sinha, *op.cit.*, p. 73.

51. Report on the floods in Lower Bengal in 1868, F.H. Rundall, Chief Engineer, Bengal Irrigation Branch, 11 December 1869.

took place to the Cuttack and Puri road about 5½ miles from Puri.[52]

In Mahanadi there was moderate flood, reading only 117.70 on the circuit house gauge. The greatest injuries occurred in the lower parts of the deltas of the Mahanadi and Brahmani.[53]

In civil subdivisional station of Jagatsinghpur there were no breaches. On the lands below that place, some 25 breaches were shown, aggregating 1,605 feet of length. The large tract was protected from inundation because the embankments were much improved. By the rivers Brahmani and Kharswan the greatest injuries were done to the embankments of Mahanadi division. Those rose respectively 6 inches and 1 foot higher than the flood recorded in 1862. It created a number of breaches. In the lower reaches of the Brahmani and the Kharswan, considerable damage was also done.[54]

The level of the flood in this locality had been higher than ever before known and the low lying tracts submerged for 8 to 12 days. The Naib of pargana Utikun asserted that 24,000 acres of paddy crop were more or less destroyed. In Killa Aul however the greatest destruction occurred. The devastation occurred in the areas situated between Kharswan and Brahmani which were exposed to the chronic flood of both the rivers. The new Aul road (which served as an embankment) got breached in several places and injury was caused from the flood of the river Kharswan. The embankments which were raised above the flood level of 1866 were over topped. The Kharswan river having risen 18 inches higher than the latter remained submerged for a long time. It was certain that 80 square miles of this tract remained uncultivated in that year. To help the flood-prone victims, rice was sent from the Government Golahs in shape of relief and work was provided in shape of repair of the embankments and roads.[55]

The flood also did a considerable damage to the country around Kendrapara and Marshaghai. The Chief Engineer of Irrigation reports thus about the flood of 1868, "By 3.00 p.m. on 11th June, the junction of the river Chitratola with the Mahanadi was reached and from that point the boats sailed across the country over which the floods were standing 6 to 7 feet deep, straight to Marshaghai, a distance of 10 miles; the country as far as the eye could reach was one vast sheet of water, the

52. A.G. Crommelin, Superintending Engineer, Cuttack Circle, to the Chief Engineer, BID, No. 1961, 9 October 1868.
53. Memorandum of Tour through the Province of Orissa by the Chief Engineer of Irrigation, see in supplement to the Calcutta Gazette, August 12, 1868, p. 570.
54. A.G. Crommelin, Superintending Engineer, Cuttack Circle, to the Chief Engineer, BID, No. 1961, 9 October 1868.
55. Supplement to the Calcutta Gazette, August 12, 1868, pp. 570-571.

tress and houses alone being apparent, and the water standing inside many of the latter; the people were seen moving off in boats, but the cattle were huddled together on the only dry spot of land visible in each village. The people said the inundation was as high as in the year 1866".[56] The total number of breaches caused in the Mahanadi division by the rivers other than the Kathjori is given below.[57]

	Breaches	*Length*
Government Embankment	203	3.6
Zamindari in Government care	133	4.6
Zamindari	5	0.6
	341	8.8

Out of this 341,81 were partial and the rest were totally destructive. The Cuttack-Kendrapara road severaly suffered due to the breaches in the right side of the Brahmani.

The southern portion of the Balasore district comprising the Jajpur subdivision was subject to the influences of the Kharswan and Baitarani. The embankments in this subdivision were injured severely and there were about 181 breaches. The greater part of these injuries was of course, caused by the Baitarani, which rose at the Akhuapada 11 inches higher than had ever been known before.[58] The Rebo Nala over topped by a depth of 6 feet, sweeping away the villages that were below its level and carrying away the villages that were below its level and carrying away thousands of cattle also destroyed the Dak Bungalow at Barripaore.[59] According to the information of the Assistant Collector of Bhadrak:

> "Villages along Rebo Nala and near Akhuapada in rains, about a dozen bodies lying on a side of road between Akhuapada and Bhadruck. I have seen this, cannot say whether the death due to drowning or cholera-cholera risen Virulent at Barripore and Akhuapada. Crop all destroyed. The trunk road breached every half mile".[60]

In the Ankura Sea Dyke, 80 breaches were reported aggregating 1.7 miles. The Busta subdivision principally affected by the Subarnarekha

56. *Ibid.*, p. 569.
57. A.G. Crommelin, Superintending Engineer, Cuttack Circle, to the Chief Engineer, BID, No. 1961, 9 October 1868.
58. A.G. Crommelin, Superintending Engineer, Cuttack Circle, to the Chief Engineer, BID, No. 1961, 9 October 1868.
59. Supplement to the Calcutta Gazette, August 12, 1868, p. 571.
60. T.F. Bignold, Offg. Collector, Balasore to the Secretary to the Board of Revenue, Fort William; No. 277, 23 June 1868.

was injured severely by the flood. About 132 breaches occurred, aggregating 6.2 miles in length. Sub-engineer O'Neil then in the service the late East India Canal Company inspected the locality which had suffered from the inundation and immediately reported that the water had swept over the province with an average depth of 6 feet and fully destroyed two-thirds of the standing rice crop and laid in ruins some 60 villages on both banks of the Baitarani and on the Rebo Nala. The affected people took refuge on the Calcutta road, and on the tops of houses, trees and the like.[61]

From Barripore onwards Balasore the injury was trifling. The road between Cuttack and Balasore was disrupted. On 18 June all communications with the north Balasore had been prevented by the flood of the Burabalang river. The Trunk road was extensively damaged for about 14 miles (between Dantoon and Rajghat). The new road at from Jaleswar to Balliaghye under construction was injured by the Subarnarekha floods for about first 8 miles from Jaleswar. Early sown rice crops were completely destroyed by this flood.[62] Advance was given from relief funds to the destitute and houseless people of Akhuapada. Some deaths took place among pilgrims Cholera broke out in Bhadrak town, which had ten or twelve death-toll. The Assistant Collector, Rampini granted advances for the purpose from the balance of the relief fund at his disposal.

About 150 persons were rescued by the police boats from the positions of considerable difficulties. The price of rice also increased. The figure given below shows the rates of rice per rupee prevailing in Balasore district.

	1st June	*17th June*
Balasore	32	21
Bhadrak	32	17
Soro	32	16

The Taccavi advances was also given to the farmers for the purchase of seed grain.[63] Much attention was not given by the Government to protect the flood affected people.

In the year 1862, 1866 and 1868 three important floods occurred in the Tahasil of Banki and caused several breaches on both right and left banks of Mahanadi. No information was found about loss of cattle, men

61. Report on the Floods in Lower Bengal in 1868; F.H. Rundall, Chief Engineer, Bengal Irrigation Branch, 11 December 1869.
62. Supplement to the Calcutta Gazette, August 12, 1868, p. 572.
63. T.F. Bignold, Offg. Collector to the Secretary to the Board of Revenue, Fort William, No. 274, Balasore, 18 June 1868.

and houses. The repairs were then carried out by Executive Engineer but the total charges were met from the revenue of this Killa. The statement below shows the cost of repairing bunds and the remission of revenue granted to ryots during the above period.[64]

Year	*Amount paid to the Executive Engineer on account of construction and reparation of bunds*	*Amount remitted to ryots*	*Total*
1862	3322-0-0	–	3322-0-0
1866	5850-15-4½	1372-3-3	7223-2-7½
1868	3625-2-8	1980-5-0	5605-7-8
Total	12798-2-½	3352-8-3	16150-10-3½

The Flood of 1872

The flood of July 1872 was the highest known since 1855 and it probably was the highest ever recorded. The reading at Naraj weir on 27 July 1855 were 93.11. While the readings on the gauge on 4 July 1872 were 93.30. On this day the floods topped the Ganjam and Puri roads and breached the embankments which protected the Calcutta road in its first mile on north of Mahanadi.[65] In Cuttack 1,135 square miles were inundated and where as in Puri 1070 square miles were inundated. Of these 2,205 square miles, about 600 were under water for 14 to 17 days and the rest from 7 to 10 days. Cuttack town was ex-communicated with the adjacent areas.[66] Cuttack town was in imminent danger and was only saved by the energy of the engineering staff who were aided by the military persons and prisoners from the Jail and they spent whole night on the earth works. The gauge readings on the Mahanadi river at 6.00 p.m. on the 29 June were 71.75 above sea level. The river continued to rise from 74.50 on 30th June to 75.85 on 4th July.[67]

Due to the communication disruption in Cuttack, during the flood, it was difficult to procure rice in Cuttack market. The nominal price was about 13 seers per rupee. The canals and embankments were seriously injured and the country was a vast sea of water stretching from Cuttack

64. Srinath Bose, Tahasildar of Banki to Mr. Walker, Superintending Engineer of Orissa Circle, 20 January 1875 (OSA).
65. *RAB*, 1872-73, p. 254.
66. *The Samaj*, 7 October 1982, Cuttack Natural Calamities.
67. *GAROD*, 1872-73, p. 2.

TABLE 1.3
LIST OF ANIMALS DESTROYED IN 1872

Name of the district	*Name of the subdivisions or police stations*	*Buffaloes*	*Cows and Bullocks*	*Goats*	*Sheep*	*Total*
Cuttack	Cuttack	107	1733	0	0	1840
	Jagatsinghpur	1308	14264	0	0	15572
	Kendrapara	994	1985	0	0	2979
	Jaipur	29	4994	0	0	5023
	Total	2438	22976	0	0	25414
Puri	Puri	1624	3094	0	0	4718
	Pipli	12	1809	0	0	1821
	Gop	500	2000	200	200	2900
	Khurda	500	3000	400	300	4200
	Tangi	50	40	0	0	90
	Banpur	314	1107	0	2	1423
	Total	3000	11050	600	502	15152
Balasore	Balasore	1765	227	0	0	1992
	Soro	571	29	0	6	606
	Basta	91	162	0	0	253
	Baliapal	0	0	0	0	0
	Jaleswar	0	0	0	0	0
	Bhadrak	0	0	0	0	0
	Basudevpur	963	769	0	0	1732
	Dhamnagar	34	28	0	0	62
	Mota	0	0	0	0	0
	Total	3424	1251	0	6	4645
	Grand Total	8862	35241	600	508	45211

to the cost, dotted here and there with a few village sites, where the people and the cattle found a temporary shelter and huddled together in the greatest distress.[68]

Puri district was also flooded by the Daya and Bhargabi rivers. Aid was given by means of taccavi advances for the purchase of seed grain.[69] Malud and Parikud of Puri district also suffered from floods. The Chilka

68. *GAROD*, 1872-73, p. 2.
69. *Ibid.*

LIST OF ANIMALS DESTROYED

CUTTACK DISTRICT

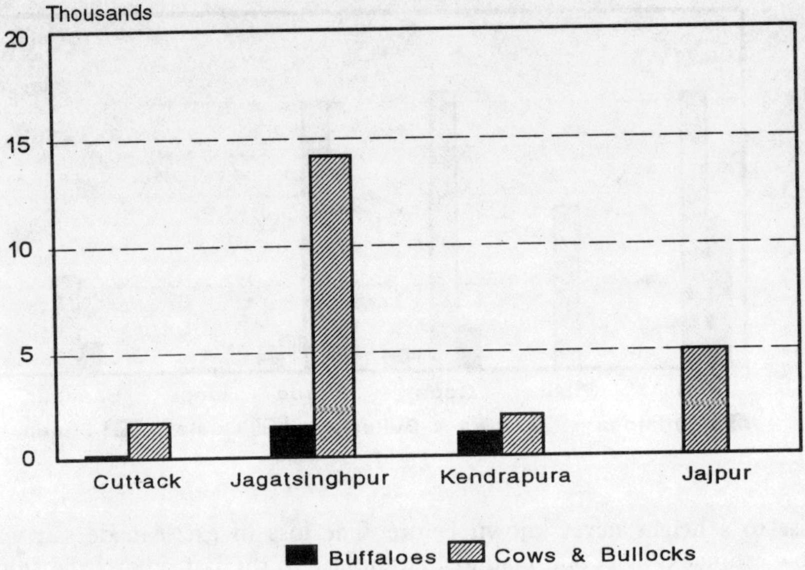

BALASORE DISTRICT

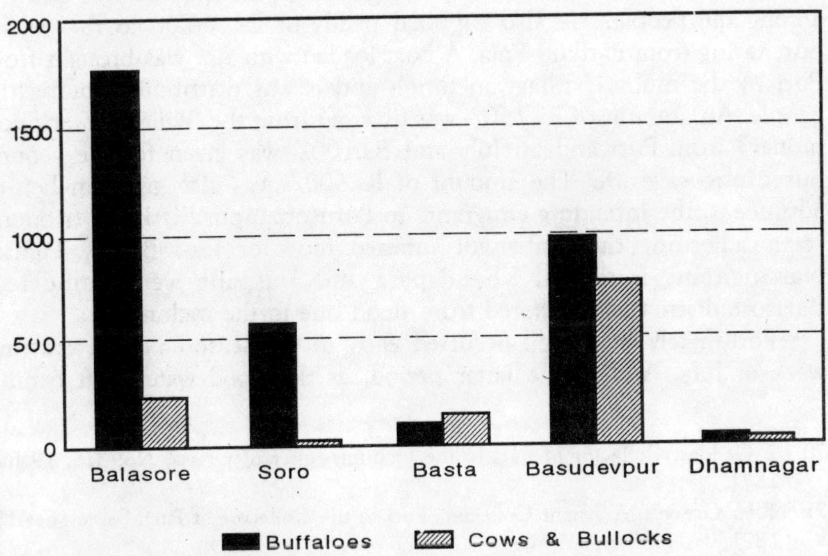

Fig. 1

LIST OF ANIMALS DESTROYED
PURI DISTRICT

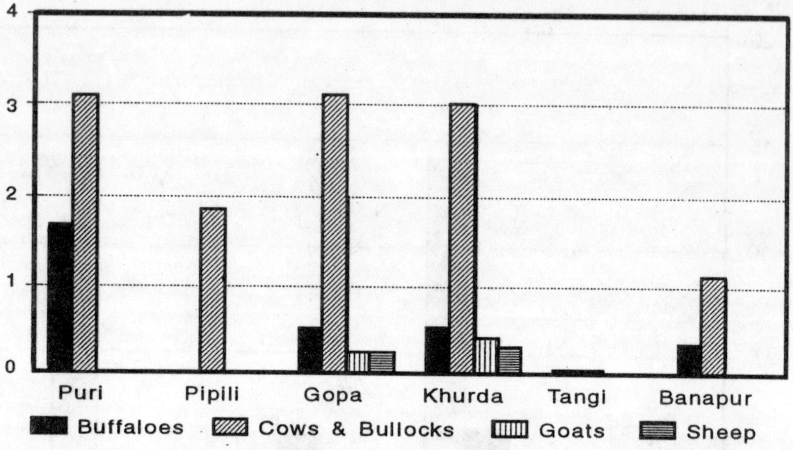

Fig. 2

rose to a height never known before. The loss in excise-made salt was now estimated at 12000 maunds. According to the last reports the stock in Kalupara godown near Tangi on the otherside of the Chilka was in serious danger. By the floods of Bhargabi, in a village near Damodarpur no less than 80 heads of cattle were lost.[70] The Assistant Collector immediately rushed to Parikud and Malud and distributed rice and dal among the people. He also supplied paddy of Rs. 60.00 to the people purchasing from Parikud Raja. A boat loaded with rice was brought from Puri by the muharir Bhagwan Singh and it was distributed among the people. An amount of Rs.250/- was diverted from the 'Relief subscription money" from Puri and 26 July and Rs.100/- was given for the general purpose to save life. The amount of Rs.500/- was also given in lieu of advance to the intending emigrants to Puruṣottampur.[71] All the tributary states adjoining the Mahanadi suffered more or less. Banki, Tigiria, Narsinghpur, Baramba, Khandapara and Daspalla were inundated. Balasore district also suffered from flood due to the cyclone.[72]

Fortunately this flood occurred early in the season *i.e.*, in the first week of July. And in the latter period, as the flood waters left behind

---

70. J. Geddes, Collector of Puri to the Commissioner of Orissa, No. 325, 19 July 1872.
71. R.H. Greaves, Assistant Collector, Puri to the Collector of Puri, September 19, 1872.
72. *GAROD*, 1872-73, p. 2.

layers of silt, a good crop was obtained from most of the inundated lands.[73] Availability of official statistics shows below the damages of animals caused by the flood in Orissa in 1872.[74]

The Naraj weir, which had been damaged by the flood of 1872, was strengthened. The Mahanadi weir was repaired and at the same time the revetment at Jobra workshop was strengthened. The old Maratha wall of 240 feet round the city of Cuttack was rebuilt. At the same time that of 325 feet was in progress with the reconstruction which fell during the year.[75] "The protective works of the city were maintained in good order".[76]

Banki suffered a lot by the floods of June and July of 1872. The flood caused a great loss of cattle and grain. The Banki and Trigiria embankments were not in a good condition to protect the people from the high flood.[77]

The Flood of 1874

In July 1874, the rivers Mahanadi and Brahmani rose to the height of flood and did some damage to the crops of low lands. Rain was heavy of 6 August, when the Brahmani and Baitarani came down in great force and damaged many embankments and submerged the whole low land crops. In the following week the Mahanadi also rose and submerged large tracts in the south and centre of the district. Throughout September the country remained flooded especially by the Brahmani and Baitarani and the former rose again in October and destroyed the crops. The crops in low lying tracts of Kanika, Aul and Kalamatia suffered a lot. The low lying lands in the south-east of Balasore district suffered severely from the inundations in the month of August by the Baitarani and Salandi.

Heavy rainfall in June and July caused great inundation and Breaches of embankments in Puri district. The crops were seriously affected by the high floods. The average rainfall in Orissa division is given below compared with that of last year.[78]

	1873-74	*1874-75*
Balasore	48.43	52.25
Cuttack	44.55	69.75
Puri	55.66	68.28
Divisional average	49.59	63.42

73. *The Samaj*, 7 October, *op.cit.*
74. *U.D.*, 1872, quoted in Bulletin No. 4, compiled by S.C.De, pp. 33-34 (OSA).
75. *RAB*, 1873-74, p. 141.
76. *Ibid.*, 1874-75, p. 305.
77. From the Superintending Engineer, Orissa Circle, to the Superintendent of Tributary Mahals, No. 428, 28 January 1873.
78. *GAROD*, 1874-75, pp. 2-3.

In Balasore fever was prevalent after the rains. Cholera broke out in many parts of the district. After the heavy rains low fever was prevalent in Cuttack district. In cholera and dysentery were the recurrent features in Puri district during the pilgrim festivals.[79]

The Floods from 1877 to 1880

In July 1877, heavy rain fall caused floods on some parts of Cuttack and Balasore districts.[80] The sudden and heavy fall of rain of 12 inches on 12 July and of 16 inches on 13 July caused the rivers to rise rapidly. The Baitarani river rose on 13 and 14 July 1877 to an unprecedented high point. The flood caused immense damage to the Trunk road and high level canal. Protective embankments were breached in many places. The Akhuapada inspection bungalow, police outpost, and bazar were washed away and no less than 21 villages between the river bank and the protective embankments were destroyed. The villagers lost stored rice, cattle and household goods of an amount of Rs. 37,923. According to the police report one human life was lost. Of course less damage was done to the rice crops.

The Collector of Cuttack gave the details of the flood in Baitarani thus:

"The river Baitarani rose unusually high from 11.00 p.m. of the 13th to 6.00 p.m. of the 15th July 1877; causing much damage to the embankments, canal, bunds, houses, crops, cattle etc., of the villages adjoining the bund. The maximum height of flood was 9 feet 5 inches, although it exceeded the ordinary flood levels but less than the great flood of 1868 *i.e.*, 11 feet 5 inches. The 2nd and 3rd ranges of the canal at Akhuapada were very seriously injured. The water submerged the village roads and the Calcutta main road also suffered and the mail was temporarily stopped. The number of houses destroyed by the flood in Thanas Jajpur, Dharmasala and Aul seemed to be 1,188 which was ascertained by the police. The Brahmani, Nuna Chitratola and Paika rivers over flowed their banks causing the rice fields to be submerged for sometime. The crops on the low land were washed away. No important damage took place to the property and live of the people".[81]

In 1878 there was a moderate flood in Cuttack district.[82] All the rivers of Orissa were in flood in August 1879. The floods were high in Mahanadi and Brahmani rivers and their branches. In Balasore the flood of Baitarani was not as destructive as in Puri and Cuttack.[83] The flood

79. *Ibid.*, pp. 3-4.
80. *RAB, 1877-78, p. 128.*
81. GAROD, 1877-78, pp. 6-7.
82. *Ibid.*, 1878-79, p. 288.
83. *Ibid.*, 1879-80, p. 6.

was higher than any other flood except that of 1855 and 1872. The Cuttack city was rescued some how but the lower part of the district suffered a lot. In Jagatsinghpur the crops suffered a lot. The embankment at Kaliabod was breached and it destroyed many houses. One man was drowned in the water and the roads were overtopped by the flood water. The people of that area reported that such flood did not occur within last twenty years.[84] In the Jajpur subdivision, much damage was done in pargana Alti by the flood water of the Brahmani and by a breach near Jenapur in parganas Bari and Olash. Over a large tract of these parganas, 12 annas of the crops were destroyed chiefly by the caterpillars which were brought on by the flood.[85] Gupta, the subdivisional officer of Kendrapara depicted the effects of flood in his subdivision in the following manner:

"The flood was severe than the usual. The rivers began to rise early in August at the rate of six inches a day, increasing to over a foot by the night of the 13th after which the water began to fall, having sunk to a depth of 9½ feet by the 24th. The next day, however, the rivers began to rise again and continued to rise till the 2nd of September. The third and last flood commenced on the 13th and with fluctuations of rise and fall, lasted till the last October. During the first flood the Brahmani breached the Zamindary bund near Bosepore and flooded Indupur and other villages lying outside the Pattamundai canals. Many houses were destroyed and numbers of people had to take shelter on the flood bank of the canal. The rivers like the Nuna and the Chitratola, were also in flood, and caused serious damage to parts of Kujang, Balubisi Sukuai and Pyna. The losses in open and unprotected tracts like Kalamatia were much greater than that in ordinary years. Nearly for a week the people of the inundated tracts were confined to their houses. Luckily, there was only one casuality in which a man was killed by being burried under a falling wall.

The sufferings of the cattle were even more intense and much more prolonged. For days together they had to stand in mud and water and were half starved for want of folder. The number of houses totally destroyed was 1,753 and of those partially damaged was 965".[86]

On 23 August it was reported that 2000 cows were washed away by the Mahanadi flood near Jobra. Two cowherds however escaped narrowly. Some details about high floods which occurred in Orissa from 1855 to 1879 are given below:[87]

---

84. *U.D.*, 16 August 1879.
85. N.N. Banerjee, *op.cit.*, p. 177.
86. *GAROD*, 1879-80, p. 7;
    N.N. Banerjee, *op.cit.*, p. 177.
87. *U.D.*, 23 August 1879.

TABLE 1.4
THE HIGH FLOODS FROM 1855 TO 1879

Name of the Place	*1855*	*1857*	*1872*	*1874*	*1876*	*1877*	*1879*
Kathjori river at Lalbagh	82'74"	82'1"	82'24"	80'24"	79'71"	78'4"	81'3"
Mahanadi at Jobra			75'11"	73'11"	73'3"	72'44"	75'54"

A high flood also occurred in Puri which was more destructive than that of Cuttack. The Sadar subdivision was fully flooded. Many embankments were breached. In Kakatpur two men were drowned. The crops were also totally destroyed.[88]

The then Collector of Cuttack Nolan ordered that the fund Rs. 1156/- collected from Kendrapara to help the draught prone victims of Madras, which could not be sent due to some unavoidable circumstances should now be distributed among the flood stricken people.[89] A very small sum was also given to Puri district as taccavi advance.[90] Due to the effect of the floods of the Mahanadi, the average price of common rice rose in 1879-80 to 21 seers 9 chhataks per rupee against 20 seers 5 chhataks in 1878-79, for the general failure of the biali and also of sarada crops in many places the prices also increased.[91] The people did not get sufficient help at the time of flood as per their expectation.

In the month of August 1880 both rain and flood simultaneously devastated the Cuttack district. The Mahanadi, the Brahmani and their tributaries remained in high spate in this district. The chief damage in the sadar subdivision was in pargana Binahar, which was caused by breaches in the Alanka embankment. Kendrapara was also affected by the rise of the Mahanadi, the Brahmani, and the Gobri, but the damage done, as compared with that of the previous year, was considerable. These rivers began to rise on the 28th of June. The Brahmani inundated a portion of the country three months later in September. The Gobri, although a small river, rising to an unprecedented height, submerged a great portion of the fertile lands and also destroyed the paddy crops.

The following figures give the rainfall at the sadar subdivision of each of the districts of Orissa during the years 1879-81.

88. *U.D.*, 23 August 1879.
89. *Ibid.*
90. *GAROD*, 1879-80, p. 8.
91. *Ibid.*, p. 13.

	1878-80 Inches	1880-81 Inches
Cuttack	61.16	66.78
Puri	54.12	87.98
Balasore	54.33	75.73

Though a small amount of local damages was done by the floods, the year was exceptionally favourable for agriculturists.[92]

The Floods of 1881 and 1882

In 1881 the north of Cuttack district and some parts of Balasore district were affected much by the floods of the Brahmani and Baitarani.[93] In 1881 flood, 45 breaches occurred in the embankments on the Kathjori and its affluent the Kuakhai and other branches; only three breaches occurred in the embankments of the Mahanadi and its branches.[94] The chief feature of the year was the repeated floods of the rivers in the north of the district. And the whole of the sarad crop on the lands, from the Brahmani in the south to the Baitarani in the north was swept away by the floods of July. With some intervals the flood continued till the first week of August and the rivers were unusually high until the beginning of September. The result was that in some parts of Jajpur and in Aul and Kanika of Kendrapara the time for replanting the crops was lost. In the Ward's estate of Kanika the greater portion of the crop was lost in 178 villages for which a remission amounting to Rs. 22,366/- had been necessary. But Ahiyas, Bantara, Barana, Baruya, Dolegram, Hodh and Olash parganas were less affected.[95] The breaches in the Brahmani also affected the western portion of the district on the left of the Trunk road. The continuance of the floods till October prevented a second sowing of rice.

Under the prevailing circumstances, many had to leave their villages for employment in Calcutta and elsewhere.[96] In Dhamnagar about 4½ annas were lost by flood and drought and the same conditions occurred in Dolsahi. In the south of Chandbali and Basundebpur the crops were destroyed. In Jaleswar, Kamarda and single in the north, about 6 annas

92. N.N. Banerjee, *op.cit.*, p. 177;
RAB, 1880-81, p. 144.
93. *RAB*, 1881-82, p. 129;
W.A. Inglis, *The Canals and Flood Banks of Bengal*, p. 236.
94. *Ibid.*
95. *GAROD*, 1881-82, p. 7.
96. N.N. Banerjee, *op.cit.*, p. 178.

of crops were lost.[97] During flood and also later the Government did not take any remedial measures to help the destitute people or did not grant any remissions or suspensions of revenue.[98]

There was in increase, in the mortality from fever in Puri due to the frequent floods in July, September and October.[99] The material conditions of the people of Cuttack during the year was not bad but continued low prices of agricultural produce even in the neighbourhood of Cuttack, where the crops were best, had left the agriculturists without much margin of earnings in money. In Jajpur there was a great amount of discomfort and temporary suffering owing to the floods which destroyed many houses and much property. The apprehensions of distress which had been at first raised, were not verified. As a result a large number of people had left their homes for work in Calcutta and other places of Bengal during the year.

In Kendrapara the condition of the people did not improve during the year. The main crop in some parts was very short; while prices were lower than in the previous year. Zamindars were in a great difficulty to collect their rents. Most of the people of Aul and Kanika went to Calcutta for Job. However embankment works were in progress to provide food for the time being.[100] On the whole Government did not take any preventive measures to protect the people from the peril of flood.

In the year 1882 there was a high flood in the Mahanadi. The level at Naraj on 26 July of that year was 92.10 and at Bellevue on the Kathjori, it was 83.30. Puri district suffered from this flood and many embankments were breached in all directions. Cuttack district was less affected. The Kendrapara canal and the Kendrapara extension canal from Marsaghai to Jambu were overtopped and breached in many places. However the damage done to the crops was not serious.[101] There was also high flood in the Subarnarekha. The embankment surrounding Bhograi and 10 to 15 parganas adjacent to it was washed away by this flood. The flood water continued to stay for 12 days and destroyed the crops. So the people were bushed into embarassment for hardly did they find any device to maintain their family after paying revenue to the Government. They also demanded to build the Bhograi embankment higher to protect the parganas from the floods.[102] But the Government did not take any preventive measures to protect the country from the effects of floods.

97. *GAROD*, 1881-82, p.7.
98. *U.D.* 13 August, 1881.
99. *GAROD*, 1881-82, p. 10.
100. *GAROD*, 1881-82, p. 12..
101. W.A. Inglis, *op.cit.*, p. 236.
102. *U.D.*, 25 August 1883; P. Mukherjee, *Irrigation, Inland Navigation and Flood Problems in North Orissa during the British Rule*, p. 47.

The Floods of 1884 and 1885

In September 1884, there was a high flood. The ordianry supplies were disrupted both at Jajpur and Kendrapara. The price of rice at this time rose from 24 to 20 seers per rupee and later on to 10 seers. The subdivisional officer of Kendrapara also noticed that the crops of Utikan and Aul parganas suffered a good deal from the inundations due to the cut of protective embankment of the Brahmani.[103] In Banki the crops were entirely swept away. This year people also faced the scarcity of rice. The sub-deputy Collector was deputed to inspect the inundated tracts. The people hoped, there might be relaxation in payment of revenue and care was taken for that. The Deputy Collector also proposed to dig 2 wells at the time of scarcity of food. Many mauza of Dampara and Khurda also suffered from the flood.[104] In Baramba and Narsinghpur some damage was caused by floods of the same year.[105]

The highest flood in the year 1885 in Mahanadi river was that of the 19th July when the gauge at Naraja read 82.50, or 8.25 feet below the highest point attained by the flood, and 8.50 feet below that of 1879.[106] It was also observed that the highest flood of the year in the Baitarani river took place in the month of September. The rever Salandi also reached its highest level in September 1885. The Table 1.5 depicts the highest flood levels in the year 1885-86.[107]

In the month of June, the highest flood of the year occured in the Mahanadi and its branches in the month of August. In the month of June 1885, a high flood visited Puri district which entirely damaged the crops on the low lands where replanting was impossible. The high flood of July caused some damage to the crops on the low lands in Banki and in the inundated tracts of the district.[108] The embankments within the Puri division suffered more severely, as the returns show 73 breaches with a joint length of 19,453 feet or 3.69 miles, took place by the flood

Mahanadi and branches	8	3,992
Kathjori and branches	39	8,175
Kuakhai and branches	50	13,283
Total	97	25,450

103. *GAROD*, 1884-85, p. 7.
104. *U.D.*, 27 December 1884.
105. *RAB*, 1884-85, p. 8.
106. R.H. Rhind, Superintending Engineer, Orissa, Circle to the Chief Engineer, Bengal Public Works Department, No. 4658, Cuttack, 12 October 1887.
107. *Ibid.*, No. 3004, Cuttack, 6 July 1887.
108. *GAROD*, 1885-86, pp. 6-7.

Flood in the year 1885-86

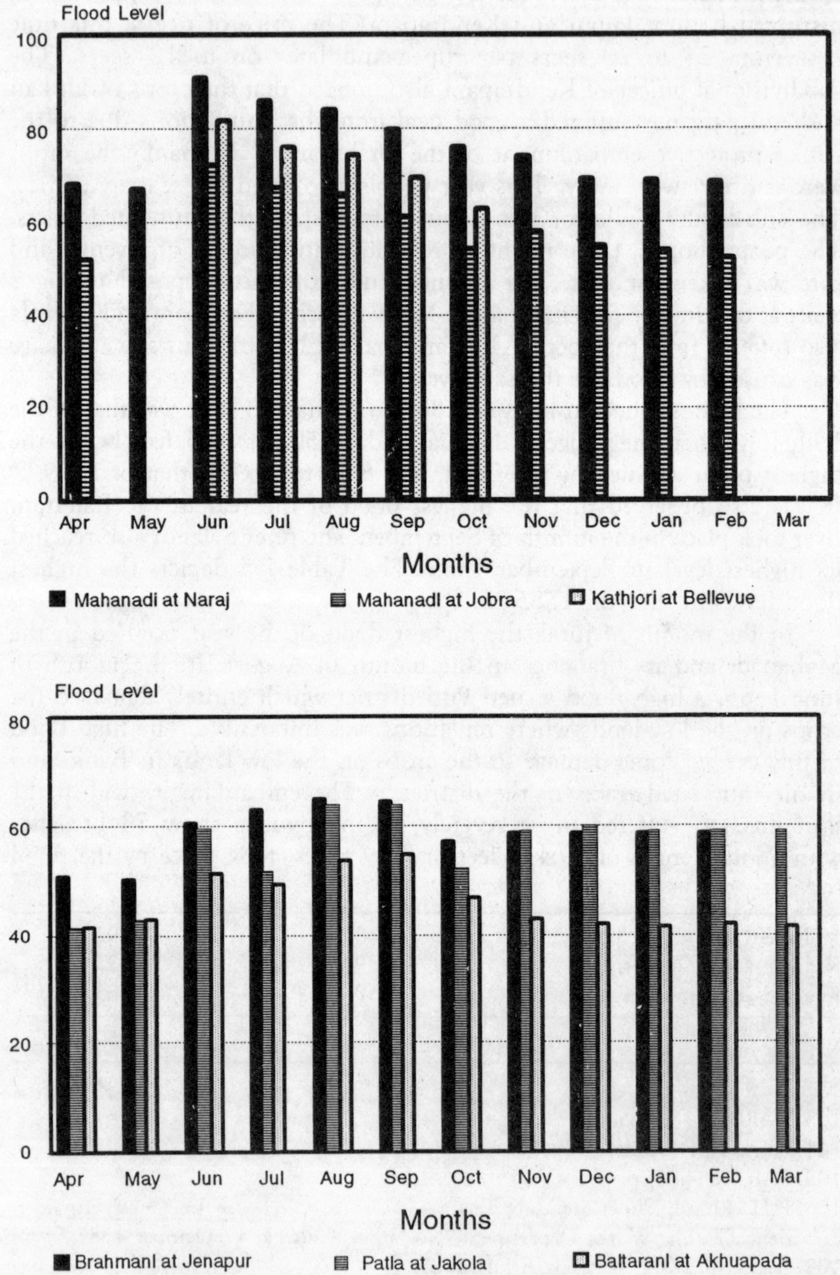

Fig. 3

TABLE 1.5
HIGHEST FLOOD LEVELS IN PRINCIPAL RIVERS IN THE YEARS 1885 AND 1986

Month and Year	*Mahanadi at Naraj above weir*	*Mahanadi at Jobra below weir*	*Kathjori at Bellevue*	*Brahmani at Jenapur below weir*	*Patia at Jakodia below weir*	*Baitarani at Akhua-pada below weir*	*Salandi at Randia*
April 1885	68.20	52.05	-	50.60	41.25	41.45	45.35
May 1885	67.20	-	-	50.20	42.80	42.50	47.40
June 1885	90.75	72.30	81.65	60.40	59.45	51.00	47.90
July 1885	86.00	67.45	75.90	62.90	51.60	49.00	48.85
August 1885	84.00	66.00	74.35	64.80	63.65	53.70	53.10
September 1885	79.75	61.25	69.55	64.10	63.65	54.50	57.65
October 1885	75.90	54.20	62.75	56.80	51.80	46.80	47.80
November 1885	74.05	58.00	-	58.20	58.75	42.70	46.02
December 1885	69.10	55.00	-	58.65	59.95	41.91	45.50
January 1886	68.75	54.00	-	58.35	58.85	41.35	45.25
February 1886	68.62	52.20	-	58.45	58.75	41.75	45.10
March 1886	-	-	-	-	58.95	41.25	45.40

of 1885. There were 23 breaches with a total length of 6,170 feet in Cuttack district. The total number of breaches which occurred in both divisions during the year under review were distributed among the three rivers in the manner:[109]

Usually when high floods occurred in the Mahanadi, Puri district through which Kuakhai and its branches passed was the worst sufferer.

About the flood of 1885 in the Mahanadi river, at Beranassi point, above Cuttack, the reading was 84.35 above mean sea level, as compared with 81.95 in the previous year and 84.37 in the high flood of 1879. The present flood was higher by 2.40 feet than that of 1884 at this place, but 0.02 feet lower than the flood of 1879. At the circuit house, above the Mahanadi weir, the flood of 1885 stood at 76.10 above datum, as compared with 73.95 in 1884 and 76.80 in 1879. It was below the recorded levels of the flood of June 1885 at several important points on the right bank of the Mahanadi river, below the weir at Jobra.[110]

The highest flood of the year in the Brahmani river occurred on the 26th of August, upon which date the readings above and below the Brahmani weir were 65.20 and 64.80 respectively. The highest levels of the water above and below the Patia weir at the left bank in the flood of

109. R.H. Rhind, *op.cit.*
110. R.H. Rhind, *op.cit.*

	1879	*1884*	*1885*
Head of the Sukhpyka	60.58	57.18	60.45
Outfall of Sukhpyka	41.89	87.73	41.85
Outfall of the cross Kathjori at Jeypore	33.35	29.71	32.95
Head of the Punkpal	22.97	19.77	20.50
Taldunda	16.66	15.32	16.45
Paradeep	10.18	7.10	10.50

1885 were 63.70 and 63.65 respectively. The highest flood of the year in the Baitarani river took place on the 24th of September, when the gauge below the Baitarani weir at Akhuapada read 54.50, or 9.29 feet below the level attained by the high flood of 1881 at that point and 3.30 feet below the highest reading recorded in the previous year, as the discharge of this river was affected by the heavy rainfall caused by the cyclone of September 1885.

No breaches occurred during the floods of 1885 in any of the embankments on the Baitarani and its branches, but some of those on the Kharswan river suffered to some extent in consequence of the cyclone of September 1885. In the Puri division the flood of June 1885 caused a considerable amount of damage to the provincial roads, as a breach which occurred in the left bank of the Kuakhai river breached the Puri road of a distance of 13 miles. In the Mahanadi division the floods caused some injury to the distributaries of the first sections of the Taldanda and Machhagan canals.[111] By the flood of 1885, Orissa division suffered a lot. It was found that 24 families from the villages of Zilla Balbhadrapur in Khurda emigrated to Runpore and Chabiskud, being tired of losing their crops so frequently from the floods of the Daya river.[112]

The Floods of 1886 and 1887

The highest flood of the year 1886, in the Mahanadi and Brahmani rivers and their branches took place in the month of July and that the highest rise in the Baitarani river occurred in the month of October, while the highest recorded flood of the year in the Salandi was that of the 23rd August 1886. The flood of that year was the lowest which had occurred in this river during the last 16 years. The Table 1.6 depicts the highest flood levels in the year 1886-87.[113]

There was no natural calamity of any exceptional character such as

111. R.H. Rhind, *op.cit.*
112. *GAROD*, 1885-86, p. 14.
113. R.H. Rhind, *op.cit.*, No. 4658, Cuttack 12 October 1887.

high floods or severe storms in 1886 and it was generally reported that the outturn of crops was larger than in any season during the last eight or ten years.[114]

The highest flood of 1887 in the Mahanadi river was that of the 26th August, when the gauge at Naraja read 87.70 a level which was lower by 3.05 feet than the flood of 1885, which rose to 90.75 at this point. In the year 1887, there were four floods in the months of July and August, which rose to a higher level than this in the Kathjori at Cuttack. The following were the readings for the four floods at the Bellevue gauge:

Flood of 16th July 1887	..	76.25
Flood of 27th July 1887	..	77.85
Flood of 12th August 1887	..	74.95
Flood of 26th August 1887	..	78.75

TABLE 1.6
HIGHEST FLOOD LEVELS IN PRINCIPAL RIVERS IN THE YEARS 1886 AND 1887

Month and Year	*Mahanadi at Naraj above weir*	*Mahanadi at Jobra below weir*	*Kathjori at Bellevue*	*Brahmani at Jenapur below*	*Patia at Jakodia below weir*	*Baitarani at Akhua-pada below weir*	*Salandi at Randia*
April 1886	68.25	51.70	-	49.60	55.75	41.20	45.13
May 1886	68.23	53.50	-	50.30	51.90	41.15	44.95
June 1886	76.00	59.00	60.12	58.20	57.30	46.80	47.78
July 1886	82.50	64.35	73.00	63.00	62.00	47.20	50.48
August 1886	80.10	63.10	70.50	59.80	60.00	50.20	53.88
September 1886	79.50	62.60	70.00	61.50	60.90	51.00	52.28
October 1886	78.25	61.65	67.22	59.40	59.10	53.60	-
November 1886	75.00	59.70	58.15	54.60	59.10	45.40	-
December 1886	73.08	58.60	-	53.50	42.70	40.65	-
January 1887	69.48	56.90	-	-	42.00	40.65	-
February 1887	68.99	55.90	-	52.40	41.15	40.63	-
March 1887	67.80	52.15	-	50.70	41.10	40.34	-

The highest flood of the year in the Brahmani river was that which took place on the 12th July, when the guage below the weir at Jenapur read 61.60. The highest reading which was observed in the Baitarani river, below the weir at Akhuapada was that of the 26th July, when the flood rose to a reduced level of 52.20. The Salandi river, however rose to a greater height than it did in the year 1886, as the reading at Randia at

114. *GAROD*, 1886-87, p. 4.

Flood in the year 1886-87

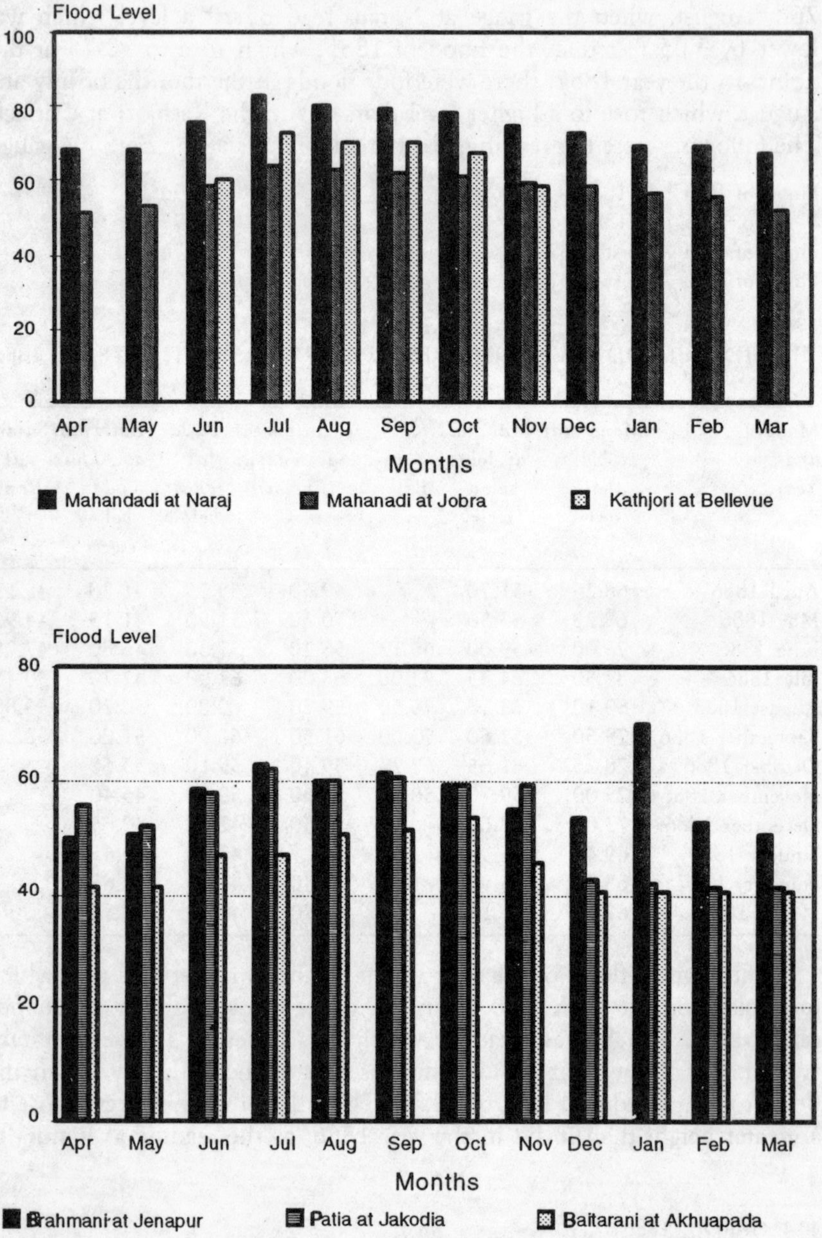

Fig. 4

the end of the high level canal, 3rd range, was 59.78 on the September, as compared with those of 53.88 in August 1886.[115] The highest flood in the Mahanadi occurred, in the month of August. The flood of July 1887 in the Brahmani was lower than the one which took place in the same month in 1886, although there was a considerable increase in the July rainfall at Jenapur.

At Naraja gauge in the Mahanadi the highest reading of the year 1887, as previously stated as 87.70 and in the Kathjori at Cuttack the same flood rose to 78.75; while at the head of the Kuakhai river the reading of the flood of 26 August 1887 was 78.18. The gauge readings in various branches of the Kuakhai in the previous years were as follows:[116]

	1879	*1885*	*1886*	*1887*
Head of the Kuakhai	80.03	81.03	71.68	78.18
Head of Kusabhadra	68.82	71.90	61.05	68.12
Head of Daya	55.00	54.67	46.97	52.67
At Kantee on the Daya	36.50	35.85	26.35	31.10
At Satpara on the Chilka lake	3.95	3.00	3.30	3.40
At Janakadeipur, on the Bhargabi branch	23.60	21.23	18.48	22.73

The floods of 1887 did not cause much damage to the material prosperity of the people.

The Floods of 1888

The heavy floods in 1888 caused by the copious rainfall in August and September injuriously affected the crops in many places in Cuttack and Balasore.[117] The highest floods which occurred in the Mahanadi, Brahmani and Baitarani rivers took place in the month of August and the Salandi rose to its greatest height during September 1888. The Table 1.7 depicts the maximum rises which occurred during the year 1888-89 in each of the principal rivers.[118]

It was also lower than the floods of 1872, 1879 and 1885. The highest flood of the year in the Mahanadi was that of the 11 August, when the gauge at Naraja read 85.80 and at Bellevue gauge in the Kathjori river at Cuttack it was 76.85. The highest flood of the year in the Brahmani river took place on the 24th August and the gauge below the weir at Jenapur then read 66.20 and the highest flood at the Baitarani

115. R.H. Rhind, *op.cit.*, No. 5907, Cuttack, 16 November 1888.
116. *Ibid.*
117. *GAROD*, 1888-89, p. 4
118. R.H. Rhind, *op.cit.*, No. 4650, Cuttack 22 October 1889.

Flood in the year 1888-89

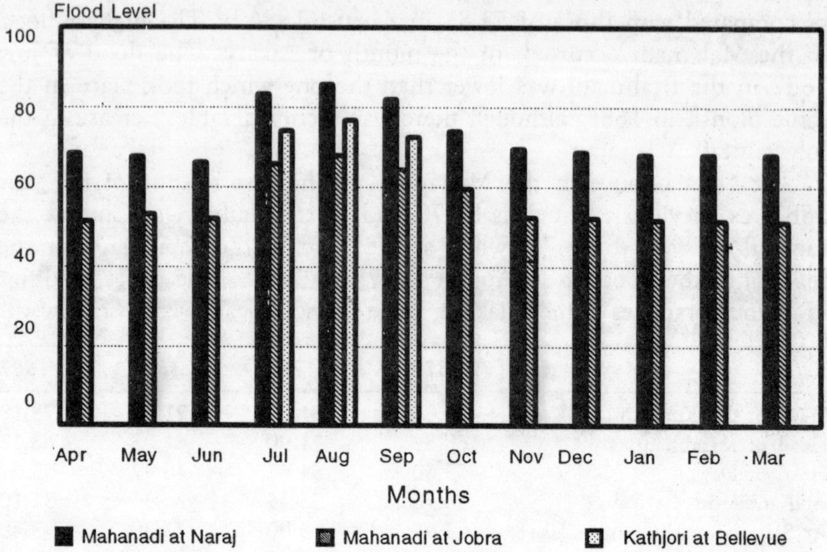

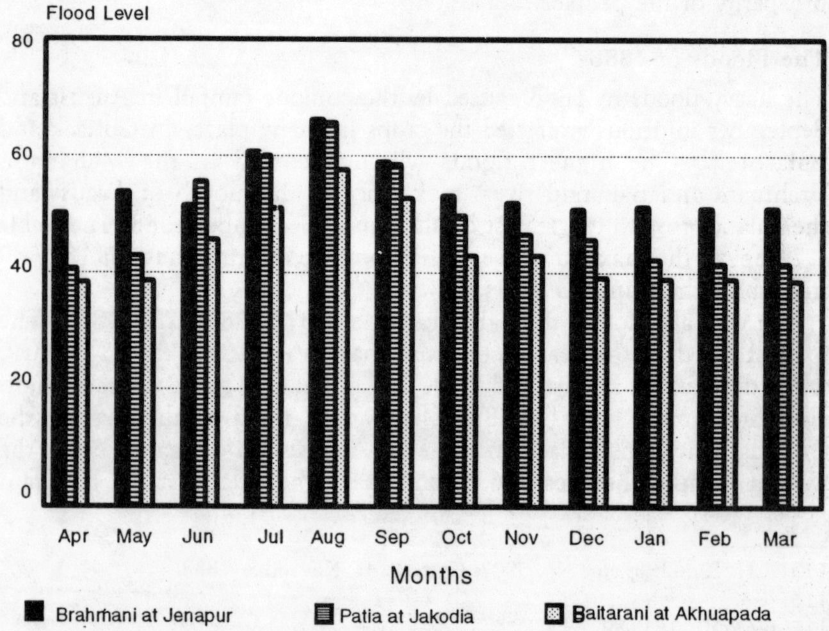

Fig. 5

TABLE 1.7
HIGHEST FLOOD LEVELS IN PRINCIPAL RIVERS IN THE YEARS 1888 AND 1889

Month and Year	*Mahanadi at Naraja above weir*	*Mahanadi at Jobra below weir*	*Kathjori at Bellevue*	*Brahmani at Jenapur below weir*	*Patia at Jakodia below weir*	*Baitarani at Akhuapada below weir*	*Salandi at Randia*
April 1888	68.50	51.45	-	50.00	40.55	38.33	-
May 1888	67.60	53.10	-	53.70	42.80	38.40	-
June 1888	66.22	51.95	-	51.35	55.55	45.50	45.20
July 1888	83.30	65.80	74.15	60.60	60.10	51.00	47.53
August 1888	85.80	68.00	76.85	66.20	65.60	57.60	55.88
September 1888	81.85	64.40	72.50	58.90	58.60	52.70	57.98
October 1888	74.10	59.50	-	53.10	49.70	42.90	-
November 1888	69.60	52.37	-	51.85	46.50	42.70	-
December 1888	68.75	52.25	-	50.80	45.50	39.10	-
January 1889	68.15	51.75	-	51.10	42.15	38.95	-
February 1889	68.10	51.50	-	51.00	41.45	38.85	-
March 1889	68.15	51.25	-	51.00	41.45	38.60	-

river, below the weir at Akhuapada, was 57.60 The flood in the river rose highest to a level of 57.98 at Randia at the end of the high level canals, III Range, on the 17th September. The figures given below show the rainfall in the principal centres of each district of the Orissa division during 1888-89 as compared with the previous two years.

		1886-87 inches	*1887-88 inches*	*1888-89 inches*
Cuttack	Cuttack	77.04	54.06	52.21
	Jajpur	66.52	52.09	62.96
	Kendrapara	66.13	60.55	46.78
	Banki	72.81	41.39	45.46
Puri	Puri	56.30	37.50	39.72
	Khurda	67.10	41.16	44.98
Balasore	Balasore	69.63	58.25	59.98
	Bhadrak	63.98	54.36	52.05

So the rain in the early part of the year retarded cultivation, while the heavy floods caused by the copious rainfall in August and September injuriously affected the crops in many places of Balasore and Cuttack.[119]

119. *RAB*, 1888-89, p. 24.

No breaches occurred during the year in any of the embankments which were under the care of the Mahanadi division, but in the embankments belonging to the Puri division there were breaches, with a total length of 1,372 feet, which took place in the branches of the Kusabhadra and Bhargabi rivers, and in the minor branches of the Kathjori. The Executive Engineer of Puri division, reported that the breaches occurred on the Bhargabi river, were caused by the flood water having risen above the crests of the embankments. As the flood of the year 1888 in the Baitarani river was a moderate one, no breaches took place in the embankments belonging to the Akhuapada-Jajpur division. The special damage which was caused by the floods of the year under study, occurred in that part of the Orisa Trunk road which lies between the Brahmani and Baitarani rivers, where some small breaches were formed in thę road, and portions of the metalling were washed away from its crest.[120]

The price of rice, which was the staple crop of Orissa, rose everywhere, and the figures given below bear testimony to it.

AVERAGE PRICE OF COMMON RICE PER RUPEE

	1887-88		*1888-89*	
	S	C	S	C
Cuttack	19	3	17	15
Jajpur	25	2	22	3
Kendrapara	27	3	22	4
Puri	21	11	19	1
Khurda	20	15	17	5
Balasore	25	5	22	3
Bhadrak	26	0	24	3

The material condition of the people was very bad. The landless labouring classes suffered more or less everywhere. In Khurda subdivision there was considerable distress and relief operations on an extensive scale were rendered imperative. Distress was also felt in Banki in consequence of a scarcity of the food supply and it had continued during the current year, necessiting the provision of relief works.[121] On account of the inundation in September, there was temporary distress in thanas Chandbali and Basudebpur of Balasore district. Private subscriptions were raised at both Balasore and Bhadrak and immediate relief measures were provided to the sufferers in these thanas and in Baliapal also. From the Calcutta Relief Fund Rs. 6000 was diverted on relief work for the above

120. R.H. Rhind, *op.cit.*
121. *RAB*, 1888-89, p. 108.

two thanas. The Bhograi tract suffered most from failure of crops where the rice crop was destroyed in an area of 50 square miles. Employments were also provided by the Public Works Department for repairing of embankments. The district board sanctioned Rs. 2000 in order to provide labour to the destitutes. The Collector also gave an advance of Rs. 4620 from the subscriptions raised, to supply food to a number of women and children owing to partial failure of crops in Balasore. A large number of men also went away to Calcutta and other places in search of work.[122] From the above description, the insufficiency of the Governments stand to relieve distress from the affected tracts could be easily understood.

The Floods from 1889 to 1891

The floods of the year 1889-90 and their maximum rises which occurred in the years in each of the principal rivers are shown in the Table 1.8.

The highest flood of the year in the Mahanadi was that of the 20th August, when the gauge at Naraja read 87.00. It was a moderate one for this river. The highest flood in the Brahmani river took place on the 18th August and the gauge reading below the weir at Jenapur was then 67.50. The Baitarani river was also at its highest point this year on the 18th August, when the reading below the weir at Akhuapada was 55.80 and in the Salandi river at Randia during the year under review was 56.73.[123]

TABLE 1.8

HIGHEST FLOOD LEVELS IN PRINCIPAL RIVERS IN THE YEARS 1889 & 1890

Month and Year	*Mahanadi at Naraj above weir*	*Mahanadi at Jobra below weir*	*Kathjori at Bellevue*	*Brahmani at Jenapur below weir*	*Patia at Jakodia below weir*	*Baitarani at Akhua-pada below weir*	*Salandi at Randia*
April 1889	67.65	51.20	-	51.00	41.30	38.43	-
May 1889	65.75	54.70	-	-	47.30	-	-
June 1889	73.75	58.70	-	60.20	59.25	44.80	51.60
July 1889	84.00	66.25	75.00	61.20	59.70	43.80	49.79
August 1889	87.00	68.90	78.00	67.50	65.70	55.80	56.73
September 1889	80.25	64.75	72.75	59.50	58.10	45.70	50.83
October 1889	78.75	62.00	68.76	56.30	52.10	48.20	46.98
November 1889	77.90	60.50	-	58.40	49.45	48.00	-
December 1889	73.05	60.00	-	53.80	42.20	40.80	-
January 1890	69.80	54.50	-	52.10	41.05	39.40	-
February 1890	69.50	51.19	-	51.40	41.00	39.24	-
March 1890	69.15	51.10	-	50.95	41.30	38.75	-

122. *GAROD*, 1888-89, p. 12.

123. R.H. Rhind, *op.cipt.*, No. 5247, Cuttack 4 November 1890.

Flood in the year 1889-90

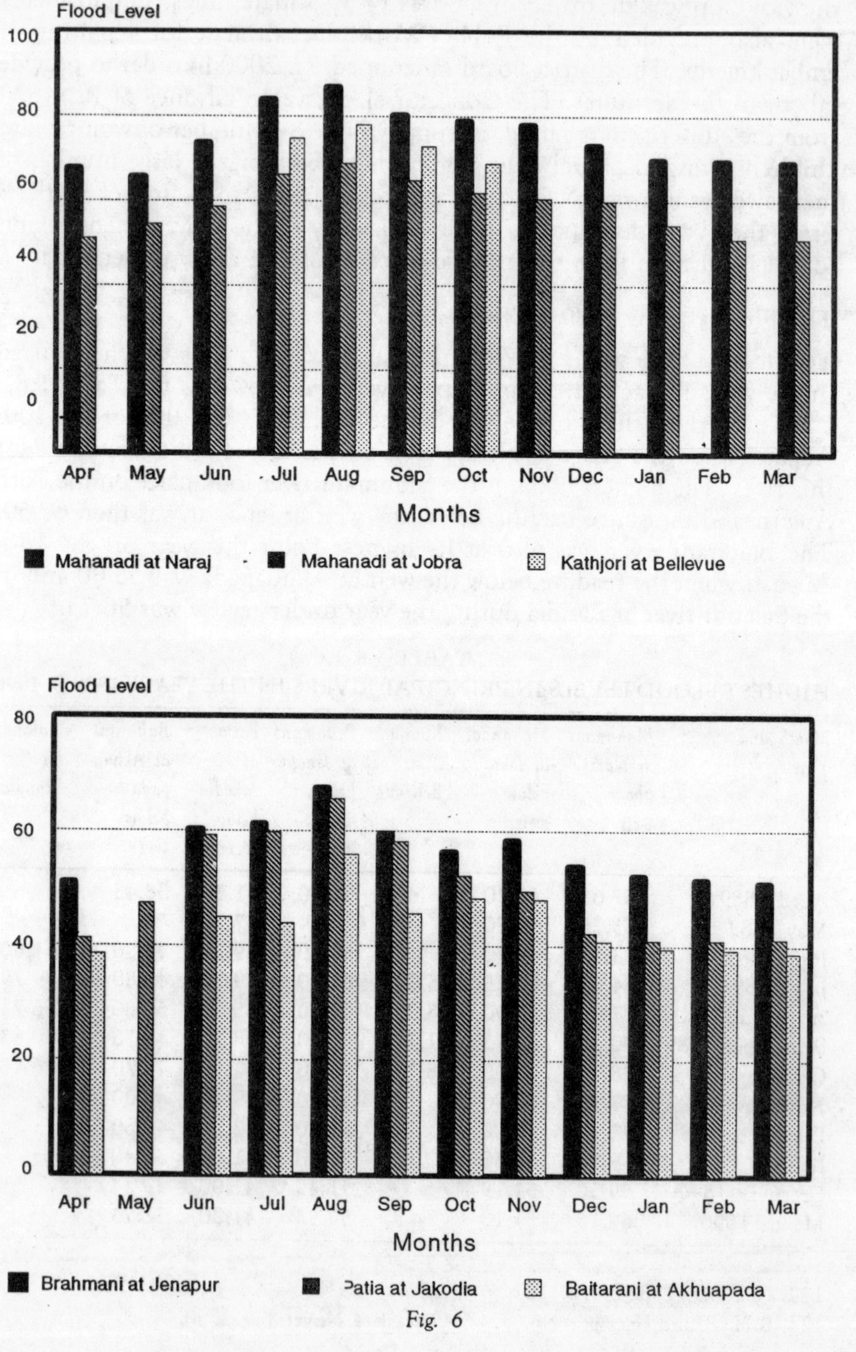

Fig. 6

The recorded levels of the flood of 1889 at several important points on the right bank of the Mahanadi below the weir are given in the following Table:

	1879	*1885*	*1888*	*1889*
Below the weir at Jobra	73.30	72.30	68.00	68.90
Head of the Sukhpyka	60.58	60.45	55.83	56.58
Outfall of Sukhpyka	41.89	41.85	35.65	36.30
Outfall of the cross Kathjori at Jeypore	33.35	32.95	27.66	29.16
Head of the Punkpal	22.97	20.50	16.36	20.53
Taldanda	16.66	16.45	12.95	15.35
Paradeep	10.18	10.15	6.45	7.20

The above readings show that the flood of 1889 was higher than that of the previous years at all points between the Mahanadi weir and Paradeep.

There were no breaches during the year in the embankments of the Baitarani and its branches on account of the low state of the river during the flood season. At the Birupa weir damage was done by the floods to the tail apron of the body of the work in several places. In the Brahmani weir little amount of damage was caused by the floods. The high flood in the Brahmani river washed away the mettaling of the causeways in the 39th and 59th miles of the Orissa Trunk Road and similar damage was done to the causeway in the 63rd mile of the same road, at the end of the branch canal to Bhadrak, in consequence of spill water from the Salandi river.[124]

The year 1889, was one of high prices for rice.

AVERAGE PRICE OF RICE PER RUPEE

	1887-88		*1888-89*		*1889-90*	
	S	C	S	C	S.	C.
Cuttack	19	3	17	15	16	8
Puri	21	5	18	3	17	15
Balasore	25	12	23	5	19	12

The general condition of the people was not so good. The price of food was high owing to the shortness of the harvest in 1888-89 and the effects of this fell seriously upon the labouring class people.[125]

The Table 1.9 depicts the maximum rises of flood level which occurred during the year 1890-91 in each of the principal rivers.

124. R.H. Rhind, *op.cit.*
125. *RAB*, 1889-90, p. 110.

Flood in the year 1890-91

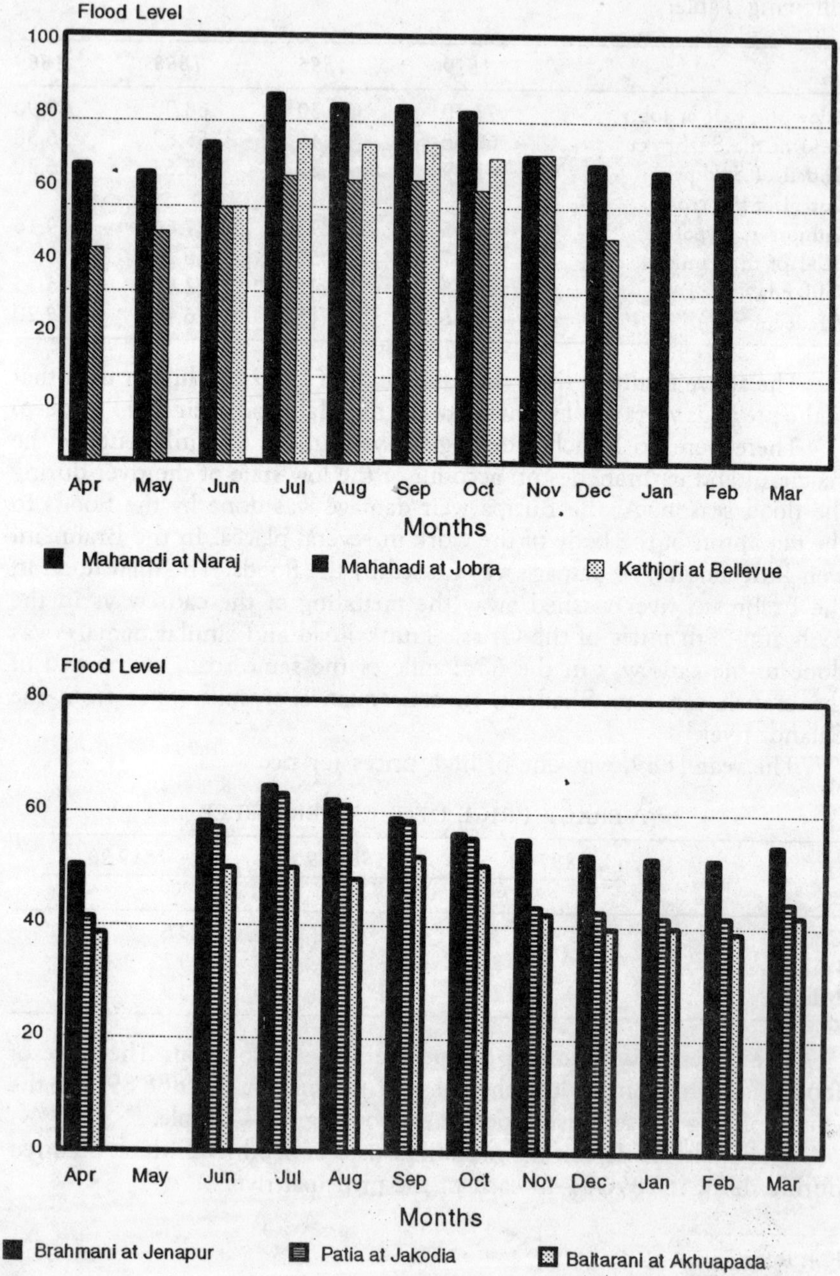

Fig. 7

The highest flood in the Mahanadi came on 12th July, when the gauge at Naraja read 85.90. At the Bellevue gauge on the Kathjori river at Cuttack, the highest reading observed this year was 75.75. The highest flood in the Brahmani river occurred on the 12th July, when the gauge below the weir at Jenapur read 64.50. The Baitarani river rose to its highest point this year on 27th September, when the gauge below the weir at Akhuapada read 52.30. The highest reading that was observed in the Salandi river at Randia the year under review was 53.58 on the 27th September. The gauge readings which were recorded at other important points upon the branches of the Kuakhai in the Puri district were as follow:[126]

	1879	*1885*	*1889*	*1890*
Head of the Kuakhai	80.40	81.03	76.93	74.43
Head of the Kusabhadra	68.82	71.90	68.20	65.05
Head of the Daya	55.00	54.67	51.97	49.97
At Konti in the Daya	36.50	35.85	30.35	29.05
At Gorodia on the Daya	24.03	21.32	17.77	16.91
At Satpara on the Chilka lake	3.95	3.00	3.80	3.70
At Janakadeipur on the Bhargabi	23.60	21.23	23.93	23.26

The flood of the year 1890 was everywhere lower then that of the previous year. There were no breaches in the embankments of the Kuakhai and Daya rivers, that year. No breaches occurred in the embankments under the care of the Executive Engineer of Mahanadi division. In the Puri division three breaches occurred in the embankments of Nuna and Monagooni rivers as compared with 24 in the previous year. No breaches occurred in the embankments under the charge of Executive Engineer, Brahmani-Baitarani division, during the year. The highest readings of the flood of 1890 at the Baitarani and Burrah weir as compared with those of previous year were shown in the following figure:

			1889	*1890*
Baitarani	Upperside		60.70	59.30
	Lowerside		55.80	52.30
		Head	4.90	7.00
Burrah weir	Upperside		60.90	59.45
	Lowerside		58.50	56.20
		Head	2.40	3.25

126. W. Connan offg. S.E., O.C. to the Chief Engineer, Bengal, No. 4944, Cuttack, 6 October 1891.

TABLE 1.9
HIGHEST FLOOD LEVEL IN PRINCIPAL RIVERS IN THE YEAR 1890 & 1891

Month and Year	*Mahanadi at Naraj above weir*	*Mahanadi at Jobra below weir*	*Kathjori at Bellevue*	*Brahmani at Jenapur below weir*	*Patia at Jakodia below weir*	*Baitarani at Akhua-pada below weir*	*Salandi at Randia*
April 1890	69.30	50.10	-	50.60	41.31	38.57	-
May 1890	67.65	54.00	-	-	-	-	-
June 1890	74.45	59.60	59.65	58.20	57.10	50.30	47.68
July 1890	85.90	67.25	75.75	64.50	63.20	50.00	50.08
August 1890	83.65	66.30	74.65	62.10	61.20	48.20	51.58
September 1890	83.35	66.35	74.60	59.00	58.60	52.30	53.58
October 1890	82.00	64.00	71.30	56.40	55.55	50.80	50.18
November 1890	71.68	75.25	-	55.30	43.50	42.20	-
December 1890	69.58	53.00	-	52.70	42.55	39.60	-
January 1891	68.40	-	-	52.10	41.55	39.80	-
February 1891	68.40	-	-	51.80	41.80	38.90	-
March 1891	-	-	-	54.50	44.20	41.90	-

In the Akhuapada-Jajpur division no breaches occurred in the embankments during the year 1890 under review. No injury occurred to the Puri and Ganjam roads in this year.[127] There was some increase in the number of deaths from fevers in all the districts, probably due to extreme heat and heavy rainfall.[128]

In 1891, high floods also came in different rivers on the following dates.[129]

Mahanadi	..	30th July
Kathjori	..	30th July
Brahmani	..	15th September
Patia	..	15th September
Baitarani and Burrah	..	14th August
Salandi	..	4th August

The embankments on the Mahanadi division were slightly damaged by the floods, and no breaches occurred in any of them. The floods in the Kathjori and Kuakhai this year were the highest since the flood of 1885 and this accounts for the larger number of breaches than in any year since 1885-86. No damage was done to the Burrah weir during the

127. W. Connan, *op.cit.*
128. *GAROD*, 1890-91, p. 5.
129. W. Connan, *op.cit.*, No. 3940, Orissa, 30 July 1892.

flood season of 1891. At the Mahanadi weir six cribs were carried away.[130] No important damage was done to the property of the people.

The Floods from 1892 to 1894

The flood of 1892 was remarkable for its intensity. This flood was due to the Mahanadi being swollen to a great height by heavy fainfall and the level at Naraj on the 26th July read 91.10.[131] The highest recorded readings of the principal rivers for the year are given in the Table 1.10.[132]

The injury to the crops was not very serious, and though the embankments in Puri district were breached in all directions, the damage done in this district was not great. The Kendrapara canal was however, breached in the 19th and 20th miles, and the Kendrapara extension canal from Marsaghai to Jambu was also overtopped and breached in many places.[133] In the year 1893, there was moderate flood.

In July 1894 there was an extraordinary flood in the Brahmani and a high flood in the Baitarani river. The flood in the Mahanadi was above the average rising to 89.40 at Naraja on the 28th July.[134] The Baitarani and the Mahanadi were all in high flood about the same time and the flood reached to maximum on 26th July. The floods seem to have been the result of the heavy rainfall accompanying the cyclonic disturbances which passed west over the hilly tracts where these rivers had their origin.[135] The highest recorded flood readings of the Brahmani and Patia at the weirs are noted below:[136]

	Brahmani weir		*Patia weir*	
1868	70.60 before construction of the weir		No recorded	
	Above weir	Below weir	Above weir	Below weir
1881	68.75	68.00	67.90	Not recorded
1894	69.60	68.60	69.10	68.70

The greater part of the district bounded by high level canal, Range II, and the Brahmani river on the south and the Bura Kharswan on the

130. *Ibid.*
131. Supplement to *The Samaj*, 7 October 1982, Cuttack, Natural Calamities, Famine of 1865-66.
132. Revenue Report of Public Works Department (Irrigation Report) 1892-93, Government of Bengal, p.8.
133. Supplement to *the Samaj*, 7 October, 1982, *op.cit.*
134. W.A. Inglis, *The Canals and Flood Banks of Bengal*, p. 236.
135. G.Stevenson, Collector, Cuttack to the Commissioner of Orissaa, No. 14769, Cuttack, 16 August 1894.
136. W. Connan, *op.cit.*, No. 5018, Calcutta, 20 September 1894.

TABLE 1.10
HIGHEST RECORDED READINGS IN PRINCIPAL RIVERS

Name of the		*1891-92*		*1892-93*		*Highest Recorded*	
River	*Locality*	*Date*	*Reading*	*Date*	*Reading*	*Date*	*Reading*
Mahanadi	Naraja above weir	30th July 1891	87.90	26th July 1892	92.10	26th July 1892	92.10
	Naraja below weir	30th July 1891	87.90	12th July 1892	92.10	26th July 1892	92.10
	Jobra above weir	30th July 1891	71.75	12th July 1892	75.95	25th July 1892	75.95
	Jobra below weir	30th July 1891	70.10	12th July 1892	74.00	26th July 1892	74.00
Brahmani	Jenapur above weir	15th Sept 1891	66.00	13th July 1892	66.40	18th July 1881	68.75
	Jenapur below weir	15th Sept 1891	65.90	13th July 1892	66.20	18th July 1881	68.00
Baitarani	Akhuapada above weir	14th Aug. 1891	62.70	11th June 1892	61.60	16th July 1881	66.60
	Akhuapada above weir	14th Aug. 1891	59.20	11th June 1892	55.50	16th July 1881	63.79
Salandi	Randia	4th Aug. 1891	56.88	3rd Sept 1892	51.10	12th Sept. 1887	59.78
Kathjori	Bellevue	30th July 1891	78.80	25th July 1892	83.30	25th July 1892	83.30
Birupa	Jagatpur above weir	30th July 1891	67.60	25th July 1892	70.40	4th July 1872	71.10
	Jagatpur below weir	30th July 1891	64.20	25th July 1892	70.40	4th July 1872	70.60

north, below the Brahmani and Patia weirs was fully inundated. All communications by the Trunk Road were blocked for a couple of days and telegraphic communication between Jajpur and Cuttack was also interrupted. This area was totally flooded due to weak embankments. Aul also suffered a lot from the inundation.[137] The damage was great, where the rivers Birupa (a branch of the Mahanadi), Brahmani with Kharswan and Baitarani were all more or less confined by embank levels that was in the tracts between the Pattamundai canal on the south and the Baitarani on the north. The Grand Trunk Road on the west and halfway between the Bara Brahmani and the sea on the east. The floods more or less swept away all the above area.[138]

The Table 1.11, gives approximate heights of the flood embankment crests over the maximum flood height, as reported by the then Executive Engineer of Brahmani-Baitarani division.

Four breaches occurred in the Bura Kharswan embankment which was under construction, three in the 8th mile at Kamalpore, opposite the Kharswan junction, each about 200 feet long, and one large breach occurred in the 9th mile 28th chain, about 600 feet long. Owing to the breaches in the Bura Kharswan embankment, five distributaries on the inundated area were damaged. In Orissa Trunk Road, four small breaches occurred, one on the 40th and the other on the 46th mile of the road.

Small damage was done to the subdivisional officer's quarters at Akhuapada where the flood rose to 6 inches over floor level, and to the Khunditar bungalow, where the flood rose to 2 feet 9 inches over floor level, and the stable and sheds of the Endulva bungalow were swept away. The Akhuapada post office had 1 foot 8 inches of flood in floor, and had been damaged.[139] The floods of the year, in the river Mahanadi and its branches, rose to an abnormal height being identical with those observed in the great flood of 1872. The embankments in the Puri division were extensively breached because the breanches of Mahanadi which passed through this district, even could not be held in tact during the year of ordinary flood. No less than 127 braches occurred in the Puri division, aggregating 4 miles 87 feet in length, while in the Akhuapada Jajpur division, there were 18 of an aggregate length of 1,577 feet. In the Mahanadi division there was only one large breach of 620 feet long and three smaller ones, and from the Brahmani-Baitarani division the number reported was four.

The resulting damage to crops was considerable. Remissions of revenue to the extent of Rs. 15,000 were reported to have been given in

137. *Ibid.*

138. G. Stevenson, *op.cit.*

139. *Ibid.*

TABLE 1.11
HEIGHT OF CREST ABOVE FLOOD

Pattamundai Canal Left Embankment				*Utikun Embankment*		*Aul Embankment*	
No. of Mile	*Crest level*	*Flood level*	*Difference*	*Mile*	*Height of crest above flood*	*Mile*	*Height of crest above flood*
27	37.55	32.50	5.05	1	2.46	1	5.33
28	37.21	31.67	5.54	2	3.94	2	5.03
29	36.38	29.58	6.80	3	3.70	3	3.85
30	35.55	30.65	4.90	4	2.04	4	3.51
31	34.15	29.96	4.19	5	1.98	5	4.31
32	33.96	29.93	4.03	6	1.33	6	4.94
33	33.91	30.00	3.91	7	2.55	7	3.19
34	32.74	28.47	4.27	-	-	-	-
35	32.05	27.61	4.44	-	-	-	
36	32.80	27.10	5.70	-	N.B. The last 4 miles of this embankment require raising.		
37	30.53	26.33	4.20	-	-	-	-
38	29.61	25.61	4.00	-	-	-	-
39	29.70	25.42	3.65	-	-	-	-
40	28.40	23.80	4.50	-	-	-	-
41	27.50	23.00	4.50	-	-	-	-
42	27.40	22.85	4.55	-	-	-	-
43	26.70	21.73	4.97	-	-	-	-
44	26.00	21.26	4.74	-	-	-	-
45	25.80	21.10	4.70	-	-	-	-
46	23.15	18.60	4.55	-	-	-	-
47-48	22.55	18.29	4.26	-	-	-	-
	21.47	17.70	3.77	-	-	-	-
Alba lock	19.60	14.50	5.10	-	-	-	-

Puri district and it Cuttack district half of the produce of the crops on 226 acres was lost.[140] To ryots of Aul Rs. 500 were given to provide aid for rabi and dalua paddy cultivation. The Raja of Aul had also advanced Rs. 700 in cash and a further sum in grain and seedings to his distress ryots within the embankment. The Raja also continued to distribute 1½ maunds of rice daily at his *anna chhatra* to the most needy and destitute people. The relief roads sanctioned by the district board afforded

140. Supplement to the Calcutta Gazette, May 2, 1894, p. 743.

employment to the destitute people of the flooded tracts.[141] Under Agricultural Loans Act for 1894-95 Government sanctioned Rs 6800 for Cuttack.[142] The relief work provided by the Government was totally inadequate to meet the distress tract.

The Fig. 8 shows the death rate per mile of the population during the year 1890-1894.

Year	*Cuttack*	*Balasore*	*Puri*	*Total*
1890	21.61	25.98	24.23	22.50
1891	23.38	26.18	27.76	25.00
1892	38.34	43.61	37.86	39.00
1893	24.26	25.91	29.02	25.80
1894	35.14	32.99	30.75	33.50

The increased number of deaths in Cuttack district from cholera, fever and bowel complaints was attributed in a great measure to the bad crops of the preceding year. The high prices of food grains also forced the people to maintain a poor life. The distress was aggravated by the high floods of July, which forced the poorer classes in the affected tracts to supplement their livelihood by jungle products. It was remarked that the drainage in some parts of the districts during the flood season was extremely bad, and this probably accounted for the prevalence of fever in those tracts.[143]

The Floods of 1895 and 1896

The flood of 1895 in the Mahanadi was little higher than that in the previous year rising at Naraja to 90.55 and on the Bellevue gauge to 81.15 on the 1st July. In this year no damage occurred on the Mahanadi proper by several large breaches occurred in Puri district alone.[144]

By the flood of 1896 the Brahmani and Baitarani as well as the Mahanadi rose to a great height almost simultaneously, but the main feature of the flood was its long duration.[145] All the rivers of this division rose after the 20th July and reached the maximum height on the 24th and 25th of that month. It was reported by R.C. Dutt, Officiating Commissioner of Orissa Division thus, "Floods were more frequent in Orissa than in other divisions. The present year had been a year of

141. H.M. Pherson, Offg. Collector to the Commissioner of Orissa, No. 1906G, Cuttack, 27/29 October 1894.
142. G. Stevenson, *op.cit.*
143. *GAROD*, 1894-95, p. 8.
144. W.A. Inglis, *op.cit.*, p. 236.
145. *The Samaj*, 7 October 1982, *op.cit.*

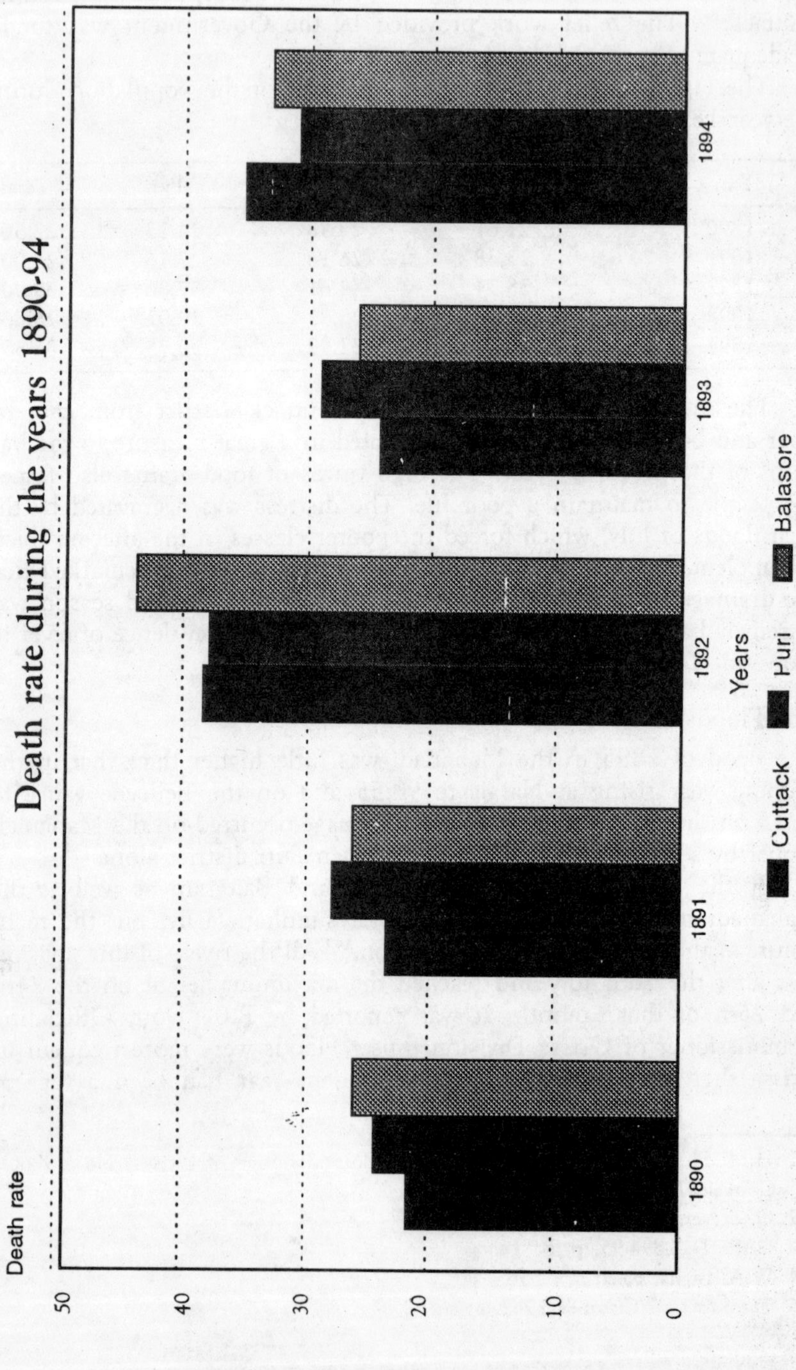
Death rate during the years 1890-94
Death rate
50
40
30
20
10
0
1890
1891
1892
1893
1894
Years
Cuttack
Puri
Balasore

Fig. 8

exceptionally heavy and prolonged floods. The country was under water for nearly a month and the loss therefore, had been exceptionally severe."[146]

The inundations were due to the rising of the Subarnarekha in the north and of the Baitarani in the south. The flood in Subarnarekha began at the end of July and when the water had subsided some attempts were made to repair the damages done by the flood. The people were again harassed by the rise of river in the last week of August. It swept away nearly all the transplanted rice. The central parts of the district along the Burabalang and Salandi suffered less than the northern tract, where about 300 square miles were inundated. But the south was seriously affected by the floods of the Baitarani river and much damage was done to the standing crops. The people lost their houses and property and there was distress in all the tracts open to the ravages of the flood.[147]

In Bhograi some embankments were breached and so there were some difficulties in obtaining supplies of food in these parts. The Collector of Balasore, De, promptly sent to the spot 50 maunds of rice, 5 maunds of dal and 2 maunds of salt purchased from the residue of a famine fund which was in his hands. Babu Kailash Chandra Rai Mahashoy, a liberal and respected Zamindar, offered to provide all the rice, dal and salt required for the distribution to his ryots in the taluk Madhupara, in the Sulsa Pant and Seth Karim Chand Premji, a Marwari Merchant and Contractor of Balasore, sent 20 maunds of rice for distribution to the people in distress. The Collector also sent boats to rescue the people in distressed tracts. When the second flood of the Subarnarekha river subsided, he allotted Rs. 200 out of the amount placed at his disposal from Babu Ram Lal Mukerji's endowment for small grants to the poor ryots for helping them towards re-building their houses and supporting their families. Under Agricultural Loans Act, steps were taken to grant them loans. Besides, the Collector made a list of the tanks, the water of which had been spoilt by the flood water, and in consultation with the civil Medical Officer of Balasore, he sent sufficient quantity of permanganate of potash to disinfect the water kept for drinking purposes. Temporary help was given to the most needy ryots in rice and pulse, and in money grants for re-building huts. There

146. R.C. Dutt. Offg. Commissioner of the Orissa division to the Secretary to the Government of Bengal, Revenue Department, No. 17PT, Camp Puri, 21 September 1896.

147. L.S.S. O'Malley, *BDG, Balasore*, p. 97.

had been very little loss of life or live-stock, although the damage to the crops had been exceptionally severe.[148]

From the 24th July to the 7th August, the Mahanadi was continuously above the level of 88.00 at Naraja except for a few hours on the 2nd August. On the 25th July it attained its greatest height of 92.10 or the same height as was reached by the floods of 1872 and 1892. The embankments were breached in numerous places and the Kendrapara extension canal, standing out like the bank of an inland sea, suffered much from the erosion of the waves breaking on it and was again wrecked. In almost all the parts unprotected by embankments the heavy floods destroyed the bhadoi and winter rice crops and extensive tracts lay under deep water for many days. Some lost their lives and property, and there was considerable distress in all the country open to the ravages of the flood.[149]

After the high flood of the 24th July Growse, the then Collector of Cuttack sent a supply of Chura and rice and straw for bullocks to some people who were stranded and rendered houseless to the south of the Kathjori river. Similarly relief was sent to two other places in the Sadar subdivision, where the people were similarly circumstanced and needed relief urgently. The sub-manager of Kujang distributed rice and salt to the great relief of those actually in distress during the high floods. A sum of Rs.400 was sanctioned in this estate for gratuitous relief, and a sum of Rs. 20,000 for taccavi advances. The Manager of Kanika had similarly got Rs. 200 for gratuitous relief and Rs. 5,000 for taccavi advances.[150]

Puri district was traversed by several branches of the Mahanadi river, of which the Daya, the Bhargabi and the Kusabhadra were the most important. The district was subject to floods from these rivers in ordinary years, but this year the floods had been prolonged and heavy, and had therefore, caused great damages. There were breaches in the embankments of the Daya and Kusabhadra rivers, flooding the whole country. The crops were destroyed, and the communication between villages and the roads were cut off. Immediately after the flood Bell, the then Collector of Puri and J.N. Gupta, Joint Magistrate of Khurda, took possible steps to establish communication by boat with isolated villages and in sending food supply to places which were entirely cut off. Bell obtained a grant of Rs. 1,000 from the District Board of Puri for immediate relief operation and also raised about Rs. 3,000 by local

148. Selection of papers, Relation to the Famine of 1896-97 in Bengal, Vol. I (October-November 1896). Calcutta 1897, p. 306.

149. *The Samaj*, 7 October 1982, *op.cit.*

150. Selection of papers, Relating to the Famine of 1896-97, *op.cit.*

subscription at a meeting at Puri.[151] The floods of the year were exceptionally heavy and prolonged, and caused much damage, hardship and suffering to the people of Orissa.

The Flood of 1900

In the second half of September 1900, there was unusually heavy rain, which caused floods in parts of Orissa division. The people of the flooded tracts in Orissa were accustomed to such calamities and many parts, the floods left a rich of silt behind, which was beneficial to the rabi crops. So, though some damage was caused to the winter rice crop, the people were not much in need of assistance of the grant made by the Government.[152] The abnormal rainfall of the 15th to 25th September caused service floods in all the rivers of the Balasore division. The flood in the Subarnarekha was nearly one foot higher than any previous records. The Bhograi and Jokee embankments were both overtopped, and numerous breaches occurred in the Jamjunda embankment.[153] The water rose 18 inches higher than the highest flood previously recorded. Prompt measures were taken for the relief of the sufferers and boats were sent out to rescue the homeless ryots whose houses had been washed away. They were brought into Balasore where they were clothed and fed until they were able to return to their villages. There was little loss of human life but a large number of cattle was drowned. The special measures were also taken to dispose of the carcases which were found lying round the villages when the flood subsided. The agricultural embankments were breached and the crops suffered severely, especially in the western part of the district. The railway line was also breached in several places and the running of trains from Balasore to the north was stopped for sometime.[154] Raja Baikuntha Nath De, Babu Radha Charan Das, Babu Karim Chand Premji and Babu Purusottam Das played important role in Balasore district for charitable efforts in relieving the temporary distress.[155]

The Mahanadi commenced to rise very rapidly on the 20th September 1900 and reached a height of 80.27 R.L. which was 0.27 higher than the previous record of 1894. The damage to crops was considerable.[156] The

---

151. Selection of papers, Relating to the Famine o 1896-97, pp. 309-10.
152. *RAB*, 1900-1901, p. 20.
153. *Ibid.*, p. 30.
154. L.S.S.O' Malley, *BDG*, *Balasore*, pp. 97-98.
155. F.A. Slacke, Secretary to the Government of Bengal to the Commissioner of Orissa division, Revenue Department, Agricultural Branch, No. 2313 T.R. Darjeeling, 31 October 1900.
156. *RAB* 1900-1901, p. 29.

Kanika estate also suffered to a great extent. The worst tract of Cuttack was that between the Kendrapara and Taldanda canals where the flood water caused total loss. Major parts of Puri district suffered from the September flood. Out of Rs. 18,500 sanctioned recently for agricultural loans Rs. 10,000 was allotted to Cuttack and Rs. 4,000 to Puri. The Collector of Balasore reported that no grant was necessary for his district for that year.[157]

From the above descriptions it is seen that each and every year the people of Orissa suffered from floods. The crops were destroyed to a great extent. Lack of good communication forced the people to remain in distress during the time of flood. The British authority could not take any long term measures to protect the people from such calamities. It only granted some remissions and suspensions which were inadequate to meet the flood disasters. So the people of Orissa, compared to those of the neighbouring states, maintained a poor life, and poverty was developed simultaneously which broke down their economic condition.

157. From the Commissioner of Orissa to the Secretary to Government, Revenue Department, No. 2476, R, 10 December 1900.

2

Cyclones in the Nineteenth Century

As it is situated in the coastal belt, Orissa is always prone to flood, famine and cyclone which contribute much to the failure of agrarian economy of the state. But among the above three curses of nature, cyclone is the most perilous one for economic devastation. Even in the years when there was no flood or famine, the ripe crops were damaged by cyclones which caused scarcity of food, and destroyed the property, life and animal etc.[1] Among all natural calamities the tropical cyclone is unparalled in its violence and devastation. Speaking at the Regional Tropical Cyclone seminar in Brisbane in 1973, A.J. Shields a leading Australian metrologist observed that severe drought no doubt caused considerable overall economic loss because of its protracted widespread nature, but no metrological event had a greater economic and social impact than a major cyclone.[2]

Vulnerable Belts

The eastern coastal belt embracing Bangladesh, Bengal, Orissa, Andhra Pradesh and Tamil Nadu (Fig. 9) is very much vulnerable to repeated hazards of surging sea waves and heavy downpours that accompany spirally moving fierce winds, mostly in the months of October, November and December. About a 25 Km. wide belt of the eastern coast of India is vulnerable to cyclonic hazards, the risks being particularly severe in the mouths of rivers. The cyclone-prone districts (Fig. 9) include Midnapur and 24 Parganas in Bengal, Balasore, Cuttack, Puri and Ganjam in Orissa, East Godavari, Krishna, Nellore, Prakasam and Srikakulam in Andhra Pradesh and Chingleput and Tanjavur in Tamil Nadu.[3]

1. Orissa History Congress, Proceeding of the XV Annual Session, 4-5 November 1989. Quoted in B. Bhatta, "The Cyclone of 1885 in Orissa : A Brief Study", p. 119.
2. *The Heritage*, December 1987, p. 58.
3. *K.S. Valdiya, Environmental Geology, Indian Context*, New Delhi 1987, pp. 352-353.

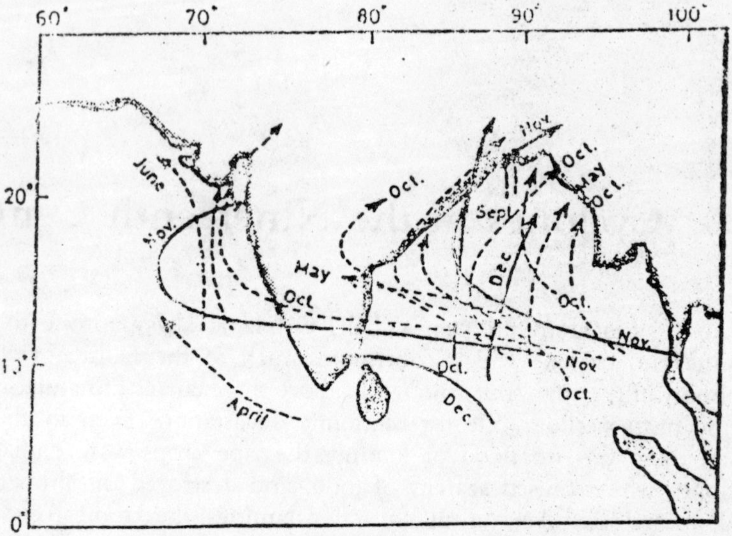

Tracks of tropical cyclones (normalized) in the Bay of Bengal, Arabian Seas and Indian subcontinent. Quotedin K.S. Valdiya, op.cit, p. 353

Fig. 9

Frequency of Cyclones

Most of the cyclones in the Bay of Bengal occur in the post-monsoon period *i.e.*, between September and December and a few take place in the months from April to June in the pre-monsoon period. The tropical cyclones are five times more frequent in the Bay of Bengal than the Arabian sea (Fig. 9). The eastern coast suffers from the hazards year after year, compared to those borne by the West Coast where northern Gujarat and Saurashtra are the most vulnerable areas.[4] The coastal belt of Orissa suffered most from the cyclones in the 19th century. The series of cyclones which hit Orissa were in-1823, 1831, 1832, 1833, 1840, 1842, 1848, 1850, 1851, 1864, 1867, 1872, 1874, 1885, 1887, 1988, 1890, 1891 and 1893.[5]

---

4. *Ibid.*
5. *The Heritage, op.cit.*, p. 59.
   N.N. Banerjee, *Report on the Agriculture of the District of Cuttack*, pp. 176-179.
   L.S.S.O'Malley, *BDG, Cuttack and Balasore*, Calcutta, 1907, Several Volumes of GAROD.

Causes of Cyclones

The area nearer to the coast is hence affected more due to the depressions arising in the Bay of Bengal. The depressions then proceed to inlands passing over the coast. The velocity of wind on land is maximum at the coast. The accompanying tidal surge is sometimes 6 to 7 meters high which inundates the coastal settlements and results in loss of life, property and crops. Though the main tract of cyclone exists on the north of Mahanadi delta its effects are profound in the area. During the post-south-west monsoon season, the cyclone phenomena prevail in many parts of the coastal region. It is during August and September when the Kharif crops are in the fields, the cyclone generally occurs and causes the maximum devastation. August and September are the mean periods for the probability of occurrence, whereas the cyclones of the winter season normally do not affect much the Orissa coast. Their effects are mostly felt in Andhra and Tamil Nadu. The intensity of cyclonic storm decreases from the coast to the interior region bringing with it heavy rainfall. The direction of the cyclonic storms is west-north-west which comes from Bay of Bengal. The intensity depends on the speed of the wind which ranges from 90 to 200 km. per hour. But the speed of 80 to 90 km. per hour can be enough for the destruction of a large number of houses. From this damage done during the high speed, cyclonic winds can be imagined.[6]

Cyclone Havoc (1803-1851)

During the first two decades, there was no severe cyclone in Orissa. On the 27th May 1823 however, there was a furious cyclone in Balasore district, which was said to have been the third calamity of the kind within eight years. The sea suddenly rose and penetrated six miles inland, carrying with it every living creature in them, not even the vestige of a human habitation being left.[7] On 31st October 1831 a terrible cyclone took place in Orissa. Twenty one lives were lost in Balasore district by the falling of houses and exposure to the gale. The sea rose twenty feet higher than usual, and rushed in a torrent over the country, carrying everything with it. This was not the case in the most exposed situations only, from the Subarnarekha to the Dhamra river, the country was inundated some places as far as ten miles from the coast. Between Balasore and Busta the torrent passed over the high Jagannath Road on one estate situated N.E. from Balasore, out of upwards of 300 inhabitants, thirteen only survived. On a property on N. bank of the Burabalang

6. Orissa History Congress, Proceedings of the XV Annual Session, *op.cit.*, pp. 119-120.
7. L.S.S. O'Malley, *BDG*, *Balasore*, Calcutta, 1907, p. 93.

river, 281 and on another S.E. from Balasore, 768 were drowned. The loss calculated may be at least about 15,000[8] of human lives and 50,000 of heads of cattle in Balasore district.[9] The irruption of the sea was but partially felt in central Cuttack, and that only five estates have suffered from the visits. Throughout the district, however, the crops would appear to have been damaged to a considerable extent by the violent wind and the excess fall of rain.[10] In central Cuttack 331 human beings were ascertained to have perished the loss of life though lamentably great, was yet small compared to other parts of the coast and the great injury had however been done to property, particularly the lower grounds bordering the coast which were tilled chiefly by Malangies. The sum of Rs. 1,226 were distributed among Malangies alone. The method of granting relief was that of giving a rupee per each family of Malangies, with a promise of another similar donation on their commencing the manufacture of salt. Another mode of relief was that of permitting a sale at low prices of grain which had been sent from Calcutta. A large sum had been disbursed to clear ponds, to prevent the people dying from diseases which might arise from drinking brackish water. R. Hunter's explanation put emphasis on adequate relief can be granted to the agricultural classes by securing to them the full benefit of any relaxation in the Government demand from proprietors.[11]

The loss incurred by the Government was as follows:[12]

Value of salt destroyed at its prime cost	:	53942-8-0
Advances probably irrecoverable	.	544-7-9
Clearing out tanks	:	1360
Boats for bringing fresh water	:	300
Donations made	:	1226
Difference between cost of repairs as by amount estimate and will now be incurred	:	2226
	Rs.	60,830-15-9

Some damage occurred to Puri district as well. Parts of the walls of the Commissioner's circuit bungalow and the Magistrate and collector's

8. S.A. Chandra Dasgupta (ed.), *The Days of John Company, Selections from Calcutta Gazette* 1824-32 (Calcutta, 1959), pp. 691-92.
9. L.S.S.O'Malley, *BDG*, *Balasore*, p. 94.
10. R.D. Mangles, Acting Junior Secretary to the Deputy Secretary to Government, Revenue Department, 9 March 1832.
11. The Board of Customs Salt and Opium Fort William, No. 32, 27 February 1832.
12. *Ibid.*

cutcherry had been damaged and the portico of the former building was nearly blown down.[13]

The number of those who required assistance at Balasore may be estimated at about the 15,000.[14] The Government gave discretionary power to the Commissioner for the relief of the agricultural classes in the northern division of the provinces.[15] He had power to extend it throughout his province.[16] The scarcity of food was felt among the sufferings who were suffered under the double loss of property and kindred. The suspensions and remissions were granted to the people but it was not sufficient to meet the needs of the people. The fury and destructions of that late gale of 1831 felt more in Balasore district than any other district.

The distress and difficulties became severe, when a second great gale visited, the Balasore coast in October 1832. It became more violent but the storm wave was less destructive.[17] The pargana Bherah was twice overwhelmed by the sea in the storm of 1831 and 1832. The village entirely swept away and nearly all the inhabitants were perished.[18] The same coast was also visited by similar gale of the 21 May 1833.[19] On 30th of April 1840, the district of Puri was visited by a disastrous storm. The dalua crops was damaged severely but as informed by the Collector it was confined to a few villagers in the vicinity of Puri town.[20] The Collector of Khurda was authorised to make taccavi advances as follows.[21]

		Rs.
Taluk Delang	:	2, 168
Taluk Kishan Naggar (in addition)	:	164
Killa Tulpuddah	:	105
Killa Durjepur	:	38-14-0
	Total Cases:	2,475-14-0

13. W.G. Bcaher, Executive Officer, Cuttack Division to Major Cheape, Supt. Public Works Province of Cuttack, 24 November 1831.
14. S.A. Chandra Dasgupta (ed.), *op.cit.*, p. 693.
15. R.D. Mangles, Acting Junior Secretary to Deputy Secretary to Government, Revenue Department, 9 March 1832.
16. *Ibid.*
17. L.S.S.O'Malley, *BDG*, *Balasore*, p. 94.
18. H. Ricketts, Collector of Balasore to the Commissioner of Revenue for the 19th Division, Balasore, 1 January 1835.
19. H. Ricketts, Collector of Balasore to Capt. G. Young, Secretary to the Military Board, Fort William.
20. *BdRP*, A.J.M. Mills, Commissioner to the Secretary to Government Judicial Department, No. 2424, 12 June 1840.
21. *Ibid.*, A.J.M. Mills, Commissioner to the Collector of Khurda, No. 2431, 12 June 1840.

The districts of Cuttack and Puri were also visited by a severe storm in October 1842[22] and October 1848.

In the latter case, the damage occurred in the large tributary Mahals of Killa Kujang and Kanika and to Certain estates in their vicinity *viz.*, Taluk Pattamundai, pargana Utikan, Nowlbisee, pargana Kaima and Kismat-kaima and Bautara in which the sarada crops which then covered the low lands were destroyed by the inundation of the sea, some damage was done by the hurricane but it was chiefly confined to trees and buildings. The crops were rather benefitted than other wise by the rain which fell during the storm as they had previously suffered from drought. The principal damage was sustained in Killa Kanika (Kunkah) where there was also considerable loss of life and cattle. This estate which was under the jurisdiction of the court of wards at the time of cyclone had since been made over to the Raja and half the sudder Jama of the past official year had been suspended under the Boards orders of the 4th ultimo No. 53. In Killa-Kujang the mufassil balances to the extent of the loss had been remitted as reported to the Board in the letter No. 482 of the 10th April last and the Collector had been directed to report whether there was any necessity for suspending or remitting any portion of the Government demand. In Pattamundai taluk the loss of crops in five division was estimated at Rs. 14,000. In this estate also half of the sudder Jama had been suspended under orders of the Board and the Zamindars had been allowed to pay the balance due on the 8 pana kist in 2 instants. In Nowlbisee the crops was supposed to have been lost almost.[23]

The Collector of Puri also informed that the storm was attended with strong wind and heavy rain. Some damage occurred to houses and trees. But is saved the district from drought.[24] In Balasore during the gale of October last the rice crops appeared to have suffered more or less all along the coast from the Dhamra to the Subarnarekha owing to the irruption of the sea water. But Ankurah and Bherah suffered the most than any other parts of the district. In these two parganas, the sea appeared to have been forced by a strong gale from the N.E. and E. across the low lands into the Kunttai river near the Kanika estate.[25] The large amounts outstanding in Cuttack and Balasore were to be ascribed mainly to the

---

22. Commissioner to the Sudder Board of Revenue, 7 October 1842, Quoted in P. Mukherjee, *Irrigation, Inland Navigation and Flood Problems in North Orissa during the British Rule*, p. 42.
23. F. Gouldsbury, Commissioner to the Sudder Board of Revenue, No. 952, 19 June 1849.
24. F. Gouldsbury, *op.cit.*
25. Sudder Board of Revenue, Misce, Mimo No. 851 1/2, 1849 (O.S.A. Sl. No. 2087).

gale of October 1848, inconsequence of which heavy suspensions and remissions of demand had been granted with the sanction of the Government.[26]

By the cyclone of April 1850, Balasore was devastated more than any other districts. The local enquiries of the northern parganas were made by a Deputy Collector and the Sirastadar of the Collector's office while those in pargana Bherah were conducted by a British officer stationed at Bhadrak.

Lands on the bank of the Muttai river towards the sea was found to be uncultivated which Brown attributed to the calamities of by gone years (for which suitable remission or suspensions have been allowed). The collector was of opinion that some relief for the current year ought to be given to the zamindar, but the commissioner could not support such a recommendation. According to him the lands in question were unproductive. In the northern parganas he also recommended the suspension of the estimated losses for the period of one year.[27] In the middle of October there was a fair prospect of a generally good harvest in Balasore, but the gale which occurred on the 22nd of that month and extended all along the coast was said to have done some damage to the standing crops upon the whole.[28] The ryots of Nauanand and Bherah pargana appealed to the Government to inspect the area which were devastated by the cyclone of 1851. The appeal of the people was as follows.[29]

Court of the Deputy Collector Hon'ble William Bonesahib, Bhadrak, dt. 29.11.1851.

The ryots and general public of parganas Dayananda and Bheda under mauza Birilo have appealed for a through investigation into the losses causes of low harvest in 1259 due to scanty rains and the storm in the month of Kartika.

Since the loss cannot be investigated without the permission of the collector, this copy is being sent for his information and necessary action.

Abhaya Charan Baral
Narahari Das

---

26. The Secretary to the Sudder Board of Revenue to J.P. Grant, Secretary to the Government of Bengal Revenue Department, No. 278, Fort William, 15 May 1850.
27. F. Gouldsbury, Commissioner to the Secretary to the Board of Revenue, L.P. No. 1210, 26 June 1851.
28. *BdRP*, F. Gouldsbury, Commissioner to the Secretary to the Board of Revenue, L.P. No. 2342, 26 November 1841
29. OSA, Vol No. 183(C), Acc. No. 191B (Rect) year 1851, p. 564.

The Cyclones from 1852-1900

The cyclone of 1864 burst on the 5th October and was of unprecedented violence. It had its origin in the vicinity of the Andaman Islands and travelling northwards and west wards, first struck Bengal on the Balasore coast. The southern and eastern parts of Balasore exposed to the full force of the storm wave and the effect was most disastrous.[30] The Orissa coast suffered to a great extent from the violent cyclonic storms in the first half of the 19th century. It also caused much destruction to the lives, and properties of the area. The frequent occurrence of cyclone devastated the healthy economic life of the people of Orissa. The British Government did not take any systematic long-term measures to protect the people from such calamities. They only granted some remissions and suspensions of revenue. But it was not sufficient to alleviate the plight of the people. Orissa again suffered from a cyclonic storm in the night of 1st November 1867. Captain A. Bond, Master Attendant of Balasore, who was on his way to Calcutta in two of the conqueror stated that he did not encounter the storm, which passed him to the north-east. He gives the following readings of the barometer.[31]

Date	*Moon's age*	*7.00 A.M.*		*Noon*		*4.00 P.M.*		*Wind & C*
		Barometer	*Thermometer*	*Barometer*	*Thermometer*	*Barometer*	*Theemometer*	
30th October	3¼	29.78	75	29.80	78	29.77	80	N. light to N.W to N.N.N. cloudy to N.E.
31st October	4¼	29.75	77	29.74	77	29.72	76	N.W. very cloudy rain to N.E. rain
1st November	5¼	29.68	75	29.58	74	29.51	72	N. rain at noon heavy rain to N.W. heavy rain
2nd November	6¼	29.72	75	29.78	79	29.80	75	W. to N. at noon N. clear with light wind

30. L.S.S.O'Malley, *BDG*, *Midnapore*, Calcutta, 1911, p. 95.
31. A. Manson, Special Assistant Commissioner, Cuttack Division to the Secretary to the Board of Revenue, L.P. No. 907 1/2, Cuttack, 26 November 1867.

"There was no loss of life or property to any great extent."[32]

From Baliapal it was reported that some damage had been done to the crops, on the Subarnarekha river and at Busta and Bherah as well. In the north side of Balasore district a few huts, were unroofed, but no life appeared to have been lost in any part. The damage done by the storm was extremely slight. The Assistant Collector of Bhadrak after personal inspection, reported from Kolho to Chandbali the force of the wind on the 1st November levelled the paddy to the grounds in many fields, and the rain which subsequently fell had rolled it. In the fields especially of guru Dhan, the ears had been emptied of their contents, and nothing but chaff remained over this tract between Chandbali and Dhamrah little injury had been done. The injury to the subdivision had been confined to the coast tract.[33]

In Jajpur subdivision no accounts of the force or direction of the wind had been received. In Ulabhur some huts were unroofted and from Aul, the crop had been injured to the extent of 4 annas or ¼, and slight injury had been to the sarada crop. The strom waves had inundated saraswats and jagula in the Bhadrak side of the Dhamrah.

At Kendrapara the wind rose from the evening of the 30th October to a gale at about noon of the 31st, it continued with some violence till evening of that day, and subsided entirely on the morning of the 1st November. The storm was accompanied by showers of rain. At both Pattamundai and Kendrapara a few old huts were unroofed. The Assistant collector wrote from personal inspection, that the parganas Tikal, Utikan, Nowlbisee, and part of Kujang, were most liable to injury from hurricane. In Cuttack town no mischief to life or property occurred. The wind was high both on October 31st and November 1st and blew steadily from the north. The Master of the False Point Light House reported that the storm commenced at 10.00 P.M. and October 31st, and blew from north-north-east until about 8.00 P.M. of November last. "He described it as the severest gale he even experienced. At Puri the wind was heavy but no damage occurred.[34] From the above records it was found some serious damage had occurred to the crops and there were no reports of loss of cattle or human life, but some injury was done to the houses only.

In July 1872 the whole of the coastal belt was completely devastated due to a severe storm accompanied by tidal eruptions.[35]

32. E. W. Molony, Famine Commissioner in charge of current duties to the Junior Secretary to the Government of Bengal, No. 967, Cuttack, 19 December 1867.
33. *Ibid.*
34. E.W. Molony, *op.cit.*
35. P.Mukherjee, *op.cit.*, p. 42.

The Cyclone commenced in Balasore from north-west, between 1 and 2 P.M. of the 1st July, and shifted round to north-north-west, north-west, and north-east by 8.30 A.M. The center of cyclone passed over and in the immediate neighbourhood of Balasore town where the very great damage was done.[36] By the cyclone the loss of human life had been very slight as the cyclone occurred during the day time when the people were able to take care of themselves. The loss of cattle however had been very severe, the heavy losses in Balasore, Soro and Basudebpur were due to the fact that in these places the cattle were taken to graze on the plains near the sea which were treeless and open so that they had no protection. The sea waves which rolled for a short time, killed a large quantity of them. No application for relief had been made on this ground. But the Collector (J. Beames) pointed out that district was poor in cattle and could not afford to lose nearly five thousand heads. It would be useless to give as there were no cattle to be brought. But the Government acted liberally by sending some cattle for this distribution from other districts. This would also improve the breed which was very poor indeed. During the cyclone in the 1st July 1872, the death toll to cattle and human beings is given below.[37]

No. of Cows	*No. of Buffalo*	*No. of Sheep*	*No. of Persons died by fall of walls etc., in the cyclone*
3424	1215	5	21

Many schools were also affected by the cyclone severely. The Collector also submitted the list of schools to the Government to grant half the sum required for the following schools:

Barabatte school, Revd. J. Sapart's Girls school, Sundaria school, Balikuti school, Bansdiha school and Soro school, etc.

The Collector before receiving a detail estimate, guessed that a grant of Rs. 20 to Rs. 40 per school or Rs. 160 in all would be sufficient for the repairing of the schools. The Dolasahi school was perhaps repaired out of the funds of the Government Khas Mahals of Nuanand.[38] The Collector was outgoing help and relief to the sufferers and laboured incessantly for some days in adding people to collect their property and get some shelter over their heads. The Burabalang river rose considerably

36. Selections from Divisional and District Annual Administration Reports, 1872-73, Calcutta, 1874, pp. 464-465.
37. John Beames, Collector to the Commissioner of Orissa Division, Cuttack, No. 432, Balasore 13 August 1872.
38. *Ibid.*, No. 360, 20 July 1872.

during the storm and flooded a good deal of low land. As the crops were not sufficiently advance to be much injured and the water passed off speedily, the loss of crop was comparatively small. The storm however, passed in a south westernly direction over Nilagiri, Keonjhar and Pal Lehara and across the hills travelling south towards Board Khond Mals, on the Madras frontier.[39]

Money was promptly asked for from Government and has promptly granted for relief of sufferers and for rebuilding and repairing the wreck of houses in Balasore.[40] The proposal of the then collector, John Beams for a wholesale remission of the town tax for 9 months following the disastrous effects of the cyclone, was turned down by the Government on the plea that there must be some rich and well-to-do people in Balasore who could well afford to bear their own town burdens. After all a sum of Rs. 1,500/- was granted as aid to the Balasore Municipality due to its distressed condition, leaving it to the local officers to carry out the partial remission of the town tax as might seem most advisable to them. The charge of Rs. 1,500/- was to be debited to the head of provincial reserve in the budget of that official year.[41]

Due to the cyclonic storms, Cuttack and Puri districts were affected by a very heavy and destructive flood which inundated the whole country for some days and the Cuttack city was in imminent danger. It was saved by the energy of the engineer staff, who were aided by the military and prisoners from the jail.[42] Some temporary distress occurred during and immediately after the cyclone and floods when supplies to local markets and particularly to Cuttack were cut off.[43]

In 1874, Balasore district was visited by a cyclonic storm which caused extensive damages in the coastal belt of that district.[44] The following account of the cyclone in Balasore district was taken from the report of the Collector, T. Norman. The barometric readings made at Balasore in the day of the cyclone, the preceding and following days, unreduced for temperature, but accompanied by thermometric readings were as follows.[45]

39. Selections from Divisional and District Annual Administrative Reports, *op.cit.*, p. 465.
40 *Ibid.*
41. J.W. Edgar, Offg. Junior Secretary to the Government of Bengal to the Commissioner of Orissa, No. 3993, Calcutta, 11 September 1872.
42. Selection from Divisional and District Annual Administrative Reports, *op.cit.*
43. *Ibid.*, p. 467.
44. P. Mukherjee, *op.cit.*, p. 47.
45. Report of the Midnapore and Burdwan cyclone of the 15th and 16th of October 1874, by W.G. Willson, Calcutta (printed at the Bengal Secretariat Press 1875), p. 45.

Date	At 7.00 A.M.		At Noon		At 4.00 P.M.	
	Barometer	Thermometer	Barometer	Thermometer	Barometer	Thermometer
14th October, 1874	29.64	84	29.68	84	29.62	85
15th October, 1874	29.53	80	20.48	80	29.23	79
16th October, 1874	29.54	83	29.63	83	29.49	84½

Along the coast line, the western limit of the cyclone of the 15th instant, which entered the country from the Bay of Bengal was coincident with longitude 87^0 85' and almost precisely coincided with the western boundary line of the Baliapal police station jurisdiction. Accordingly, the only portion of the district which fell within the track of the cyclone had been northern most police station jurisdictions and Baliapal and Jaleswar, excluding the pargana of Futiabad on the west bank of the Subarnarekha, which forms of north western corner of the district. A gale, with moderation occurred in the south of the district on the 15th instant, the intensity of the gale continued for six hours *viz.*, from 3.00 A.M. to 9.00 A.M. The direction of the wind was north and north by west. The strength of the gale was only moderate and no damage was done.[46]

No damage was done in this neighbourhood, except a few walls having collapsed by the heavy driving rain. At Jajpur it was simple bad weather. All the appearances indicate, however, that a heavy storm of a cyclonic character had passed up by the Bay of Bengal, and that it affected an usually large tract as far as breadth is concerned.[47] Baliapal during the period had a population of 69,416 souls and Jaleswar a population of 45,722. Here the ravages of the storm had been almost indescribably disastrous.[48] According to the returns prepared by the police, the number of persons killed by the cyclone was 105 and the number of cattle nearly 10,000. The houses which came within its tract were demolished. The injury done to the standing crops was surprisingly moderate. The houseless people suffered a lot due to eight or nine days heavy and incessant rain.[49]

46. Report of the Midnapore and Burdwan Cyclone, *op.cit.*
47. Report of the Midnapore and Burdwan Cyclone, *op.cit.*, p. 46.
48. *Ibid.*
49. *GAROD*, 1874-75, No. 433, Cuttack, 17 June 1875.

The Government gave aid to the people, local subscriptions were raised, and a portion of the SOSO Relief Fund, unexpanded last year, was utilised in helping the people to rebuild their houses. The loss of crops though local was very severe, and the people were still in a very impoverished state.[50] The northern parts of Balasore, and the main tracts affected by the cyclone, did not enjoy the general immunity from diseases. The people were weakened by exposure and privation, attendant on loss of houses and crops fell victims to a very severe outbreak of cholera, which continued until May. More than 781 deaths were reported.[51]

The most remarkable feature of the cyclone on its western side, was, as Norman points out, the abruptness of the line of demarcation between the violent and destructive part of the hurricane and a moderate gale outside.

In the year 1885, the most noticeable storm of the year was a small but extremely violent cyclone which was generated to the north west of the Andamans on September 18th and 19th and travelled rapidly in a north-westernly direction crossing the Orissa coast on the morning of the 22nd September. The centre of this storm passed over False Point light house at about 6.30 A.M.[52] It was accompanied by a storm wave rising to a height of about 22 feet above mean sea-level, which at once submerged the village of Jambu at terminus of the Kendrapara canal to the north-west of False Point and then rolled on in north-westernly direction till it lost itself in the Brahmani river.[53] But its violence, and by the severe storm-wave by which it was accompanied, did much loss of life at that station and in other parts of Orissa.[54] Some important and severe cyclones in India were given in Table 2.1.

The cyclone caused serious damage to the crops, and the loss was very keenly felt in the Jajpur and Kendrapara subdivisions. The loss of human life, cattle and destruction of houses and property was very great. Large fruit-bearing trees were blown down, and the crops totally swept away in many parts. The storm wave was 16 to 18 feet high and carried away everything before it.[55] In Jajpur subdivision no less than 2,447 villages were affected and nearly 50,000 houses were destroyed; about 300 human lives were lost by falling trees, walls and homesteads, and 2,973 cattle were killed.[56] Since at that time in the town, the price of

---

50. *Ibid.*
51. GAROD, 1874-75, *op.cit.*
52. *RAB*, 1885-86, Calcutta Secretariat Press, 1887, p. 101.
53. L.S.S. O'Malley, *BDG*, *Cuttack*, 1938, p. 135.
54. *RAB*, *op.cit.*
55. *GAROD*, 1885-86, Pr. 24, p. 8.
56. L.S.S. O'Malley, *op.cit.*

common rice was 8 local seers per rupee and daily wage of a coolie was half anna many people were incapable of rebuilding their residence in order to stay therein. The cyclone which made its headway into this area destroying the ripe paddy crops absolutely, had rendered the people unable to avail rice in a cheap rate.[57] The loss of human life caused by cyclone was computed at about 5,000 in the Kendrapara subdivision which suffered most and two of its parganas *viz.*, Kerara and Kaldip were submerged under the storm wave. The whole of cultivation in Kaldip and about three-fourths of Kerara were swept away and the loss of cattle was estimated at 10,000 heads.[58] These parganas which included 290 villages with a population of about 26,000, suffered more severely than any other part of the district and a total area of about 250 square miles was submerged. Eleven villages were completely swept away. About 150 more villages were levelled to the ground, though a considerable part of the population managed to escape.[59] The Kanika estate, which included a considerable part of the affected sea-board, suffered most severely and many villages than destroyed had not yet been inhabitated. The salt deposited on the lands by the tidal wave affected the crops for about five years.[60] A sum of rupees 4,876 was spent in Cuttack for repairs of the river embankments of the Kanika estate. The Muharir in charge of the work with his coolies was swept by the cyclone of the 22nd September last.[61]

The cyclone was also accompanied by a tidal wave which swept over False Point Harbour, knocking down all the houses before it, and completely submerging Jambu.[62] The locke was drowned with whole family and the dead body of postmaster was found. All others also faced the same disaster. Out of 9 souls only two females and one child survived, who had taken rest in two strong buildings there. All the steamers and boats present there were completely destroyed.[63] At Jambu, out of a population of 150 only about ten were saved.[64]

A Batighar (Light House) the velocity of wind was too intense and sea water intruded but it a matter of happiness that no life was lost. The Government meteorological calculations predicted about this storm a day before. That day the rain and thunder storms started which violently intensified on 22nd morning but no human life was lost. One ship had

57. *U.D.*, 3 Sept. 1885.
58. *GAROD*, *op.cit.*, p. 8.
59. L.S.S.O'Malley, *op.cit.*
60. *IGI*, Provincial Series, Bengal, Vol. II, p. 248.
61. *GAROD*, 1885-86, Pr. 140, p. 31.
62. L.S.S.O'Malley, *op.cit.*
63. *U.D.*, 26 August 1885.
64. *Ibid.*, 3 Sept., 1885.

TABLE 2.1
SOME SEVERE CYCLONES IN INDIA

Date	*Landfall Point*	*Maximum Wind Speed (km/hr)*	*Minimum Pressure (mb)*	*Cyclone Tract speed (km/hr)*	*Storm surge height (m)*	*Loss of Life*
October 31,1831	Balasore (Orissa)					20,000 (lives lost) 50,000 (cattle heads)
October 15-16,1847	Contai (Bengal)	226			3	75,000 + 6,000 (cattleheads)
July Ist, 1872	Balasore (Orissa)					21 (lives lost) 4,645 (cattle heads)
Nov.24-Dec.1, 1876	Bakerganj (Bangladesh)				3-12	10,000 (drowning) 1,00,000 (epidemics)
September 19-23, 1885	False Point (Orissa)	243	919	21	6.4	5,000 (lives lost) + 10,000 (cattle heads)
November 3, 1946	Narasapuram (A.P)	130	965	11	3-5	750 + 30, 000 (cattle heads)

Sources : K.S. Valdiya, *op.cit.*, p. 357; L.S.S.O.' Malley, BDG, Balasore, p. 94; John Beames, Collector of Balasore to the Commissioner of Orissa Division, Cuttack, No. 432, 13 Aug. 1872, N.N. Banerjee, Report on Agriculture of the District of Cuttack, p. 178.

been thrown into the jungle but no sailor died. A rice loaded French ship had completely been destroyed.[65]

No trace of the remains of the houses, which stood at Hookeytola had been found. Along the coast hundreds of dead-bodies were lying along the sea-face. The bodies of seven monks were discovered some 40 miles away from Hookeytola.[66] The cyclone of the 1885 had done little mischief in Balasore except in the south-east corner of the district.[67] The Grant's

65. *U.D.*, 3 Sept., 1885.
66. Commissioner Office, Orissa Division, to Under Secretary, Government of Bengal, Revenue Department, No. 840, 7 May 1886.
67. *GAROD*, 1885-86, Pr. 29, p. 10.

(Collector of Balasore) report gave detailed damage caused by cyclone on the northern twenty miles of the coast of his district. According to the Collector it was found that the estate Birso had lost most of crops and cattle than any other parts of Balasore. Half of the crops of this estate was lost, about one-fourth of the whole seemed safe and the rest was doubtful. Credible persons affirm that Erem was not safe.[68] After the crops had been harvested it appeared that most of the tenants in Government State (Birso) had lost whole crop or at least three-fourth of it.[69]

In the small portions of the Basudebpur and Chandbali thanas, where the wave managed to penetrate inland of the canal, the loss was put at about half of the crop. The mischief done to the district as a whole was very slight indeed as regards the crops. What they felt most was the loss of cattle, for the wave came while the cattle were on the sea-face grazing grounds and about 14,000 heads were destroyed in all. The district escaped very lightly from what would have been a most grave calamity had it not been for the coast canal embankment.[70]

According to the report of the Khas Tahasildar, Nuanand also suffered from the effects of the cyclone. But there was very little loss of paddy crops in this estate.[71] The pargana Ankurah and Bherah of district Balasore suffered most by the effect of the late cyclone and stormy waves of the year 1885. The average loss of crops in this area was about 14 annas and the loss of cattle was also more than ¾ of the whole. Many houses were damaged and only 6 lives had been lost: others narrowly saved their lives by utmost care. From the east bank of coast canal down to the embankment raised by Zamindars there was not a single paddy plant because all were decomposed by the effects of the sea waves. The cattle suffered much from want of fresh water.[72]

The great cyclone of September did not affect much the Puri district except Dandimal which suffered a little.[73] The storm also passed into the Garjats travelling into Keonjhar at Nilagiri. Due to the pass of gale, the destruction of tress were many which completely blocked the road.[74]

Immediately after the disaster the Government officials visited the devastated area and distributed food to the survivors.[75] Measures were

---

68. Letter of Commissioner of Orissa, *op.cit.*
69. *Ibid.*
70. *GAROD*, 1885-86, Pr. 29, p. 10.
71. Letter of Commissioner of Orissa, *op.cit.*
72. Balasore District Loose Records, Collection 14, Miscellaneous No. 105, 15 January.
73. *GAROD*, 1885-86, Pr. 21, p. 7.
74. Letter of Commissioner of Orissa, *op.cit.*
75. C.E. Buckland, Bengal under the Lieutenant Governors, Calcutta, 1901, pp. 822-23.

taken with the advice of commissioner for the relief of the surviving distressed people by sending down rice for gratuitous distribution and for establishing grain depots.

Taccavi advances were also given to enable the people to reconstruct their houses and purchase cattle. These advances were made available from the funds of the Kanika ward's estate.[76] Two depots were established at Hansua and Rajnagar, from where allowances were doled out at the rate of ½ a seer for each adult and ½ seer for each child.[77] It was found from records that 564 bags of rice had been sent directly to Rajnagar.[78]

The storm wave of the September, did serious damage at Kujang and left many ryots homeless and destitute. In this devastation they were mainly assisted in money by the officials of Court of Wards. But the Maharani of Kujang did not spend a single rupee or relieved a single ryot. The distressed peasantry would hardly be inclined to deny that the court of wards on that occasion stood forth as the landlords in responsible possession of the estate.[79]

In Balasore district less damage was done by the storm wave. It was stopped by the embankment of the sea-coast canal which thus saved hundreds of square miles of country from being submerged by salt water. As a protection against similar visitation, a strong place of refuge was constructed on the highest ground available at False Point.[80]

In the way of relief the people of Birso asked for firstly the remission of the interest for the fasli year 1293 (1886), secondly the postponment of the unpaid 3 annas kits for the year 1292 (1885); thirdly, a taccavi advance of Rs. 1,000 at the time of harvest. Of these proposals T.J.C. Grant admitted to second proposal and the Commissioner of Orissa also agreed with him that it would be unexpedient to grant remission of past arrear on account of unforseen prevailing calamities which at best only temporary in their effects. The first and the third proposals were recommended to the board for sanction on 18th March last.[81]

The Governor-General in Council expressed regret for the considerable sufferings and the great loss of life caused by the cyclone in Orissa. But the prospects of the present seasons were greatly excellent due to the steps taken by the Lt. Governor and by the officers acting

76. *GAROD*, 1885-86, Pr. 25, p. 8.
77. N.N. Banerjee, *op.cit.*, p. 178.
78. Board of Revenue Loose Records, No. 424/2, Sept. 1885.
79. H.J.S. Cotton, Secretary to the Board of Revenue, L.P. to the Secretary to the Government of Bengal, Revenue Department, No. 3584, 5 May 1886.
80. C.E. Buckland, *op.cit.*, pp. 822-23.
81. Letter of Commissioner of Orissa, *op.cit.*

under His Honour's order to alleviate distress. The efforts made by private charity for the relief of distress were extremely gratifying.[82]

The public health suffered from the effects of the seawave and cyclone on 22nd September 1885.[83] The following Table 2.2 shows the total registered mortality from different chief diseases in Cuttack district occurred during the year 1884 and 1885.[84]

TABLE 2.2
RATE OF MORTALITY IN CUTTACK DISTRICT DURING THE YEARS 1884 AND 1885

Year	*Cholera*	*Smallpox*	*Bowel complaints*	*Fever*	*Injuries*	*Other causes*	*Total*
1884	7,482	1,014	4,045	15,964	905	9,236	33,646
1885	10,307	826	4,208	15,520	3,127	7,729	41,617

The mortality form cholera, bowel complaints and injuries probably occurred in coastal tract due to the damage of food and salt water after the storm wave. The Commissioner also visited the affected tracts and consulting with the magistrate of the district, adopted measures to prevent the spread of these disease by having the tanks emptied and filled in with fresh water. The tanks were also dug and medicines supplied to the sufferers. Some thousands of people were washed away and from statistics it was known that the number of deaths swelled from 905 to 3,127.[85] In Balasore district fever and cholera had broken out due to the injuries done by the cyclone.[86]

The unprecedented disaster of the cyclone altered the condition of the people living in the southern and southwestern parts of the district of cuttack and Balasore. The sea wave carried away several thousands of people and the survivors were left in a most miserable condition from the total or partial loss of their houses, cattle and the implements of agriculture. In parts of the country, especially in the Kanika wards estate of the Cuttack district, where the effect of the seawave had been most seriously felt, the people were still in need of help.[87]

82. C.S. Bayley, Under Secretary to the Government of India, Revenue and Agriculture Department to the Secretary to the Government of Bengal, No. Fam. 2-43, Calcutta, 8 January 1886.
83. *GAROD*, 1885-86, Pr. 31, p. 11.
84. *Ibid.*, Pr. 32, p. 11.
85. *GAROD* , 1885-86, Pr. 33, p. 11.
86. *Ibid.*, Pr. 40, p. 13.
87. *GAROD*, 1885-86, Pr. 40, p. 13.

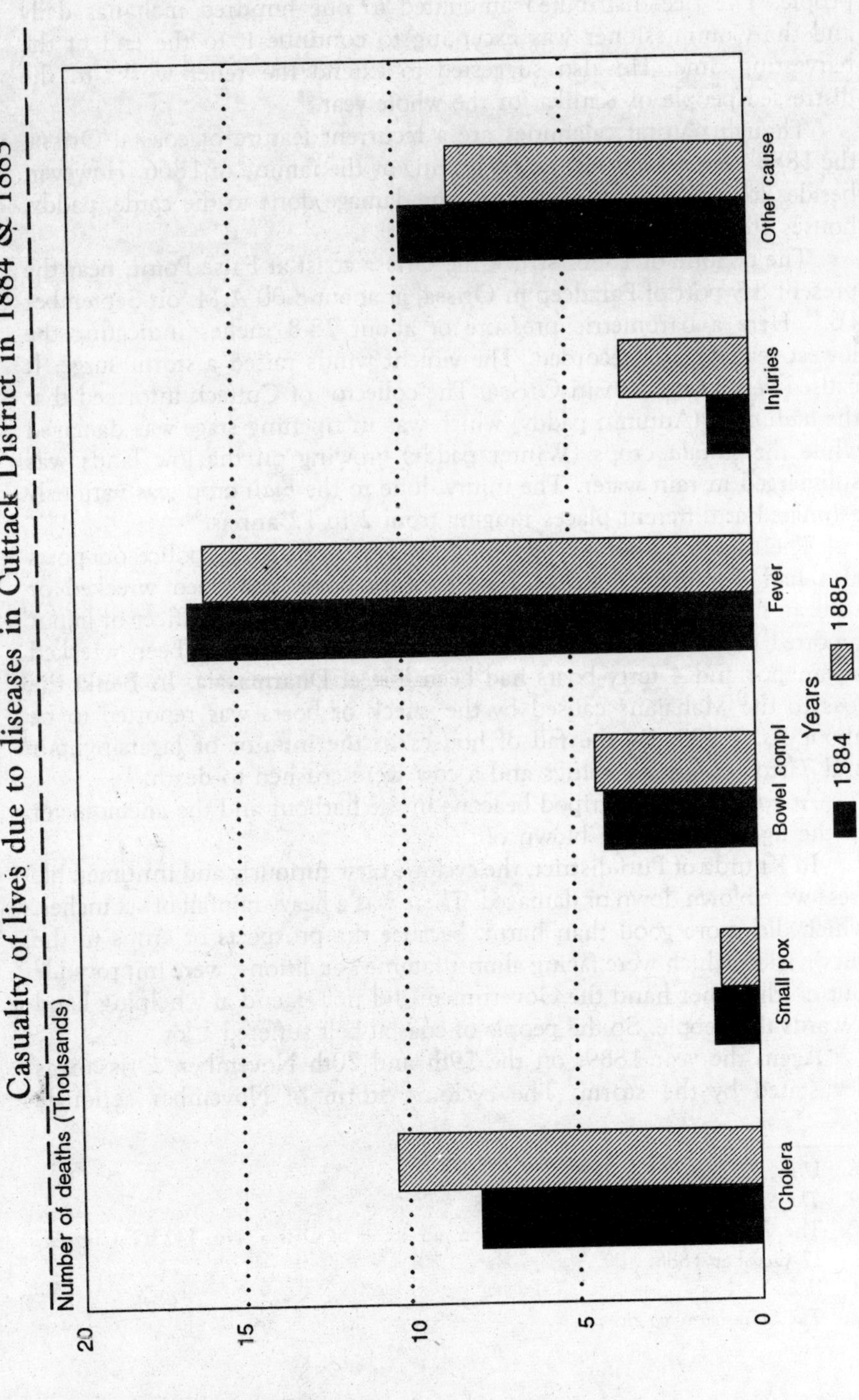
Casuality of lives due to diseases in Cuttack District in 1884 & 1885
Number of deaths (Thousands)
20
15
10
5
0
Cholera
Small pox
Bowel compl
Fever
Injuries
Other cause
Years
1884
1885

Fig. 10

The Commissioner extended his all possible help to the distress people. The rice distributed amounted to one hundred mahanas daily and the Commissioner was excepting to continue it to the end of the harvesting time. He also suggested to extend the relief works to the distressed people of Kanika for the whole year.[88]

Though natural calamities are a recurrent feature of coastal Orissa, the 1885 cyclone was not as devastating as the famine of 1866. However, besides loss of many human lives, the damage done to the cattle, paddy, houses etc., were quite extensive.

The cyclone of 1888, struck the Orissa coast at False Point, near the present day port of Paradeep in Orissa, at about 8.00 A.M. on September 16.[89] Here a barometric pressure of about 28.8 inches indicating the lowest reading was recorded. The violent winds raised a storm surge. It caused very heavy rain in Orissa. The collector of Cuttack informed that the *biali* crop (Autumn paddy) which was in ripening stage was damaged while the *sarada* crops (Winter paddy) growing on the low lands was submerged in rain water. The injury done to the *biali* crop was variously estimated at different places ranging from 2 to 12 annas.[90]

The thatched roofs of houses were blown off. Many police out-posts also had lost their thatches. The country boats had been wrecked or sunk in many places, some with cargo. The subdivisional officer of Jajpur reported that six boats laddened with *dhan*, rice etc., had been wrecked at Janapur and 4 ferry boats had been lost at Dharmasala. In Banki the loss to the Mahajans caused by the wreck of boats was reported to be about Rs. 2,000. By the fall of houses in the interior of Jagatsinghpur and Tirtol, 8 human beings and a cow were crushed to death.[91]

At False Point the tripod beacons in the harbour and the anemometer in the light house were blown off.

In Khurda of Puri district, the cyclone blew furiously and innumerable tress were blown down or damaged. There was a heavy rainfall of six inches. which did more good than harm, because the prospects of crops in the subdivision which were facing almost famine conditions, were improved.[92] But on the other hand the Government did not extend any helping hand towards the people. So the people of coastal belt suffered a lot.

Again the year 1889, on the 19th and 20th November, Orissa was devastated by the storm. The cyclonic storm of November seriously

88. *U.D.*, 21 November 1885.
89. *The Statesman*, 17 September 1888.
90. The Collector of Cuttack to the Commissioner of Orissa, No. 1423G, Cuttack, 27 October 1888.
91. *Ibid.*
92. *The Statesman, op.cit.*

damaged the crops of the Cuttack and Puri districts.[93] The Collector of Cuttack reported on 26th November regarding the damages done, to the crops that the rabi crops, the biri, mug and jaba had suffered considerable damage, with 10 to 12 annas being totally lost. Somehow the crop kulthi had been benefited. About the paddy, 4 annas of *laghu sarada* and 6 to 8 annas of *guru sarada* crops in Cuttack district were destroyed.[94]

Though the rainfall was normal throughout the whole of Balasore district, yet it was heaviest in the south-eastern parts. The bumper harvest expected in Bhadrak and Chandbali was reduced to the category of an average one. The poor crop in Sadar subdivision became poorer. It was reported that the ripe crops had been thrashed out by the rain and the flowering crops had already lost their productiveness.[95]

The seawaves in the coast of Puri rose to a height of 15 to 20 feet. The Chilka lake was swollen and inundated the agricultural fields. In Paikerapur village in paragana Bajrakote all the inhabitants left for Parole in the Ganjam district. In Malud, Bajrakote and Parikud, the private embankments had been partially destroyed and so submerged the fields. In the Khurda subdivision and Chilka tracts some lives were lost. On the sea shore and in the Chilka tracts loss of cattle was very heavy. Immediately after the storm the collector visited the affected areas and took steps to alleviate the suffering of the inhabitants as far as possible. All communications were interrupted for two days; no mofussil carts which were supplying rice to the town, could not come there. So the merchants closed their shops.[96]

The year was marked by an unhealthy situation due to the increase in mortality in each district and the list is given below:[97]

TABLE 2.3
INCREASE OF MORTALITY IN ORISSA DIVISION DURING THE YEARS 1887-1890

	NUMBER OF DEATHS		
	1887-88	1888-89	1889-90
Puri	27,833	18,460	43,767
Cuttack	30,708	36,892	51,413
Balasore	22,772	20,751	36,604

93. *GAROD*, 1898-90, p.4.
94. J.A. Hopkins, Offg. Commissioner of the Orissa Division to the Secretary to the Government of Bengal, Revenue Department No. 2205R, Cuttack, 9 December 1889.
95. J.A. Hopkins, Offg. Commissioner of the Orissa Division, *op.cit.*
96. *Ibid.*
97. *GAROD*, 1889-90, p. 5.

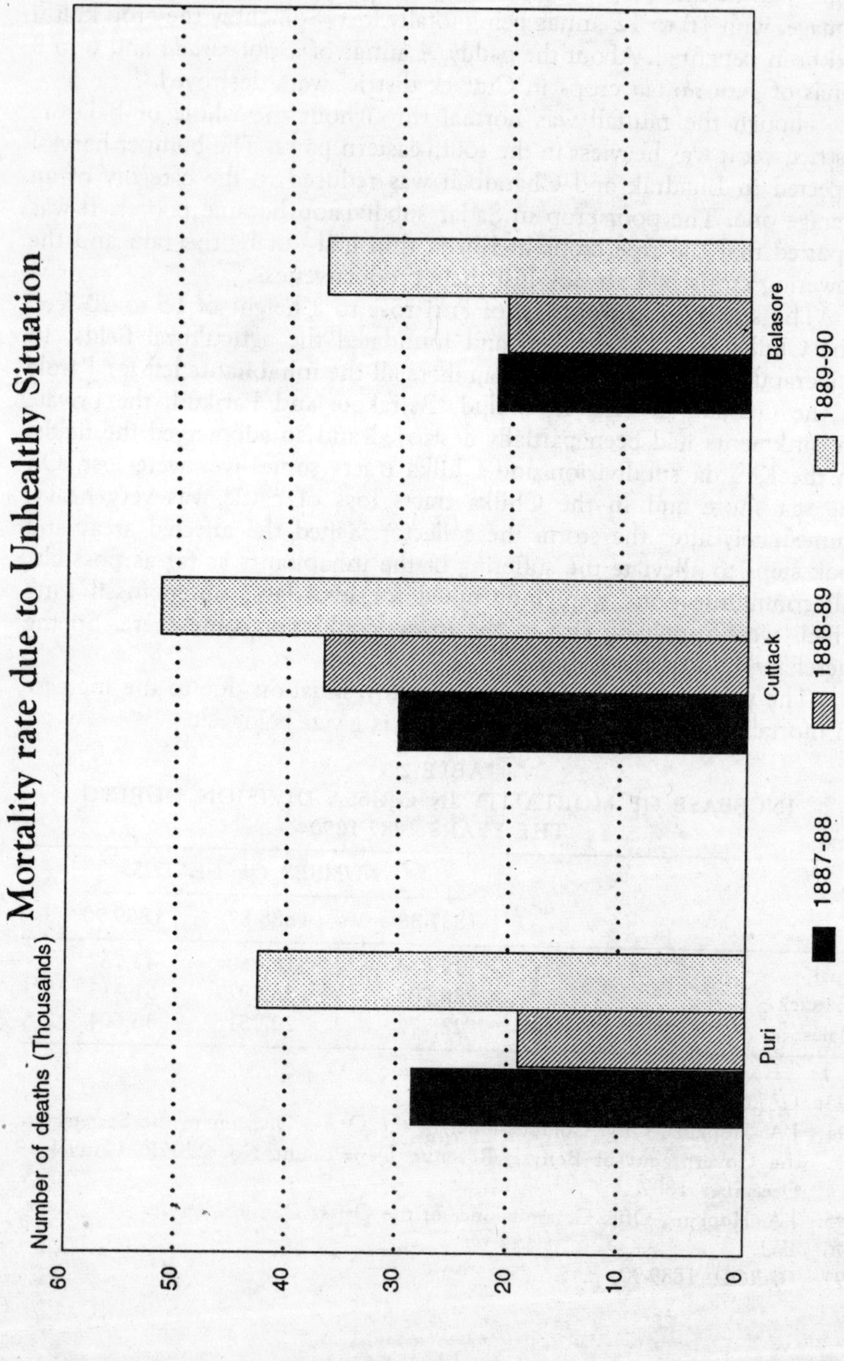
Mortality rate due to Unhealthy Situation
Number of deaths (Thousands)
60
50
40
30
20
10
0
Puri
Cuttack
Balasore
1887-88
1888-89
1889-90

Fig. 11

The heavy rainfall and the high prices of food grains were the main cause of the general unhealthiness of the year.

The number of deaths increased in the Puri district due to the excessive rainfall, which accompanied the cyclone in November. In the Puri town Small-pox broke out after the November cyclones and 54 patients were admitted to hospital.[98] The material condition of people was not prosperous in the year 1889. More or less the landless classes suffered from high prices of grain. The condition of the people of southern Chilka tracts deteriorated due to the reduction of the salt trade, loss of half of their crops and a number of their cattle in the November cyclone.[99]

There was no evidence available to show that the Government took any preventive measures to alleviate the distressed condition of the people from the effects of cyclone. Again in 1890 a storm wave caused considerable injury to the lands lying between Jambu and other creeks to the north of the Kendrapara Canal.[100] The standing crops had been swept away, and all the tanks and wells were filled with brackish water. After four months of tidal wave, the Manager of the estate reported that nearly nine-tenths of the people had remained in distressed condition because they had lost the power of purchasing grain. Many people migrated to other places with a view to seeking employment. Taking this view into consideration the Government sanctioned for constructing bunds which might protect an area of 12,000 mans of this tract liable to sea-water inundation.[101]

Another cyclone hit the Orissa coast on the 4th and 5th November of 1891. The cyclone commenced at Puri at 10.25 P.M. of the 4th and lasted till 1.30 P.M. of the following day. It was violent along the shore from False point down to Puri. The height of the storm coincided with low water and its rose high enough to sweep the low parts of the country as far as Tikri, the headquarters of Kujang Estate in Cuttack district. It caused damages to the paddy fields near the mouth of the river Devi and breached some embankments in Parikud and Malud in Puri district.[102]

The storm struck down thousands of tress and numerous houses. In Balasore the doors windows of the light house the roof of the godowns, dwelling houses, thermometer shed, and other out-offices in Shortt's Island were seriously damaged. In Cuttack district, the outpost office buildings of Erma, Mohakalpara, Shamagole, Pawhpalli, Balikunda, Nuagaon and the

98. *Ibid.*, pp. 5-6.
99. *Ibid.*, pp. 6-7.
100. P. Mukherjee, *op.cit.*, p. 42.
101. N.N. Banerjee, *op.cit.*, p. 179.
102. The Commissioner of Orissa Division to the Chief Secretary to the Government of Bengal, No. 2192R, Cuttack, 12 December 1891.

out-houses of Tirtol and Jagatsinghpur Police Stations were blown down. The dak bungalow at Taldunda and the Kujang estate office at Tikri had been laid in ruins and all the Kutcha buildings at Hookitolla and Jambu were blown down away. In office districts Astrang outpost, Gop Canungoe's office, post office, police station Balighai, public works bungalow, out houses of the town station, Kakatpur Canungoe's office, police outpost, post office and Older Canungoe's office came down and some records in the record room and the treasury buildings were damaged by rain water and the anemometer and the storm signal were blown down.[103]

About 343 human beings and 3592 heads of cattle in Cuttack district and 205 human beings in Puri district were reported to have lost their lives, while no casuality relating to loss of life was reported from Balasore district. The Board sanctioned Rs. 4,050/- out of the Burdwan Ward's Estate to the sufferers of the Cuttack district. The Collector of Cuttack issued parwanas to the Zamindars to postpone the collection of rent from ryots. The application of the Zamindars for the postponement of the next kist was to be considered favourable if it was proved that they had helped their ryots. The District Board also sent a civil hospital assistant with drugs to visit these affected tracts. The crop of course suffered most wherever the sea-water came in and in affected tracts, not more than 4 anna crop was expected to be harvested.[104]

In the year 1893 again Orissa coast suffered from a cyclonic storm. The storm lasted for 4 days *i.e.*, from 23rd to the 26th May. Owing to its effect, the rain was heavy in Bhadrak and Chandbali. No loss of human life or cattle was immediately noticed. About 5000 old houses were reported to have been destroyed, mostly in Dhamnagar and partly in Basudebpur thanas.[105]

The rainfall was very heavy in Cuttack district. The velocity of winds was high along the coast and heavy wind caused the mud walls to collapse. Several rivers were flooded too. The river Gobri at Kendrapara was in high flood and great part of Kendrapara town was submerged. A few cattle were drowned in the floods or killed by the fall up mud walls. The crop in low lands were heavily injured. The roads and bridges in Kendrapara subdivision had been damaged. At False Point the cyclone was severe but fortunately no damage occurred.[106] In the Kujang estate

---

103. *Ibid.*

104. The Commissioner of Orissa Division to the Chief Secretary to the Government of Bengal, No. 2192R, Cuttack, 12 December 1891.

105. From the Subdivisional Officer, Bhadrak to the Collector of Balasore, No. 412, 18 June 1893.

106. G. Stevenson, Collector of Cuttack to the Commissioner of Orissa Division, No. 1018G, 7 June 1893.

the Cutcherry houses were very much damaged by the cyclone of May 1893. No work was done for several days and postal communication was disrupted. In Kanika estate paddy stocks suffered.[107]

The Government spent a sum of Rs. 24,000 in the Kanika estate in Cuttack for the repairs of the embankments which were destroyed by the cyclone. A scheme of complete embankments on the sea side of the Kujang estate was prepared with the approval of the Irrigation Department.[108]

A severe cyclonic storm occurred on the Orissa coast in November 1901 and the rainfall accompanying it was more in quantity than what ordinarily fell in November. As far as rainfall was concerned, False Point reported about 10 inches, Gopalpur 7 and Puri 4. As a result, heavy loss was confined to Orissa coast.[109]

Hence from the above analysis, it is clear that throughout 19th century Orissa suffered from chronic disease of cyclone. No doubt, the colonial Government took some measures to redress the moribund condition of the people, but that was meagre in quantity as per the requirement. They did not take any long term measures to protect the country from the severity of the cyclones. Being repeatedly devastated by it each and every year, the people of Orissa were mortified to see their economic condition deteriorated day by day and made little efforts to cope with the hazard. At the same time, the geographical position of Orissa also contributed a lot to the occurrence of frequent cyclones and the destruction of lives and crops in its wake.

107. Supplement ot Calcutta, Gazette, October 24, 1894, p. 2395.
108. *Ibid.*
109. Supplement to Calcutta Gazette, December 18, 1901, p. 2064.

3

British Policy Towards Floods and Cyclones

Of the different forms of natural calamities, floods and cyclones are the most frequent and had recorded a perilous impact on the economic history of Orissa. In the 19th century the severity of floods and cyclones had drawn the attention of the then British rulers. The Britishers realised that the floods and cyclones are the major contributory factors for the poverty of the people of Orissa. They brought about several measures for ameliorating the economic scarcity caused by floods and cyclones. It was during the British period that major irrigation works were constructed. They also introduced a comprehensive storm warning signal service system for protecting the people and the sea-going ships from cyclone. It is in this context that the present chapter is designed to yield a comprehensive analysis of the various control measures undertaken by British Government against floods and cyclones.

(A) Flood Control Measures

One of the greatest dangers to agriculture is flood. The chief rivers of Orissa namely, Mahanadi, Subarnarekha, Brahmani, Baitarani, Burabalang and Salandi bring devastating floods at frequent intervals. It causes extensive damages to rice crops. The problem of flood is one of the causes responsible for the economic instability of Orissa and appalling poverty of its masses.[1] Inundation in the detail area is considered to be natural phenomena and as such there has been a perpetual struggle against nature to protect the populated and cultivated areas from floods and destruction. The construction of embankments has been the natural outcome of this struggle.[2] Some embankments are constructed to afford

1. Jadu Nath Mohapatra (ed.) *Orissa in 1936-37 to 1938-39*, (Cuttack, , 1941), p. 145
2. Floods in Orissa Rivers during 1955 and 1956. Final Report, Government of Orissa, Revenue (Special Relief) Department, Bhubaneswar.

protection to the cultivators against floods. It was only after the devastating flood of 1866-67 that the necessity of embankments drew the attention of the Government. Thereafter, the Government took up the construction and repair of embankments as the funds permitted.[3]

There are three major schools advocating divergent views. Some want to confine the extra water within the limits of the river channel and not to allow any surplus water to spill over the delta. But this will mean permanent damage to the country side and the channel itself. Of course, if this process is followed, the mouth can be kept free from sand bars but the rivers beds will further rise with levee formation. In case of subsequent breaches heavy damage to life and property will be caused. This was proved during the floods of 1955. Then, again it is difficult, if not impossible to check the floods by this process since the embankments are not percolation-free. Moreover, embankments have to be raised to keep pace with the rise of the river-beds, consequently at the maximum point breaching will be more frequent. This, therefore, is no permanent solution.[4]

Stirling in 1822 A.D. wrote that the town of Cuttack was first planted on the present site in about 989 A.D. by Nrupa Kesari and that the reign of Markata Kesari was distinguished for the construction of a stone embankment in 1006 A.D. to protect the new capital from inundations. Historical evidence has however led to various controversies about the time when the stone revetment, a great work of engineering was executed. The `Madala Panji' an old almanac preserved in the temple of Jagannath, mentions about the establishment of Cuttack and the construction of the revetments during the Kesari periods. But it is said to have no corroboration from contemporary sources.[5] However the existence of the strong embankment from very early times could not be denied and it can also be assumed that this fortification was entirely to protect the town from inundation.

Harris Committee Report

Frequent occurrence of floods in Orissa created problems to the Government. By the recommendation of the superintendent of embankments. Lt. Harris was appointed on special duty to survey the Mahanadi and generally to investigate the question of the disposal of the flood waters. According to Harris, it was certain that for the considerable period prior to 1855 the volume of flood had been increasing in the Kathjori branch and lessening in the Mahanadi main channel. The result

3. Jadu Nath Mohapatra (ed.), *op.cit.*
4. B. N. Sinha, *Geography of Orissa*, New Delhi, 1971, p.76.
5. Floods in Orissa Rivers, *op.cit.*, p.36

was that the town was liable to be severely flooded from the Kathjori, while it was fairly secure on the Mahanadi side.[6]

It had received some attention previously, and the superintendent of embankments in his letter No. 1439, dated 24 September 1855, to the Chief Engineer, lower provinces wrote –

> "A stone weir across the Katjuri head is the first great work to be constructed. It will then I think, be necessary to place a weir across the Kokhai head, for it is not desirable to shut up the Katjuri"[7]

Lt. Harris in his report referred earlier observed that the danger to the town of Cuttack was due mainly to the increased volume of water then flowing into the enlarged bed of the Kathjori as a measure against which he proposed a remedy by the construction of a stone spur or groin at Naraja, and it brushwood spurs along the revetment in the bed of the Kathjori. The aim of the former was to cause the Mahanadi main channel to deepen, and so take a greater relative volume of the flood.[8] However, Lt. Harris was of opinion that for permanent safety of the city a complete weir from Naraja to the head of the town of Cuttack would be more desirable.[9]

J.P. Beadle's Modification

The superintendent of embankments (J.P. Beadle), lower province, Bengal, however suggested some improvements in the proposals of Lt. Harris, and preferred to have a continuous weir across the basin connecting Naraja with the head of the town by a "curvilinear bank of rubble stone over which high floods would spill." This he through would divert the water along the deep channel at the Mahanadi and would clear the Birupa which had silted up so that as Lt. Harris observed "It (Birupa) would be the best channel to make navigable". In support of his proposal J.P. Beadle observes in 1858, brought in a complete change of outlook and based his suggestions on the fundamental proposition that "the regulation of waters of every country depends incomparably more than upon anything else". The spur at Naraja, as suggested by Lt. Harris in 1856 was started in 1857 and Col. Arthur Cotton observed, "The small groyne or spur began at Naraj point has also had great effect causing a great deposit at stand along the west side of the Katjori and also scouring the head of Mahanadi. So that difference at level of two rivers at Cuttack had already

6. W.A. Inglis, *The Canals and Flood Banks of Bengal,* Calcutta, 1909, p. 205.
7. Selection from the records of the Government No.XXXV, Papers relating to the Cuttack Rivers, Part-I, Calcutta, 1860, Pr.20, p. 84.
8. W.A. Inglis, *op.cit.*, p. 206.
9. Floods in Orissa Rivers, *op.cit.*, p.38

diminished". He suggested some improvements by extending this spur towards the head of the delta and to clear the head of the Mahanadi to effect unrestricted with this kind to work and observed that "These works cannot however possibly relieve the sufferings of Orissa."

He suggested a more ambitious scheme while observing that "The only thing that will be effective, the only thing that will prove to the people that they are under a beneficient and able Government; the only thing that will enable Orissa to bear its proper share of the burden of general Government and of its own protection, the only thing that will wipe off the terrible disgrace of the district on degree worse than it was under the former distracted native rule, is a system of works that will completely regulate the waters of the province." Cotton was the person who first suggested the construction of an elaborate system of canals as the only remedy against the droughts and floods to which the district was subject and it was an excellent report on the river Mahanadi. He[11] gave a scheme consisting of –

(1) Weirs across the Mahanadi, Brahmani and Baitarani rivers.

(2) Irrigation channels, completed for navigation throughout the whole deltaic tract.

(3) Drainage channels between all the irrigating channels.

(4) Embankments to all the rivers.

(5) A high level canal for navigation to Calcutta, which would also irrigate extensively.

Colonel Arthur Cotton tried to establish that his scheme, while controlling floods, would provide navigation and irrigation and thus bring about an increases in the revenue. This system of works would completely regulate the waters of the province, which was similar to those in the Godavari and Krishna deltas.[12] According to Colonel Cotton :

"The question of the control of the Mahanadi is not a question of the preservation of the town of Cuttack containing 35,000 inhabitants, it is a question of the preservation of the province of Cuttack and Puri, containing probably 1¼ million".[13]

In pursuance of the policy, construction of the spur at Naraja which started in 1856-57 ultimately developed into a complete weir across the Kathjori head by 1863. The Barang river which took off on the left bank just below Naraja and flooded into the Kathjori was cut off by an embankment at its head in about 1857. In 1860, the rocky spurs on the

11. Quoted in N.N. Banerjee, Report on the Agriculture of the District of Cuttack, Calcutta, 1898, p. 10; Floods in Orissa Rivers, *op.cit.*, p. 40.

12. Note by Lt. J.W. Ottley, R.E. 10 December 1874.

13. *Ibid.*

left bank of Mahanadi were removed by blasting to encourage the flowdown of the Mahanadi river.[14]

The East India Irrigation and Canal Company (a private company) undertook the work of canals in 1863. The Mahanadi and Birupa annicuts were started this year and completed in about 1869. The company failed in 1868 when the works were incomplete and thereafter the Government took over and finished the works earlier than was originally contemplated. The weirs at Jenapur on the Brahmani and Akhuapada on the Baitarani were commenced by 1869-70 and were completed by 1874-75.[15]

Other Surveys

The menance of floods however continued and during the period from 1858 to 1856 there were four floods occurring in 1859, 1872, 1892 and 1896. In 1872, R.H. Rhind, Executive Engineer, Puri survey division made an extensive survey of the main river and of its various branches. According to Rhind, the maximum volume of the flood of 1872 was 1,503,637 cubic feet per second, the maximum flood discharge observed in 1834 and 1855 were 15,70,622 cubics and 5,43,431 respectively. His observations recorded in the report upon the floods of the Mahanadi during the year 1877 start out as important fundamental hydraulic data for technical undertaking relating to flood protectivion.[16]

Since the year 1855 many special enquiries started with a view to preventing or diminishing the intensity of these floods. In the majority of cases attention was focussed on problems of Mahanadi river which chiefly affected, the Puri and Cuttack districts. But the floods of 1920 drew special attention to Brahmani and Baitarani and other rivers which caused severe damage in Cuttack and Balasore.

Except for the general inquiry held by Rhind in 1872 and two more committee reports the Bengal Government under whose administration Orissa remained for long, hardly undertook any ameliorative measures to check the severity of floods or bring them under effective control. People strongly criticised the step-motherly attitude of the Government. In 1908, M.S. Das was moved to agitate for the redress of the problem and invited a few Europeans including Dr. Rutherford (MP) to witness and derive direct knowledge of the horrors of floods in Orissa. Later for the first time a resolution demanding immediate attention to the problem was moved and piloted by Gopabandhu Das Brajasundar in the old Bihar Council in 1920 but to no effect.[17]

---

14. *Floods in Orissa Rivers, op.cit.*, pp. 40-41.
15. N.N. Banerjee, *op.cit.*, pp. 10-15.
16. Lal Mohan Patnaik, *Resurrected Orissa*, Cuttack, 1941, p. 199.
17. W.A. Inglis, *op.cit.*, pp. 222-224.

Policy Deferment

Though recurrent floods had severely affected the state economy in the 19th century major policy responses in this direction came in the 20th century. A thorough survey of the whole coastal tract was made between the years 1920 to 23 and a committee appointed at the instance of the Legislative Council, investigated the question of possible palliatives and reported in 1924. But there had not so far been an authoritative review of the flood problem as a whole by recognised experts. The Governor in Council considered that the first essential to any concerted remedial action was "a reasoned statement of the problem by a body of men who are experts in dealing with river action and who are qualified to advise as to which of the many factors in operating are of prime importance and in what direction remedial action can be sought with great prospects."[18]

Accordingly a committee of four persons (Mr. C. Addams Williams, Chief Engineer to the Government of Bengal as Chairman, Rai Bahadur Bishnu Svarup, Chief Engineer to the Government of Bihar and Orissa and Mr. D.G. Harries, Consulting Engineer to the Government of India as the Member and Mr. J. Shaw, Assistant Executive Engineer, Public Works Department, Irrigation Branch, Bihar and Orissa as Secretary to the constituting committee) was formed to examine the problem of flood in the spot.[19]

The expert committee set up by the Government of Bihar and Orissa in 1928 recommended that in 8,000 square miles of the deltaic area, the protection should be afforded by providing embankments against floods and irrigation by canals. In the semi-protected areas which are protected to a greater or lesser degree from floods by embankments but not irrigated by canals, all obstacles against free flow of floods to the sea should be removed as far as possible without deteriment to the maintenance of the population. They recommended the abandonment of the Orissa· coast canal a part of Dudhei canal at the high level canal system which they through served little purpose for irrigation or transport but did obstruct free flow of flood water. They also assigned specific reasons in particular cases, suggesting opening of estuaries, cutting the sand dunes along the coasts to allow free flow of water and prevention of private reclamation along the tidal basins and in the bed of the Chilka lake. These were altogether 70 items of recommendations. Most of the proposals were investigated into and the less costly ones were carried out to some extent, while some were examined and abandoned as expensive and undesirable and on the whole there was no measure of expediency in the giving

18. Resolution No. 4741/XC-6-27-1. 25 November 1927, Government of Bihar and Orissa.
19. Resolution No. 4741/XC-6-27-1. *op.cit.*

effect to the said recommendations.[20] Except for a few minor proposals entailing less expenditures, the main body of the findings was never given effect to. The limit was reached when the Bihar Government turned down the major recommendations on the main plea of inadequacy of funds among other reasons.[21]

In 1937, the Government secured, free of cost, the services of Sir M. Visheswaryya, one of India's ablest engineers, to study the flood problem and convey his considered opinion on the subject. He submitted a thorough, thoughtful and thrashing report[22] which was more or less intended for the guidance of the Orissa Flood. An Advisory committee, in the mean times was constituted in the year 1938 with three senior engineers and a special executive division was set up for flood investigation work. The committee submitted its final report in February 1942. The major recommendations of the committee are –

(1) Conservation and improvement of main rivers by a system of adequate embankments and by the provisions of maintenance of efficient outlets to the sea to enable the rivers to carry their normal flood discharge for which the slope is made.

(2) Prevention of breaches in the embankments which led to deterioration of the main rivers.

(3) Provisions of high level escapements so designed as to pass only the finder grades of silt and spill water in excess of predetermined figure, over the adjacent land.

(4) Control of deforestation in the catchment areas.

The post-war development schemes assumed importance especially during the days of the Congress Ministry in 1946-47. Mahanadi valley project was undertaken not only to protect the Mahanadi valley against the floods of the river Mahanadi but also to irrigate it, but diverting the water of Mahanadi through canals. It was intended to confer immense economic benefit on the people of Cuttack district in North Orissa and presently Sambalpur* district in Western Orissa.[23]

The Congress Ministry had succeeded in preparing the background for the construction of multipurpose dam in Orissa with the help of Government of India as the first step towards its economic prosperity.

The Orissa Flood Committee of 1928 also took a very pessimistic

---

*Sambalpur is now district in Orissa.

20. Floods in Orissa Rivers, *op.cit.*, p. 42.
21. Lal Mohan Patnaik, *op.cit.*, p. 200.
22. *Ibid.*, p. 201
23. Orissa Legislative Assembly Proceedings, Vol. II, 1946, p. 121.

view on the construction of reservoirs on the river Mahanadi. It opined that in the absence of proper hydrographs it is not possible to say exactly how large the reservoirs would have to be. It is most improbable that a site would be found which would permit the storage of a huge volume of water. Even though such a site exists the cost would run into many crores of rupees. But the gravest difficulty in many schemes of this nature is the fact that the lives of the reservoirs would be extremely limited and the silt laiden water trapped by the dams would deposit its sediment in a comparatively short and the storage capacity of the reservoirs can be reduced to such an extent as to render the work useless.

Sir M. Visheswarayya in his preliminary note of 1937 on the above question viewed that this type of a reservoir will be of value to hold up floods temporarily and release them gradually so as to run the waste at harmless rate.

It was on the basis of these remarks that the multi-purpose development scheme of the Mahanadi valley comprising the Hirakud Dam project came out successful to protect the province from the ravages of the flood water of Mahanadi river. However it was unfortunate that none of the aforesaid committees laid any special emphasis on the protection or control measures in respect of the rivers Brahmani and Baitarani which played important role for unaccountable loss. The Multipurpose reservoir on the Mahanadi came out successful only in the second half of the 20th century.

(B) Protective Measure Against Cyclones

No doubt, Orissa suffered a lot in the 19th century due to the wrath of nature, particularly in the form of cyclone, yet the authorities did absolutely nothing to frustrate the natural rampage. Rather the British authorities in India were very much concerned about making the meteorological department more efficient and to warn the whole population of the approach of cyclonic visitations. This is evident from the correspondences between the Secretary to the Calcutta Trades Association and the Under Secretary to the Government of Bengal, Junior Secretary to the Government of Bengal and the meteorological committee and *vice-versa*. The recommendations to meet the exigencies are known from these correspondences. They are –[24]

(1) Cautionary reports should be sent on the occasions of threatening weather to the chamber of commerce, the Traders' Association, and some conspicuous building in Chowringhee

24. From H.F. Blandford, ESQ, Secretary to the Meterological Committee, to the Junior Secretary to the Government of Bengal, No.296, 18 December 1867.

(such as the Asiatic Society's building) at which signal posts are or may be erected also to the newspaper offices, to enable the editors, if so disposed, to issue `extra' notices to their subscribers.

(2) That two forms of day signals be adopted, a black double cone and drum, (or triangular and square flags of the same colour)' the one to be used as a cautionary signal, the other to indicate the actual approach of a storm. These should be kept in readiness at each of the buildings specified, and hoisted on due notice given from the meteorological office. Further every care should be taken to make the public sufficiently familiar with the idea of cautionary signals as distinct from danger signals.

(3) With reference to the night signals the authorities first decided to make use of guns with prior permission of the military authorities. But the difficulty lies in the fact that the guns would scarcely be heard in most parts of Calcutta as the wind blows from north-east or east north-east direction to lamps are to be employed according to the fitzroy method at some places of higher altitude.

(4) Further, perhaps the most important suggestion to take the challenge of cyclone is to make the meteorological department more efficient and to consolidate as much as possible the work of the department. Thus a uniform meteorological system is pertinent to obviate the possible confusion, delays, and errors arising from divided responsibility.

(5) Again, it is also recommended to furnish additional instruments viz., vacuum black bulb thermometers for solar radiation, minimum radiation thermometers for grass, earth thermometers, anemometers and evaporation gauges. However great care must be taken that all these instruments should be issued after thorough testing. In this sphere also, in checking these instruments the responsibility should be undivided and unified.

(6) Another measure recommended to the Government is that the meteorological observatory be established in some clear space not surrounded by buildings, the effect of which is greatly to influence the thermometric and hygrometric readings, while the necessity of erecting the anemometer and wind-vane on the summit of a lofty building practically removes the former from the eye of the observer.

(7) Again the using of the agency of the police in conveying warning of impending storms, as well as against needlessly alarming the town in general in cases where the event will frequently fail to justify such alarm.

These measures will render the meteorological department very much more effective, by placing the administration more in the hands of one officer and so concentrating responsibility, by ensuring a degree of accuracy and reliability to the records of observation and by removing existing caused of delay in the communication of urgent information to the meteorological reporter and of warnings from him to the shipping and mercantile public.

Besides droughts and floods, Orissa is liable to a third form, and perhaps that is the most appalling form of natural calamity, the cyclone. Cyclone does immense damages to life and property and causes total destruction of crops over wide areas and as an effect of the salt wave for some years huge areas of land have been put out of action. So it playes an important role in the agro-economic life of the people of Orissa. The coastal belt of Orissa is always prone to cyclonic devastation due to its geographical position. But the important question is how to protect the people from such natural calamities, particularly from cyclones which are unavoidable.

Report of the Bengal Meteorological Department (1887-88)

Alex Pedler* in his report (1887-88) to the Government of Bengal has vividly analysed the content and processing of the then meteorological report by the meteorological department. In this report he proposed far reaching changes in the prevailing storm warning signal service.

The first important aspect of the report was the change in the timing for the submission of the report. As per the new schedule, the meteorological reporter is to submit for two years only brief accounts of the principal points in connection with the administration of his department, while every third year he is to prepare full, detailed and comprehensive reports for the three yearly period.

The most significant change analysed in the report was the change in the storm warning signal service. In the old system the Meteorological Reporter was expected specially to give notice of the occurrence of storms in the Bay, which were likely to affect the ports of Calcutta and Chittagong which he was used to give general information as to the existence of storms in the Bay. In practice the reporter telegraphed the message regarding existence of storms to various port points likely to be affected and the message had no official status.[25]

Besides, it was purely the discretionary power to the Bengal reporter to issue such warnings to any ports except those above named. A major

---

*Officiating Meteorological Reporter to the Government of Bengal.

25. Administration Report of the Meteorological Department 1887-88, published in Supplement to the Calcutta Gazette, July 18, 1888, p.1494.

drawback of the system was that the authorities did not allow the message to be displayed and, even though allowed, it was too late for the sea proceeding ships to apprise the situation. Hence, many a time it was not possible on the part of the ships to confront a stormy weather.

In the new system, comprehensive changes were introduced in the reporting practice. The previous practise of hoisting the signals in the river approaches to Calcutta was extended to the port of Calcutta itself. It also introduced a "bad weather preparatory signal" system to inform about the intensity and magnitude of storms formed in the Bay. The duties of the Meteorological Reporter were extended to the warning of the Orissa ports (Puri, False Point, Balasore and Chandbali) and he was empowered to order the hoisting of the storm signals at all the ports on the coasts of Bengal. But subsequently a uniform method of conveying warning was devised and the Bengal Reporter was to give full information of the formation, and growth and line of march of cyclonic storms in the Bay to the port offices of various ports likely to be affected. Also the responsibility to order hoisting of signals was entrusted to the port offices of the concerned ports. All this managements had substantially increased the responsibility of the Bengal Reporter. However, it is to be noted that the storm warning signal systems prevailing in Burmah and Madras ports were more satisfactory than those in the Bengal ports.[26]

In order to render information at the disposal of the Bengal Reporter for working the storm warning system as complete as possible under existing circumstances, sanction was accorded by the Government of India to the inclusion of a larger number of reporting stations in those sending telegraphic information to Calcutta for the daily report. An observatory at Puri on the Orissa coast was established before the close of the official year. But there had been a little delay in establishing three new stations on the Madras coast at Nellore, Cuddalore and Bimlipatam. The cost of this extension of the storm signal service was Rs. 12,500 annually, but almost the whole of this sum (about nine-tenths) was simply for the cost of telegrams when these new stations had started functioning the information at the disposal of the Bengal Reporter.[27] From the 1st April 1888 the weather report of Bay of Bengal was to be introduced daily.[28]

The number of stations reporting observations to the meteorological department during 1887-88[29] was –

Ist Class Imperial Observatory	1
2nd Class Imperial Observatories	2

26. Administration Report of the Meterological Department, *op.cit.*, p.1495.
27. *Ibid.*, p.1496.
28. *Ibid.*, p.1497.
29. *Ibid.*, p. 1148

3rd Class Imperial Observatories	21
3rd Class Provincial Observatories	28
Other Stations reporting for the storm warning service only	10
4th Class Stations or Stations, where records of rainfall only are made	250

To make the observers more careful, a system of fines had been employed for sometime. The observers who had been most frequently punished during the year ending March 1890, were those at Balasore and Puri.

In past years the condition of the lines connecting Diamond Island and False Point with the mainland had been the subject of comment. During the year 1889-90 there was no serious stoppage at either station. But the weather was never very stormy during the monsoon season, so that they were not put to the same test as in other years. The telephone line between Hookeytollah and False Point Lighthouse was thoroughly overhauled, and the telephone replaced by Morse instruments which will soon be in use. The number of rainfall recording stations was increased during the past three years. These stations generally despatched their returns with great regularity.[30]

The alien Government took measures to mitigate the cyclone's effects, by establishing storm signals. But lack of quick steps were also responsible for the considerable damage by the cyclones. Nature was also responsible for the material damage of the province. The cyclones caused heavy down pours over the delta first, and next over the catchment area. The water of the catchment and of the cyclone combined to create greater floods. But due to lack of sufficient preventive measures Orissa suffered most from the effects of cyclones. If following measures had been taken during the period under study Orissa would have not suffered most.

Coastal Hazard Mitigation Measures

The first step in a coastal hazard mitigation programme is the identification and demarcation on maps areas or belts prone to cyclones and attendant surge storms. In coastal Orissa a 24 km. wide belt in the following districts such as Cuttack, Puri, Balasore and Ganjam has been identified as a hazard zone by the cyclone review committee. The wind damage may extend over a much wider belt up to 100 km. inland and the tidal bores may sweep deep inside the land through the mouths of rivers as happened in the Mahanadi river in Orissa (1920).[31]

---

30. Administration Report of the Meterological Department, 1889-90, *op.cit.*, p. 1641.
31. K.S. Valdiya *op.cit.*, pp. 361-62.

Developing Warning Systems

Meteorologists, based in ground observatories, in ships or on oceanographic research vessels, take note of several cyclone indicators for prediction: (*i*) the eye and the surrounding walls of cloud together with characteristic cloud structures. (*ii*) the drop in pressure, and (*iii*) the maximum wind velocity. These parameters and monitored and the cyclone field mapped (with pressure and speed values). The direction of the cyclone is tracked in order to predict whether and where and when precisely it would strike the land. Also required is the advance knowledge of the speed of winds and magnitude of the storm surges they would generate.

Air craft can be used to problem the cyclones at higher altitudes and measures various meteorological parameters, as done in U.S.A. and Japan. The air craft-probing provides the most accurate and detailed information of the eyes and the intensities. Through the geosyn chronous INSAT-IB satellite, cyclones can be continually monitored and their behavioural pattern determined.

The most efficient and effective method of forecasting cyclone tracks is using the technique of radar to track them continually. The S-band radar has been found to be most useful in watching and tracking cyclones.[32]

Reduction of Risks in Vulnerable Areas

Advance warning of the impending disaster or hazard allows people to evacuate the threatened areas and reach suffer places. But warning alone in not enough; people must have adequate perception of hazards and a willingness to adjust. Even though Bangladesh, Orissa and the Andhra coasts have been repeatedly devastated by cyclones for thousands of years, the people have made little efforts to cope with the hazard. There are no integrated plans for adjustments and there never have been any attempts at modifying dwellings. In Andhra Pradesh the fishermen have made significant adaptations in their huts to cope with the high winds.[33]

Coastal hazard managements involve developing an effective and efficient system of monitoring the movements of cyclones through satellites, radar, and air craft and giving advances warning to enable the people to evacuate threatened areas. Adopting modifications in the construction of a design that would strengthen structures to withstand the onslaught of fierce winds, surge waves and floods, and developing a massive wall of multi-storied forests along the coast are two very important measures that should receive greater attention from the governments and the public alike.[34]

---

32. K.S. Valdiya, *op,cit.*, p. 362.
33. K.S. Valdiya, *op.cit.*, p. 362-63
34. *Ibid.*, p. 364

From the foregoing analysis it is obvious that the control and protective measures adopted by the British Government were not adequate. Their approach towards natural calamities were partial and oriented to their interest. Since the then Orissa was not a substantial revenue earing province for the Britishers, they looked after the development of the those ports which served British trade the most. As regards flood control, though the Britishers were much concerned, nothing concrete was done. Except some minor irrigation works and embankments, the major aspects of flood control were not touched upon. However, the various committees such as Harris Committee Report. J.P. Beadle's Modification and Arthur Cotton's Report etc. set up by the British Government were a positive efforts in this direction. The findings and recommendations were of much help in future formulation of policies as regards flood control.

As regards cyclones, the Britishers were fully aware of its frequency and severity. The Bengal Government had established a full fledged meteorological department for issuing warning signals to various ports and cyclone prone areas. It is noteworthy that there was a comprehensive storm warning signal service system for getting early signals about an approaching storm. The meteorological reporters had been assigned the responsibility of communicating such information to different storm prone points. However, the system was not as responsive as warranted by the prevailing situation.

4

Famines in Orissa From 1803-1864

Orissa like most other parts of India is predominantly agrarian. Before the modern times, agriculture was solely dependent on monsoon. This led to the frequent occurrence of crop failures and in turn scarcities and famines which were aggravated due to the growth of inevitable poverty.[1] The poverty of the people, added to the severity of famines. In Europe nearly 450 famines occurred over a period of 850 years from 1000 A.D. to 1850 A.D.[2] After 1850 when Europe became the leader of commerce and industry achieving highest material prosperity, famines and scarcities were hardly seen.[3] It shows that prosperous and richer nation is less affected by famines and scarcities. It creates a coherent relation between famine and poverty. The economically backward and poor, are more frequently menanced by famines and it never affects the richer nation or rich sections of the society.[4] But in the past there was no correlation between famines and poverty. Some terrible famines in the World History occurred in ancient India, Egypt, China, Greece and Rome when they were economically prosperous.[5]

Before British rule a major famine occurred in almost every 50 years. From 11th to 17th centuries there were 14 famines in India and from 1765 to 1858 there were 12 famines and four scarcities. During the period between 1860-1908; India experienced 20 famines.[6] The recurrent famines deteriorated the living condition of the people and also increased the poverty of the masses.

Famines during Maratha Period

The Marathas took possession of Orissa in 1751 and they continued

1. B.M. Bhatia, *Famines in India*, Bombay, 1963, pp.7-13.
2. Southard, "Famines", *Encyclopaedia of Social Sciences*, Vol. VI, p. 85.
3. *Ibid.*, pp. 85-86.
4. B.M. Bhatia, *op.cit.*, pp. 1-2.
5. B.M. Bhatia, *op.cit.*, pp. 1-2.
6. A. Love-day, *History and Economics of Famines in India*, (London, 1914), p. 25; Report of IFC, 1901, p. 1.

their rule till 1803 in northern parts of present Orissa, consisting of the districts of Cuttack, Puri and Balasore. This period of nearly half a century is usually considered as a dark period for the economic prospects of the province. Like the Mughals the Marathas were not helpful to the peasants of Orissa but were mere tax collectors. They were criticised for this reason that though they had been supposed as very good administrators in other parts of the country, particularly near their capital, they could not pay sufficient attention to far off provinces like Orissa. Another criticism regarding their administration was though they are "often hailed as liberators of their homeland from Muslim oppression, they do not always appear in such a role in other parts of India, and their rule was not always an unmixed blessing'. The Marathas not only contributed to the deterioration of economic condition of the province but also destroyed the basic foundation of the economic structure. People were afraid that if they produced more, the Marathas might come and loot their property. There was no question of accumulation of wealth and that might invite problems. Though there are many who praise the Marathas for their liberal views in other parts of the country, their rule in Orissa, as a matter of fact, was sad and unfortunate.

There occurred three famines during the Maratha rule *i.e.*, in 1770, 1780 and 1792.[7] As in other parts of Bengal the great famine of 1770 A.D. which was of the most devastating nature, was grievously felt throughout Orissa. This famine caused widespread havoc and it left behind a dark trail of death, misery and disorder in the administrative system.[8] About 10,000,000 souls perished of starvation and diseases and one-third of the cultivated land became waste.[9] Afterall, the living condition of the people during the Marathas was grievous, for they very often offered from famines and scarcities.

Famines during British (1803-1864)

The British conquest of Orissa began in 1803 and within the next twenty five years the whole of Orissa had come under their control. A famine occurred in 1803, on the very first year of the British occupation.[10] It was also followed by a number of calamities which occurred frequently in the nineteenth century Orissa; and it is opined that this was the most important factor that contributed to the poverty of the agricultural

7. H.K. Mahtab, *History of Orissa*, Vol. II, Cuttack, 1960, p. 446.
8. Griffiths Sir Percival, *The British Impact on India*, London, 1952, p. 184.
9. P.E. Roberts, *History of British India Under the Company and the Crown*, (Oxford, 1983), p. 167.
10. H.K. Mahtab, *op.cit.*
    F.M. Senapati, *Lacchame* (Oriya), pp. 23-25.

population. The occurrence of famine increased with the advancement of the rule and became recurrent feature in every 3 to 4 years. The famine after flood became a regular incident and hence Orissa suffered from a series of natural calamities* which were beyond the control of the people. The Government on the other hand also failed to check these calamities. Due to frequent visitation of famines the economic condition of the people deteriorated.[11] Both famines and poverty were the chief causes of people's suffering during the 19th century.

In Orissa the constant variation of climate and its peculiar morphological existence acted as an impediment to the agricultural prosperity for the farmer was not conducive to put in hand physical labour.[12] The poverty of the people aggravated the severity of famines in Orissa. In the first half of the 19th century Orissa witnessed a series of famines in almost every year which broke down the morals of people in general and agriculturists in particular. The table shows the famines in the first half of the 19th century in 3 districts of Orissa from 1803 to 1864.

TABLE 4.1
FAMINE YEARS IN ORISSA FROM 1803-1864

1803, 1806, 1807, 1809, 1817, 1828, 1834, 1836, 1837, 1839, 1840, 1863.

Sources: L.S.S.O' Malley *BDG, Puri, Cuttack* and *Balasore*; W.W. Hunter, *History of Orissa*, Vol. II; G. Toynbee, A *Sketch of the History of Orissa (1803-1828):*

The first half of the period under study was full of calamities like famines and scarcities. The untimely rainfall and floods were the immediate causes of scarcities in the first half of the 19th century. The providence of Cuttack, observed the Court of Directors, "is subject to seasons of extreme uncertainty liable to the most remarkable vicissitudes of drought and inundations".[13] The immediate cause of drought was the repeated failure of monsoon.

The crops were destroyed due to drought in the year 1806, owing to the failure of the rains between 17th September and 11th November.[14] As a result of the partial failure of the rice crop in 1809 the princes rose from 8 to 10 seers higher than usual and all the former difficulties were revived. The merchants, profiting by experience, bought up all the grain

---

*Years of Natural Calamities are given in Appendix-A,B and C

11. S.N. Das, *Unabimsa Satabdir Orissa* (Oriya), Vol. I, (Cuttack, 1969), p. 66.
12. B.S. Das (ed.), *Glimpses of Orissa*, (Calcutta, 1986), pp. 276-277.
13 *BdRP*, Revenue, Org. No. 157, Issue, p.33.
14. G.Toynbee, A *Sketch of the History of Orissa* (From 1803 to 1828), Calcutta, 1873, p. 87.

on which they could lay their hands. The then Magistrate, in the hope of avoiding previous difficulties, advanced sicca Rs. 1,000/- from his own pocket to purchase supplies for the use of the troops. The grain dealers industriously circulated a report, when they had this news, that the person appointed by the Magistrate to purchase grain in the interior had an absolute monopoly to control the whole supply of the province. Then the Beparis declared that they would not come with grain to the town unless this practice was put to a stop. At last the Governor-General in Council issued orders, prohibiting the interference of any Government officers with the grain market.[15]

Again in the year 1813 there was drought and acute scarcity prevailed in the vicinity of Cuttack. The distress was so great that the poor inhabitants died for want of food.[16] On the 31st October 1831, the severest disaster occurred in the Balasore coast and nearly 22,000 were perished in this district. The whole coast was submerged,[17] and the flood washed away all the standing crops and every article of food in stock. There was acute scarcity of rice in Balasore district and the poor people suffered a lot. These calamities were followed by a drought in 1833. In successive three years 50,000 human beings were destroyed by drowning and starvation.[18]

In 1836-37, a severe drought occurred in the province and Rs. 4,52,532 of the revenue was remitted.[19] In 1837-38 similar calamity also desolated the country and Rs. 5,87,146 was remitted by the Government.[20] Rice was selling in the Cuttack bazar at 10 seers a rupee and the dealers were hoarding up their stores in consequence of the protracted drought as soon as the rains set in which may be daily except, the price will fall and abundant supply be poured into the market.[21] The Commissioner of Orissa wrote to the Collector of Cuttack, "There having become so exceedingly scarce, I am apprehensive that in a few days we shall not be able to procure any evey at the high rate at which it now sells. Under the existing scarcity Government would have the risk of sustaining a tripling loss".[22] Any interference on the grain market in the part of the Magistrate

---

15. G. Toynbee, *op.cit.*, pp. 87-88.
16. J.W. Sage, Magistrate to Secretary to Government, Ist September 1813.
17. L.S.S.O 'Malley, *BDG*, *Balasore*, p. 94.
18. *Ibid.*
19. *BdRP*, *op.cit.*, p. 34.
20. *BdRP*, *op.cit.*
21. Cuttack Collector's office to H. Ricket Esq., Commissioner, 19 Division, Balasore, 17 June 1837.
22. Letter from B. Roope, Commissioner of Cuttack to Collector of Cuttack, 17 June 1837.

was not only impolite but was strictly prohibited. He made his best endeavour to persuade the principal zamindars and dealers to bring grain but failed.[23] Thus the laissezfaire attitude cf the Government aggravated the condition.

In 1839-40 Orissa also suffered from natural calamities. The floods and famines were so severe that the Company Government was forced to remit revenue. The whole of zamindary estates suffered a lot from drought. In the commencement of the season for preparing the *sarada* crop the fall of rain was abundant and seasonable to a greater degree. In consequence every plough and every grain of seed that was available was employed and although great losses had been suffered by inundation last year and the means of the cultivators were straitened, the cultivation was remarkably extensive, the rain became scarce towards the end of August but the cultivators made strenuous exertions to save by irrigation the very promising crops they had raised. Their effects however were in many instances fruitless. In the month of November there was rain for three or four days, but it was of no avail where the crops had not been saved by irrigation. The average loss of *sarada* crops on the whole district was about 10/16. In many places it was not practicable to sow any rubee seeds. The average loss was about 12/16. The total average would be about 7/16ths. The *dalua* crops was also deficient owing to scarcity of water in streams and pools.[24]

The price of rice rose in January and February and it sold at 14 seers per rupee and so there was difficulty in collecting it. It was just impossible to distinguish the effects attributable to the drought of 1836-37, the inundation of 1839-40 in the province. The effect of all these losses upon the tenantry was necessarily heavy. Many have changed their habitations to avoid the annoyance of the creditors whom they cannot satisfy than to improve their condition. Many of the poorest classes who had bound themselves for a term of service to liquidate advances made to them in 1837 have been provided for by their employers, but many who would have been free thrown back by this fresh calamity. No Asiatic tenantry can be expected to withstand such a succession of calamities.

There has not yet been a single drop of rain and in consequence the land has no where been ploughed for the crops which ought to have been by this time considerably advanced. Many of the Zamindars have

---

23. From A. J. M. Mills, Collector, Zilla Cuttack to B. Roope, Collector Commanding 19th Regiment, Cuttack, 17 June 1837.
24. From James K. Ewart, Collector, Puri to A.J.M. Mills, Commissioner for the 19th Division, Cuttack No.105, 7 April 1840.

also filed detailed statements of the distribution of the suspensions which will afford on additional protection to the ryots and ensure to them the full benefit of the remission.[25]

In 1840, there was excessive drought in the province. So the Commissioner of Cuttack (A.J.M. Mills) proposed to sanction the remissions of revenue amounting to Rs. 587,146-9-5¼ on account of loss occasioned to the crops in the province of Cuttack by the early cessation of the last periodical rains. Mills also recommended for suspending for one year the demand of the balance of taccavi advances still due in Zilla Balasore and also suggested to take long term measures to check the country from similar disastrous effects of drought in future.[26]

The Sadar Board of Revenue agreed to the recommendation of the Commissioner and authorised the remissions of the sums (Rs. 587,146-9-5¼) and also sanctioned the recommendation for suspending for one year, the demand of balance of taccavi advances still due in Zilla Balasore. The Board also requested with reference to annexed extract para 10th from their address to Government of the 17th ultimo, "You will immediately communicate with the several collectors and surveyors in your division to prepare a well digested plan for obviating similar disastrous effects of drought in future".[27]

The revenue remitted on account of droughts of 1841-42 amounted to Rs. 2,09,290.[28] In 1842-43 the province of Cuttack also suffered from an early cessation of the periodical rains, and the revenue of Rs. 4,86,625 was also remitted.[29]

In 1845 drought occurred in the northern part of Balasore district followed by inundation in 1846. A drought occurred in Orissa in 1849-50 and it was also followed by another drought in 1851 and the revenue remitted on account of this amounted to Rs. 18,465/418.[30] During the 35 years, from 1831-32 to 1866-67, Government had to remit £257,939 of its Orissa rental for droughts alone or £455,365 for

---

25. From James K. Ewart, Collector, Puri to A.J.M. Mills Commissioner for the 19th Division, Cuttack, No. 105, 7 April 1840.
26. From J.H. Young, Deputy Secretary to the Government of Bengal to E. Currie, Secretary to the Sadar Board of Revenue, No. 978, Fort William, 7 July 1840.
27. From Secretary, Sadar Board of Revenue, Fort William to the Commissioner of Revenue for the Division of Cuttack, No. 282, 17 July 1840.
28. Droughts in Orissa during 1954-55, Final Report, p. 3.
29. Selection from the records of the Bengal Government No. III, papers on the Settlement of Cuttack and on the State of the Tributary Mahals, (Calcutta, 1851), p. 27.
30. Droughts in Orissa 1954-55, p. 3.

the combined effects of droughts and floods.[31] In the first half of the 19th century Orissa suffered much from famine. The Government did not take any long term or short term measures to prevent country from such calamities. It took some remedial measures such as only remission and suspension. Thus first half of the 19th century was full of calamities and the people suffered hard under the British Government which led to gradual impoverishment of the people of Orissa. The Court of Directors remarks about the province of Cuttack, "much of the distress which has been ascribed to over assessment, may perhaps be more justly regarded as the inevitable consequences of calamity of session in a country where from want of capital, every partial failure must be likely to produce the most lamentable effects".[32] The sad effects of the failure of the potato crops in Ireland in 1845-49 might be compared with similar results of famine in Orissa. Many parents sold their children for a scanty pittance, many were abandoned by these famine stricken fathers and mothers and many wandered in hopes of obtaining the means of subsistence but never met again.[33] Throughout the first half of the 19th century Orissa suffered from terrible famines which show its inevitable economic decline.

The Hindu kings in ancient and medieval periods accepted the responsibility for providing relief to the destitutes at the time of famines.[34] The people of Orissa were not facing any trouble, at the time of famines that had occurred in Orissa during the reign of indigenous kings. But now they had to many troubles under the alien rule. The kings were trying their best to save the people from famine. The people were not as poor as today. Day by day the people of Orissa had become poorer and had lost their power of tolerance with the establishment of foreign power in Orissa.[35]

So famines could not play havoc and people were saved due to their self help. The famine policy of the British marked the rejection of active intervention to alleviate the distress. The British rule and the progressive growth of poverty made the people of Orissa cruel victims of calamities. The following table shows the average price of rice in different periods, which depicts gradual deterioration of the condition of Orissa people:

31. W.W. Hunter, *Orissa*, Vol. II, (London, 1872), p. 184.
32. *BdRP*, Revenue, Org. No. 157, p. 36.
33. A. Sutton, *Orissa and its Evangelization*, (London, 1850), p. 227.
34. Lallanji Gopal, *Economic Life of Northern India, 700-1200*, (Delhi, 1965), p. 249.
35. Pt. S.N. Das, *op.cit.*, p. 67.

TABLE 4.2
AVERAGE PRICE OF RICE IN ORISSA (IN SEERS)

Year		*Rice per rupee*
1836-46	..	48
1846-56	..	58
1856-66	..	29
1866-67	..	5 (Na-anka-Durvikhya famine)
1869-70	..	2
1875	..	1½
1866-76	..	27
1876-87	..	22
1886-96	..	19

Sources : S.N. Das, *op.cit.*, p. 67. Maddox Report, Vol. I, p. 119.

During these years prices of rice increased rarely more than 3 times while income of people who were mostly agriculturists decreased many fold. Thus high prices which made the people poorer led to hunger and deaths. The people's material well being declined and the poverty grew to an alarming level.

In addition to natural calamities there were a number of administrative factors which contributed to the economic hardship of the people of Orissa. There was political disturbances which was a feature from the very beginning. The Paik rebellion of 1817 proves that the Oriya people did not accept the British rule without resistance.

British Policy responsible towards Famines

It was the province of Orissa which was formerly called Cuttack province. The province which consisted of the regulation districts of Balasore, Cuttack and Puri[36] was attached to Bengal for administrative purpose and the British rulers tried to prevail here all the systems they had adopted in Bengal. As agriculture was the chief occupation of the people of Orissa, the greedy rulers tried to extract revenue out of it. Since the beginning of their rule, their revenue policy proved detrimental to agriculture and greatly crippled the economic life of the people because they were ignorant about the condition of the province.

The first and the foremost task before the Britishers in Orissa was the land revenue administration. The British introduced zamindary system in Orissa because there were zamindars as were found in Bengal. In 1773 Warren Hastings decided to sell the right to collect revenue which the East India Company had gained from the Mughal Emperor by the

36. The three districts were formed at the end of 1828.

Dewani granted in 1765 to the highest bidder or the zamindar for one year. Later Lord Cornwallis introduced the permanent settlement by which the Government fixed permanently the annual land revenue to be paid by the zamindar.[37] This zamindary system, was also introduced in Orissa. Under the zamindary system, the zamindars agreed to pay a fixed amount annually as land revenue to the Government. On the other hand there was no fixed amount in real terms of the revenue payable by the peasants to the zamindar. The zamindars raised the rate heavily under the permanent settlement and the peasants lost their ownership of land and maintained the life of poor tenants.

About twelve such permanently settled estates were constituted according to the finest regulations introduced by the British in Orissa. Then the system was also extended to some of the killajats in Balasore and Cuttack districts.[38] Subsequently, the Company Government in Orissa did not consider permanent settlement to be economically beneficient to themselves and thus they introduced a new system in Orissa by which they could periodically raise the revenue payable by the zamindars to the East India Company. By this policy, the only benefit of zamindari system *i.e.*, non-increase of land revenue was denied to the people of Orissa. Also ordinary settlement was done in major parts of Mughalbandi,* which covered an area of 6000 square miles (including Khurda).[39] Henceforward the Kanungoes, Taluqdars, Rent Collectors, village headmen and holders of resumed jagirs, who were the officers in charge of revenue collection before the British rule were recognized as proprietors of huge landed estates and became zamindars.

The proclamation of September 1804 declared that at the end of 1815 a permanent settlement would be made of "Such lands as may be in a sufficiently improved state of cultivation to warrant the measures, on such terms as the Government shall deem fair and equitable". But certain changes were made in the resolution in spite of its introduction and several short settlements were provided. The proclamation of 1804 got confirmation in 1805, 1812, 1815, 1816 and 1818. Now the Government increased the assessment at each settlement without looking the real value and capabilities of the estates. As a result, the Oriya proprietors were harassed due to heavy arrears and their valuable properties (defaulting

---

*The Mughalbandi–which comprised all that plain and open part of Orrissa from the Subarnarekha to the borders of Khurda which paid a regular assessment to the Mughal Government.

37. Baden Powell, *Land Systems of British India*, Vol. I, pp. 299-304.
38. G.C. Patnaik, *The Famine and Some Aspects of the British Economic Policy in Orissa 1866-1905*, p. 3.
39. Maddox Report, Vol. I, p. 1.

estates) were sold to Bengali speculators at a low rate. Automatically absentee landlordism became a permanent feature of the revenue system of this land. The discontented people became dissatisfied by over assessment and mismanagement which became one of the causes of the rebellion in 1817.[40] Between 1805 and 1820 the revenue rose fitfully from about 11 lakhs to 13½ lakhs.

The question of introduction permanent settlement in Orissa was closed by Government because the land was not fit for that purpose. Then the regulation VII of 1822 marked the beginning of a new phase in the history or land revenue administration in Orissa by enunciating the change of policy of Government.[41] The existing Cuttack settlement extended for 5 years until 1826-27 by the new regulation. The settlement also provided for detailed measurement and settlement of the lands. The regular settlement was made in 1838,[42] and was to continue for 30 years in Orissa.

No the people of Orissa became aware of the British Government policy because starting from 1804 the Government had repeatedly promised in different proclamations, for an effective permanent settlement which was not introduced but the promises let to an adverse effect on agricultures in province.[43] The immediate effect of the expiry of a settlement had been to discourage agriculture. The people were in a chronic state of anxiety as to face the state of things to come and they had been extremely distrustful to the intention of the Government. The people had still belief for the introduction of the permanent settlement after all culturable land was cultivated. The settlement of 1837 provided for heavy assessment of revenue leaving two-thirds to Government and one-third for profit and expenses to the zamindars. But the zamindars were not well treated as they were poor and improvident. It is true that some remissions had been granted by the Government from time to time on the occurrence of great calamities, but these were not timely and commensurate with the injury sustained.[44]

The revenue policy impoverished the Indian peasantry. Unable to meet the requirement of the whole year, generations of peasants faced many difficulties. By 1837, the Government had acquired possession of some estates known as Khasmahals and managed those estates through Tahasildars. The cause may be stated that due to increase of revenue demand in course of short settlements many proprietors had lost their

40. G. Toynbee, *A Sketch of the History of Oirssa*, pp. 22-23.
41. B. Powell, *Land System of British India*, Vol. I, p. 475.
42. B. Powell, *op.cit.*
43. *BRP*, November 1877, Henry Ricketts to Secretary of States, 19 November 1866.
44. H. Rickets, *Report on Midnapore and Cuttack*, 1858.

estates.[45] Under the Mughals and Marathas the tax collection was not so much rigid as under the British.

The British trade and commerce policy had forced a large number of town and village artisans out of that profession increasing the pressure on land. The condition of the poor tenants became precarious as the assessment was heavy. They did not know about their rights and rate of rent. Though regulations were passed for the protection and preservation of the rights of ryots yet they were not effective due to lack of legislative enactment. The zamindars considered themselves as absolute owners of the lands and cultivators as poor reckrented tenants of the soil. Though the Act X of 1859 was passed in order to improve the condition of the tenants yet the provisions were met satisfactory to provide adequate protection to their life and property.

Since earliest times Orissa had a rich tradition of salt manufacture. And fine salt manufacture in Orissa had become a sort of cultivation and a natural industry through the ages before the coming of the British.[46] In the pre-British period salt manufacture of Orissa was controlled by the coastal zamindars in the northern part of the province. In the south this was carried out by the ryots *i.e.*, peasants-cum-Malangis on their own account on payment of a land rent, to the proprietors of the salt lands. The whole position considerably changed with the advent of the British as rulers of this province in 1803. They took over the salt affairs of the province in 1804 by making salt a subject of Government monopoly which compelled the industry for its ruin.

By the time of Lord Cornwallis the East India Company had established a monopoly both over manufacture and sale of salt in Bengal. The salt monopoly was extended over a portion of Orissa to the north of the river Mahanadi after its conquest. So extension of manufacture was undertaken by a phased programme with respect to the different part of the province. By 1812, several salt manufacturing centers were either revived or newly opened in the two districts of Balasore and Cuttack. It was impressed upon the Government that a revenue worth more than five lakhs of rupees would be deprived for a management cost of one lakh of rupees on extending salt manufacture under Government to the southern part of the province, which was accomplished in 1814. As a result, there were twenty four centres working in the three coastal districts of Orissa, eight in Balasore, seven in Cuttack and nine in Puri. Thus the whole of Orissa came under the salt regulations of Bengal and the revenue derived from salt monopoly exceeded the total amount of land rent of

45. Maddox Report, Vol. I, pp. 164-165.
46. S.N. Choudhary, *Economic History of Colonialism*, New Delhi, 1979, p. 113.

the state. The Government yielded about three lakhs from the sale of salt in this province along with the largest amount of nearly fifteen to sixteen lakhs annually, when salt was exported to Calcutta for salt.[47]

The price of salt increased and people felt difficulty in procuring salt even at such rates. The cause lies in the introduction of salt monopoly in Orissa in 1804[48] by which the flourishing inland salt trade to the north and westward of this province declined to the lowest ebb. Also the British authorities in Orissa gave emphasis to the sea-borne salt trade for supplying the Bengal market with Orissa salt. The inland salt trade of this province was neglected and subjected to restrictions in sharp contrast to the emphasis given to the sea-borne trade under the suspices of the Government salt monopoly. The salt monopoly like that of land revenue was disastrous to the pople as it was conducted by the fatal policy of a too sudden leap from one extreme end to the other.[49] The spirit of the revolt against salt monopoly was also found during the insurrection of 1817 in the northern division of Orissa. The insurrection of 1817 opened the eyes of the British Government to the realities. The salt department now sought to reorganise the salt monopoly by a suitable system. So efforts were made in the post insurrection period to redress the popular discontent against the salt monopoly. The price of salt was reduced but it was not reduced to the extent at which it could have induced regular maximum consumption. Several attempts were made after 1844 to stimulate the consumption of salt and thereby to increase the revenue by means of successive reduction of duties. Still the price was very high even after reduction. The Government manufacture of salt was long carried on the coast of Orissa and it provided employment not only to a large number of people of that area but also to the people of other parts of the country.

By fixing the wholeasale price of salt and by admitting the imported foreign salt to competition with the home made salt, all the damage was done to the indigenous salt trade. The sea-borne salt trade with Bengal in north was destroyed and it automatically led to economic ruin of Orissa in general.[50] Thus it was decided to discontinue the practice and to introduce instead, a combined system of customs and excise. In 1863 the manufacture was closed throughout Orissa, throwing a large number of manufactures out of employment.[51] After cessation of the Government manufacture, there remained considerably stores of salt previously

47. A. Striling, *An Account of Orissa Proper or Cuttack*, (Calcutta, 1904), p. 37.
48. Ewer's Report, 13 May 1818, Pr. 135.
49. G.T. Toynbee, *op.cit.*, p. 70.
50. S.N. Choudhury, *op.cit.*, p. 113.
51. G.N. Barlow, Collector of Puri to Commissioner, No. 272, 27 November 1865.

manufactured. The condition of the manufacturers became precarious because of unemployment.

The province of Orissa frequently suffered from the opposite evils of floods, inundation and droughts. Subjects to great variations the rainfall was precarious. There was not any provision for purposes of irrigation except some sort of water supply made by ryots. There was also made no attempts to improve the lands due to periodical settlement.[52] By an Act of Parliament in 1861 the East India Irrigation Company and the Secretary of State executed a contract for the construction of works for irrigation, navigation and supply of water and other purposes in the districts confined to the delta of Mahanadi and the adjoining region.[53] By 1866 (great famine) these works had not progressed to the satisfaction.

The province suffered from twin evils of flood and drought. In the floods of Mahanadi, Kathjori and Kuakhai hundreds of square miles of the state were devastated and heavy losses were sustained on the people. In great floods hundreds of square miles of the country were devasted in this manner, and the loss on this account had been as frequent as those on account of drought.[54]

Along with the heavy losses due to floods and inundations, the recurrent droughts made the condition of the people worse from time to time. The scanty rainfall laid to an automatic little yield which resulted in great disaster. A number of droughts and famines appeared on the soil of this land in the first half of the nineteenth century.

In the first half of the 19th century there was no system of canals and irrigation. Though the East India Irrigation and Canal Company had undertaken a project since 1861, the task had not progressed till 1866. This work had further been given importance by the historic famine that had poured upon the Govenment to expedite the work which was given importance by the Famine Commission. It was aimed at making a link between Calcutta and Puri.[55] The British Government made no attempt to improve agricultural practices on scientific lines. Better types of tools, fertilizers and manures which were known in England were not utilized either in India or in Orissa.

The Province of Orissa also suffered from geographical isolation. The country was full of hilly tracts. There was only a rotten traffic with Sambalpur by boat in the rainy season. The nature of the coast and the sea was such as effectually to stop all native traffic for the major part of

52 *RIF*, 1866, Vol. I, Evidence No. 52.

53. Orissa and Project, Contract between the Secretary of the State and the East India Irrigation, November 28, 1861.

54. *RAB*, 1871-72, Orissa scheme, p. 249.

55. Maddox Report, Vol. I, p. 22.

the year. The rivers were not used for the purpose of communication. They were inaccessible to the ordinary type of European vessels.[56] There was no protected anchorage of any kind for such vessels on 12 to 14 feet of water even at the worst season of the year provided they entered with the aid of steam.[57] The Dhamara port was declared one of the important ports of Orissa in 1858. It was a useful port even at the time of British occupation in 1803 wherefrom rice and salt were exported to Bengal.[58] No attempt was made by the British to improve the inland communication in the province.

There was not any communication by road so to say in the scientific manner. There were no roads in existence in Cuttack when the province of Orissa was taken over by the English in 1803.[59] There was only one mud and dust road, used in summer times but it was difficult to use during rainy season which passed form Midnapore through Balasore and Cuttack to Puri was probably the Jagannath Road. Some portions of the road was damaged and so it became impossible to cross it by wheeled carriages for which pack bullocks were used.

The railway line was not introduced in Orissa. This province was not prosperous enough as it lacked operations in the field of trade and commerce. There were no trading classes in Orissa. The only horns and hides were exported to Tamuluk by land and to Calcutta by water route. After 1854-55 export of salt from Orissa to Calcutta was stopped, because the Government of India allowed the import of foreign manufactured salt in order to be sold in the Bengal market. The people were idle to search for markets in order to sale their surplus grains. There were some export of grain by land from Southern Orissa to the district of Ganjam and the port of Gopalpur and from Balasore to Midnapore, Hidgelee and Calcutta.[60] In spite of the all round economic developments of the province its people were harrassed by the drain of wealth by the oppressive land revenue policy of the British and Orissa got nothing from the trade facilities which was granted to the British merchants in the province.

The province of Orissa also suffered from the defective British administrative set up. The Bengal Presidency included not only Orissa division, but also the provinces of Bihar, Assam and Bengal. Till 1853 these provinces were administered by Lt. Governors[61] who were neither assisted by council nor by superior secretaries and their works were

56. G.C. Patnaik, *op.cit.*, p. 11.
57. Kartikeswar Patra, *The Ports in Orissa*, (Bhubaneswar, 1988), pp. 180-181.
58. G.Toynbee, *op.cit.*, p. 88.
59. N.N. Banerjee, *Report on the Agriculture of the district of Cuttack*, p. 150.
60. G.C. Patnaik, *op.cit.*, pp. 12-13.
61. C.E. Buckland, *Bengal Under the Lt. Governors*, Vol. I, p. 2.

overburdened from the administrative point of view. So he had no time to look after the administration of a little division like Orissa. A Commissioner was appointed to supervise the administration of Orissa. A large number of both judicial and executive powers were vested in the hands of Commissioner of Orissa and simultaneously also the Superintendent of the Tributary Mahals of Orissa. So he could not give proper attention to each corner of the province as far as administration was concerned. "The most difficult problem that the administration had to face, is the liability of the province to loss of crops from natural calamities"[62]

There was not any permanent land revenue system and the periodical settlement differed from time to time and the province was cursed by natural calamities. And the Government showed much reluctance in granting remissions in times of calamities. "From 1827, previous to which date there are no separate records for this district up to 1831 no remissions were allowed".[63] Thus the remissions from Government revenue only were not 'timely' commensurate with the injury sustained by the people.[64] From 1832 up to 1867 the remissions on the ground of inundation and drought were about equal, the total remissions on the former ground being Rs. 6,25,844 and on the latters Rs. 6,18,660 making a total of nearly 12½ lakhs.[65] On the other hand strict rules and regulations were enforced to extract revenue from the people without understanding their real condition by which the material prosperity in general and economic condition in particular of the province deterioted during the period under study.

Famine was inevitable in the event of a drought when the people were poverty-stricken and where no single great public work was undertaken to enrich the province. Lack of communication facilities aggravated the economic life of the famine stricken people. Lack of proper effective administration, and climatic disturbances also contributed a lot to ruin the agricultural economy of the people. Famine was regarded as a calamity which was difficult to mitigate.[66] In the first half of the 19th century there was not any single newspaper to draw the attention of the public. During such calamities Orissa suffered a lot without much knowledge to the outside world.

Colonel Cotton was the first person to suggest the construction of

62. Maddox Report, Vol. I, p. 138.
63. Maddox Report, Vol. II, p. 441.
64. G.C. Patnaik, *op.cit.*, p. 15.
65. Maddox Report, *op.cit.*
66. G.C. Patnaik, *op.cit.*, p. 15.

an elaborate system of canals as the only remedy against the droughts and floods. Finally the Government made a compact with a new Company known as the East India Irrigation Company. It was offered to take a large irrigation works in preventing the country from the threefold object of the recurrence of drought, of protecting the harvest from floods, and of opening up communications.[67] The Company undertook by the private English enterprise to do for the Orissa peasants what none of its dynasties, native or foreign had ever ventured to attempt, to free it from the chronic peril of drought and famine. But before the Company could finish a single one of their canals, the terrible disaster of 1866 fell upon the province. And now the Government realising the responsibility of preserving the Orissa people from death by starvation, undertook the whole works of irrigation in the years 1868.[68] The colonial policy was changed by the great famine of 1866. So all the remedial measures adopted by the British were only after the famine of 1866. However, the great famine taught a good lesson to the Government and it was also made a guideline for the remedy of future famines.

67. N.N. Banerjee, *op.cit.*, p. 10.
68. W.W. Hunter, *Orissa*, Vol. II, p. 190.

5

The Great Orissa Famine of 1866

The natural calamity like famine has caused widespread devastations in India in all ages. In spite of the development of science and communications so easy the danger of famine is still there.[1] Orissa was also not exempted from it. Till 1866 no famine of that magnitude (of 1866) had ever ravaged the socio-economic set up of Orissa. The Orissa famine (Famine of 1866) was the most devastating natural calamity of the century which could only be compared with that of 1770.[2] This famine surpassed all the previous famines in its character and it clearly exhibited the defects of the Bengal administration, and lamentable neglect of the vital problem of the development of Orissa.

The Famine of 1866 is called the Famine of the 9th Anka (occurred in the ninth regnal year of the Puri Raja, Divyasingha Deva) who, however, gave little help to alleviate the distress of the people.[3] The horrible picture of this famine has been described by the historian, late Pyarimohan Acharya, who was an eye witness of its havoc, in the following words :

> "One feels stunned when he remembers the shocking events that took place at that time. It is quite impossible to give a faithful picture of the horrors of the famine that came accompanied by death itself. The towns were filled with the sorrowful shrieks of thousands of men, women and children who had been reduced to mere skeletons. The crematory grounds near the towns and villages were full of innumerable dead bodies and upon them the vultures and jackals feasted to their hearts' content. Men and women forshook their natural instincts owing to the unbearable pangs of

---

1. *OHRJ*, Vol. VIII, October 1959 and January 1960, Nos. 3 & 4, G.C. Das, "A Note on the Famines of India", p. 209.
2. *Maddox Report*, Vol. I, Pr. 195, p. 139.
   The mortality was estimated by the Lt. Governor at one-fifth, and by the Famine Commissioner at one-fourth of the whole province (*RIF*, 1880, Part-I, Pr. 52)
3. Report of G.N. Barlow, Collector of Puri to R.B. Chapman, Member of Board of Revenue, 26 November 1865.

hunger. Parents cast away their starving children before wild animals to be devoured by them. Some even ate the dead bodies of their own children like demons. Social evils such as murder, suicide, etc., became a very common thing at the time. Some people tried to live upon wild shrubs and inedible materials".

Among all the calamities the worst was the famine of 1866, which was the most devastating in its effects, the severity of which has gained a historic reputation and which is still remembered in Orissa with a feeling of horror.[4] The Famine Commission of 1866 marked,

> "The famine in Orissa stands almost alone in this, that there was a almost no importation, and the people, shut up in a narrow province between pathless jungles and an impracticable sea, were in the condition of passengers in a ship without provisions".[5]

The famine affected the whole east coast from Madras to Bengal but it was chiefly intense in the 3 districts of Orissa (Puri, Cuttack and Balasore) and some parts of tributary states. It covered the largest portion in the recorded history of India. But the area most affected by this famine was about 12,000 square miles with a population of about 4 millions.[6] Its severity was a widespread sea of calamity. It was reported that a famine stricken famished woman at Mahanga was in the habit of eating away raw human flesh.[7] The folklores also highlight how mothers deserted their children and some even were thrown away for non-availability of food.[8] Such famine in terms of severity, magnitude and sufferings surpassed all other previous famines and took away heavy toll of lives. Dr. Mahtab, a great historian of Orissa, observed,

> "Unfortunately this famine was not a visitation from above but was purely a man-made one, and the then officers of the British Government were solely responsible for it".[9]

Several factors were responsible for the outbreak of such great catastrophe, none of which was sufficient to cause the appalling calamity.

Causes of Famine 1866

Famine has many causes. Walford listed 12, dividing them into natural

4. H.K. Mahtab, *The History of Orissa.*
   Radha Kumud Mookerjee, Endowment Lectures, 1947, Lucknow University (published), p. 135.
5. *RCF* 1866, Vol. I, p. 21.
6. Report of *IFC*, 1880, Part-I, Pr. 51, p. 17.
7. *OHRJ*, Vol. IX, October and January 1961, Nos. 3 & 4, p. 72.
8. K.B . Das, *Palli Geeti Sanchayan*, Vol. III, (Cuttack, 1974), pp. 73-74.
9. H.K. Mahtab, *op.cit.*, p. 135.

causes beyond human control and artificial causes within human control. Drought, excessive rains and flood, tidal waves and other high winds and crop failure due to insects and plant diseases etc., are under the domain of natural causes. The artificial causes commonly political include warfare (siege or blockade or destruction of food stocks or growing grain) difficulty in the production of food grains and distribution and its import and export etc.[10]

The great famines of the world have been due to natural forces frequently intensified, however, by political factors. Sometimes, economic or demographic situations, prevalence of poverty, including unemployment and many landless labourers in a densely populated area are regarded as causes of famines.[11] The great Orissa famine however exhibited the defects of the administration and the inaction of the Government for the development of the province etc., come under the domain of artificial or man-made cause. So the famine of 1866 occurred due to more of unnatural causes than natural and may be called a man-made catastrophe.

1. Cessation of Rainfall

The main natural causes of famines have been deficiency of rainfall (drought) or excess of rainfall (flood).[12] The main cause of the famine in Orissa was the premature cessation of rains of 1865 throughout the lower provinces of the Bengal presidency in the midle of September 1865. The total quantity of the rainfall for the year 1865 was not usually small. Much rainfall early in the season before the usual time of sowing while the latter rains, which were usually expected in the end of September and October failed.[13] In Cuttack district, there was heavy rainfall during the previous season.

In the Balasore district "the rains were very heavy in July and August and the cultivators fearing that the crops would be damaged by heavy rain, let the water run out of their fields". After August not an inch of rain fell. Thus, the rains of 1865, besides being unfavourable for sowing in proper time, suddenly ceased and the winter rice crop on which the people mainly depended failed. So the deficiency of two-third of ordinary rainfall caused widespread damage to the rice crops and brought the famine.

The rainfall records of 1865 in the Orissa division (Cuttack, Puri

---

10. David L. Sills (ed.), *International Encyclopaedia of the Social Science*, Vol. V, Macmillan Company and the Free Press, 1968, p. 323.
11. David L. Sills (ed.), *op.cit.*
12. *Ibid.*
13. J.K. Samal, *Orissa Under the British Crown*, Ch. I, pp. 1-2.

and Balasore) which the Famine Committee held to be more or less reliable are shown below:[14]

TABLE 5.1
RAINFALL IN ORISSA DIVISION IN 1865

Months	*Cuttak*	*Puri*	*Balasore*
January	1.1	-	0.25
February	2.3	-	1.35
March	3.6	-	5.75
April	0.7	-	5.70
May	7.4	13.0	11.55
June	8.1	5.6	4.25
July	12.2	4.3	5.90
August	7.7	5.6	8.25
September	7.5	5.2	9.30
October	0.0	-	0.30
November	-	-	
December	0.8	-	0.6
Total	51.4	36.3	52.60

In the famine of 1865-66 the district of Puri was the worst affected area and that is evident from the rainfall records of 1865 for the district.

Lack of Irrigation Facility

The waters of the rivers were not properly utilised for the purpose of irrigation till the year of famine. At that time the whole province was "without artificial irrigation whatever beyond that to be drawn in an unusual crisis of drought from natural water courses and the petty tanks and water lodgements of the country". The successs of rice crop therefore depended solely on the supply of rain from the above. So lives of millions of people were threatended due to failure of rice crops because of the failure of the timely rainfall.[15]

Heavy Export

The famine enquiry committee of 1866, observed "throughout the famine from the very first it was symptomatic in character as rather due to scarcity of grain than scarcity of money".[16] The food stock was largely inadequate at the time of the failure of crops in the month of October 1865. This

14. Drought in Orissa during 1954-55, Government of Orissa, Revenue (Special Relief) Department, Bhubaneswar, p. 12.
15. Pt. S.N. Das, *Unabimsa Satabdir Orissa*, Part I, p. 71.
16. Drought in Orissa 1954-55, *op.cit.*, p. 13.

was both because of export had been usually brisk of late, and because the people had not been thought to protect themselves by retaining sufficient stores at home.

In 1865, the country was empty of its buffer stock of rice. It was only in 1866 that it was discovered that there was an alarming shortage of food stocks. The crops of 1863 were not below average and that of 1864, though poor in Puri, were good in Cuttack and particularly good in Balasore, but the export trade of Orissa had been considerable, which had no doubt depleted the stocks. The export trade averaged 20,000 tons of rice a year during the six years preceding 1865. In the year 1863-64 the export was only 5,49,516 maunds or 19,625 tons. In normal years the export from the state ranged up to 1,00,000 tons and sometimes touching 1,25,000 tons in peak year under controlled conditions.[17] The table shows the total export of rice from Orissa in the year 1864-65.[18]

TABLE 5.2
TOTAL AMOUNT OF RICE EXPORTED FROM ORISSA (1860-65)

Years	*Balasore (Maunds)*	*Cuttack (Maunds)*	*Puri (Maunds)*	*Total (Maunds)*
1860-61	3,50,074	23,049	83,936	4,57,059
1861-62	3,27,504	60,880	46,780	4,44,164
1862-63	4,07,622	86,696	4,816	4,49,134
1863-64	5,20.052	29,464		5,49,516
1864-65	8,06,576	72,128	58,824	9,37,528

The province became increasingly a major source of supply of rice and to the increased demand drained large quantities of rice. Agents were spread through the length and breadth of the district purchasing rice and paddy from the cultivators. Everyone was eager to sell his stores and the sales were easily affected. Though the people themselves had no undertaken any large merchantile operations, their surplus grain had been sought by others because the price of the rice remained cheap and compared with most other provinces up to the end of the year 1864. During this period there was food shortage in southern India and the Telinga Kumuti of the Madras Territory was busy enough to collect Orissa grains for sale to an enterprising French House Messers Robert Chariol and Co. exporting through False Point.[19] The quantity exported was usually high *viz.*, 33,000 tons of which Balasore alone sent away 28,000 tons.

17. Drought in Orissa during 1954-55, *op.cit.*, p. 13.
18. *RCF* 1866, Vol. I, Part-I, Pr. 47.
19. *RCF*, Vol. I, p. 13.

This had no doubt depleted the stocks to a considerable extent.[20] The people who were eager though to sell their crops, had forgotten their usual caution to keep reserve stock to counter balance a bad harvest. The stocks of rice in the Balasore district were already low when in September 1865, an alarm was felt about the rainfall. When the *sarada* or winter crop failed there was nothing else for the people to fall back upon.[21]

Low Wages and Lack of Saving Capacity

Prices of the grain and low wages were too much judged by a metropolitan standard and were on that basis supposed to be reasonable when they were really extreme in relation to the ordinary local prices.[22] Most of the Orissa people were poor and daily-labourers. Their income always fell short in relation to their expenditure due to the low wages. So saving for future was out of question and that's why they lacked staying power to withstand calamities. Whenever crop fails it severely affects the poor agricultural landless labourers and scarcity becomes severe.[23]

The saverity of scarcity was aggravated more in Orissa dure to the non-availability of food stock, frequent rise of prices, unemployment problem and low wages. So any rise in the price of food grains was felt more quickly and acutely by the low paid labourer there than by the better paid one elsewhere.

Problem of Unemployment

The people suffered a lot due to the unemployment problem on the eve of famine. The unemployment among the wage-earners in salt factories (golas) created a havoc when the manufacture of salt was abandoned in Orissa by the Government, the means of subsistence of the people of Malud and Parikud became most precarious.[24]

The geographical proximity of the sea was in fact a boon in disguise for the Orissans. It provided an additional source of income, *i.e.*, through salt manufacturing. Thus salt industry was complementary to the agricultural economy of Orissa. There was less unemployment after harvest due to utilization of summer for salt manufacture. It was a blessing in disguise for the inhabitants of Orissa. The table shows the number of salt workers in 1853 in different districts of Orissa.[25]

20. *RIF*, 1880, Part-I, p. 41.
21. P. Mukherjee, *History of Orissa*, Vol. VI, Cuttack, 1964, p. 361.
22. *The Star of Utkal*, 8 September, (Cuttack, 1908), p. 278.
23. Pt. S.N. Das, *op.cit.*, p. 72.
24. Supplement to the Calcutta Gazette, No. 20, 1866, p. 335.
25. Pt. S.N. Das, *op.cit.*, p. 75.

TABLE 5.3
NO. OF SALT WORKERS IN ORISSA IN 1853

District		No. of Employed
Balasore	..	15,684
Cuttack	..	5,417
Puri	..	15,443
Total	..	36,544

It has already been noticed that this was the time of decay of salt trade in Orissa. At the peack period in salt trade, about 2 lakh people were engaged in salt trade. The decay of salt trade brought more unemployment in Orissa and this was the primary cause of Orissa famine. Moreover the wages were very low in Orissa compared to that of other states and on the other hand there were large number of wage labourers. They remained jobless due to the non-availability of employment. Many migrated to other areas or became victim of calamities.[26]

Lack of Communication

The peculiar geographical position of the province rendering it difficult for the rest of the world to communicate with it,[27] was the main factor for the outbreack of the great famine in Orissa. There were no good roads in Orissa and the only road that connected Orissa with Calcutta through Midnapore, which was intersected by large rivers and liable to inundation, was unmetalled and unbridged.[28] There was very little communication by sea. Lack of communication was the main hindrance on the part of the trading class of Orissa and outsiders to procure food grains for the people and trade was carried out only in the month of fare weather.

Defective Trade System

The condition became worse due to the laissez-faire policy of the Government over the private traders who in their turn had no other interests except their personal gain.

T.E. Ravenshaw the then Commissioner of Orissa "informed that any interference in the natural course of trade has been most carefully avoided.[29] Had there been official control over the movement of food grain the condition would not have been worse. The Commissioner of Orissa made

26. Pt. S.N. Das, *op.cit.*, p. 72-76.
27. Supplement to the Calcutta Gazette, *op.cit.*
28. *RIF*, 1880, Part-I, Pr. 51, p. 17.
29. T.E. Ravenshaw, Commissioner of Orissa to Government of Bengal, No. 407, October 27, 1865, RCF, Vol. II, p. 24.

a great blunder when he informed the Government of Bengal and the Board of Revenue about plenty of food stock with the Orissa grain dealer without thorough inquiry about it.[30] The Government did not try to procure food grains for the people during the early course of famine.

Defective Administrative System

The famine Commission pointed out that one of the main causes of the famine of 1866 was certain inherent defects in British administration in Orissa. The executive had little contact with the mass and knew little about their material condition. It stated "the system of administration caused a defect of information and an unwillingness to take direct action on the part of the Government which materially retarded measures of relief and which could not have occurred in any part of India."[31] At that time Orissa was under the Bengal Presidency and governed by judicial officials with little knowledge of executive functions. The civil officers in Orissa at that time had no previous knowledge of Orissa. Muspratt, Magistrate and Collector of Balasore had joined early in 1865. In the year 1866, February a new Collector, Cornell had joined in Cuttack. In July 1865, Commissioner T.E. Ravenshaw had joined. The only officer having considerable experience in Orissa at that time was G.N. Barlow, an officer of 10 years standing who had been for 4 years magistrate and Collector of Puri. He however, did ample justice to his duties till his departure in October 1866.[32] Neither these officers nor the officers in the higher service had any special experience in dealing with the famine. The laissez faire attitude of T.E. Ravenshaw, the then Commissioner of Orissa, Sir Cecil Beadon, the Lt. Governor of Bengal and Groate, President of the Board of Revenue aggravated the condition and thus were responsible to a great extent "for the suddenness of the extreme collapse in regard to the food supply", which occurred in May 1866.

Lack of any Agency

When the famine began there was no single agency (newspapers) to inform the Government about the distressed condition of the people. The famine appeared at first in Puri district. But too much delay was involved in submitting these reports to the Government.[33] The missionaries played in important role in sending information to England.[34]

30. John Boulton (translated) *Atma* Jivan Carita of Phakir Mohan Senapati, (Cuttack, 1985), p. 29.
31. *RCF*, Vol. I, Prs. 410-415.
32. *RCF*, Vol. I, Part-I, Pr. 61.
33. *Ibid.*, Pr. 235.
34. *Ibid.*, Prs. 19-20.

Uncertainty of Settlements

The 30 years settlement which was somehow responsible, was just expiring and no new arrangment started till 1865. Among the people; there prevailed shadow of uncertainty among the cultivators and contraction of assessable area owing to fear of enhancement of rent.[35]

Growth of Population and Stagnancy in the Yield of Crops

The inhabitants of Orissa do not get the amount of food material that an individual requires to live. Annual expenditure for each class in Orissa ranges from Rs. 50 to Rs. 80. It is impossible to maintain from the income that one gets from 1.2 acre of land with very low yield. In addition to it, the population of our country is growing continuously and compare to it there has been no increase in the area of agricultural lands and yield of crops.[36] With the population growing on the basis of geometrical progression, the food grain production continued to grow on the arithmetical progression. Thus the country as a whole was heading towards a Malthusian trap, Oissa was no exception to it. The table depicts the growth of population in Orissa.[37]

TABLE 5.4
INCREASE OF POPULATION OF ORISSA BETWEEN 1843-1900

Year		*Population*
1843	..	2,500,000
1865	..	3,000,000
1867	..	(a) 2,500,000
1872	..	3,000,000
1881	..	3,600,000
1891	..	3,800,000
1900	..	(a) 4,200,000

(a) Estimate

The amount of land and agricultural produce available for the support of each individual has thus been reduced in the ratio of 100 to 79. The population now averages about 700 per square mile cultivated in Balasore about 570 to the square mile of cultivation in Puri and nearly 800 to the square mile of cultivation in Cuttack, while in some places the density is much greater.[38] It is such a horrible affair that it is beyond description.

35. *RCF*, Vol I, Prs. 410-415.
36. Pt. S.N. Das, *op.cit.*, p.71.
37. *Maddox Report*, Vol. I, p. 141.
38. *Maddox Report*, Vol. I, p. 141.

According to Andrewyule, "a nation which face this situation has to tolerate acute shortage of food and that nation demolished gradually". This was actually true to the normal year. In famine of 1866 that was happened and denied the famine stricken people to survive any longer.

Poverty and Ruin of Cottage Industries

Poverty and decay of industries and crafts in Orissa simultaneously with the famine played an important role to hit the economic backbone of the people of Orissa, with the coming of British to Orissa; their indigenous industry gradually declined. The village level industries, crafts and absence of trade and commerce for the benefit of the people made them poorer and they finally depended upon agriculture which was a non-productive industry in Orissa. Thus the people of Orissa suffered a lot by the famine of 1866 and also it took away a heavy toll of lives.[39]

The people of Orissa in particular were much poorer than of any other province of India. The zamindars were poor and on the other hand also improvident. Poverty and miseries of the Oriya ryots increased by the illegal exaction of the zamindars. There were no any trading class and the foreign settlers or merchants settled in important stations of Cuttack, Puri and Balasore.[40] As the income of the people was low they did not have any storage capacity to meet the challenge of natural calamity.

Duty of a Government

It is the duty of every civilized Government to plan how to stop the difficulties faced by people due to famine. The Government is fully responsible for the death of a man due to starvation. During the British rule, the Government and its workers had not done their duty, if a proper investigation is made into the number of famines occurred. Lacs of innocent people had died due to negligence of this duty by the Government. The famine committee of 1866 reveals how the Governmental officials remained passive to such a terrible famine of that year.[41]

Education

Educationally the people of Orissa were lagging behind. There was the need of the enlightened people who could forewarn the Government about the prospects of famine and insist on them for carrying out remedial measures. So lack of public consciousness also allowed the famine to

---

39. S.N. Das, *op.cit.*, pp. 74-75.
    B.M. Bhatia, *Famines in India*, Bombay, 1963, pp. 58-101.
40. *RCF*, Vol. I, Prs. 19-20.
41. Pt. S.N. Das, *op.cit.*, p. 72.

occur to shatter the peaceful economic life of people.[42] All these factors however were responsible for the outbreak of great Orissa famine and to ruin the economic life of the Oriya peasants.

Course of the Famine

The course of Orissa famine of 1866 may be divided into three phases. The first instances continued from October 1865 to November 1865. The second phase progressed from November 1865 to May 1866 and the last phase started from May 1866.

The First Phase

The first symptoms of severe distress appeared in Puri in the Acutumn of 1865.[43] The country-wide panic over the loss of agricultural products was felt towards the middle of October. The merchants stopped rice trade and shops were closed suddenly in towns of Puri and Cuttack on October 26.[44] The food shortage was experienced by everyone but the intensity of famine was ignored by T.E. Ravenshaw and he reported to Government of Bengal that the grain dealers created artificial scarcity to earn greater profit and that would be easily averted if there would be no Government interference of their trade.[45] It was also accepted by the Government of Bengal.

Ramakhya Chatterjee, Deputy Magistrate of Puri informed G.N. Barlow (Magistrate of Puri) about the acute scarcity of food in almost all parts of Puri including mufassil areas. They were reduced to the greatest misery, lived on fruits and roots of different kinds of trees and many people were leaving their houses with their family for Cuttack with the hope of being employed in Irrigation Department.[46] The whole district of Puri, particularly the localities of Nubbah, Gop, Pipli and the land laying between the Chilka lake like Malud, Parikud and Bhusandpur were worst sufferers.[47] The Collector (Mr. Barlow) recommends for the purchase of food by Government and also suggested for a ship-load of grain be forwarded direct from Calcutta to Saindeeghat at Malud. This was not supported by the Commissioer and called the attention of both

42. P.C. Das, *The Economic History of Orissa in the 19th Century*, New Delhi, 1989, p. 86.
43. Supplement to Calcutta Gazette, June 20, 1866, p. 335.
44. T.E. Ravenshaw, Commissioner, Cuttack Division to Offg. Secretary to the Government of Bengal, No. 407, 27 October 1865; *RCF*, Vol. II, p. 24.
45. T.E. Ravenshaw, to Government of Bengal, No. 7, October 22; *RCF*, Vol. II, p. 22.
46. R. Chatterjee to G.N. Barlow, No. 68, 25 October 1865; *RCF*, Vol. II, p. 10.
47. G.N. Barlow to Commissioner, Orissa, 8 November 1865; *RCF*, Vol. II, p. 14.

the Raja and Zamindar to their burden duty to support their ryots and alleviate the distress.[48]

Balasore Collector, Musprat, also informed the Commissioner about the worst conditions of the cultivators and the zamindars. He also forwarded the petitions of certain zamindars who prayed for time concession for the payment of their rents due to the prevailing scarcity in the whole of Balasore.[49] The Commissioner of Orissa forwarded over the petition of the zamindars for the rejection on the ground that the improvidence of the ryots should not be the consideration for any subsidies in regard to the payment of rent in time.[50] The rise in prices of food grains in Balasore forced the vessels of Vizagapatam to return from the river-mouths because they found no prospects of getting rice.[51] "Grain is now so scarce in this district that the crews of this vessels with difficulty are able to obtain rice sufficient for their own consumption".[52] In Balasore at Buttesur, a zamindar named Nettro Sennapaty showed a slip of paper at the police station which had threatened that his house would be burnt down if he did not sell his rice.[53] From this it could be easily understood the gravity of the situation.

Cuttack district also suffered a lot. The greater portion of the crop on all the higher lands perished from drought. Prices of rice began to rise, the situation became serious, the whole district was panicky. All the grain dealers closed their shops.[54] At that time the selling of rice varied from 6 seers to 8 seers per rupee. It was also notices that one grain-dealer opened his shop but all of his rice was carried off without any payment.[55] Food became so scarce that complaints from different quarters reached the Commissioner. The troops were not getting grains. The judge complained that all the Amalahs and Vakils (Lawyers) of his court were not able to procure rice.[56] When the Government officials were unable to get rice including the cantonment officials, the condition of other

48. T.E. Ravenshaw, Offg. Commissioner of the Cuttack Division to the Offg. Secretary to the Government of Bengal, No. 280, 14 November 1865.
49. H. Muspratt, Collector of Balasore to the Offg. Commissioner, Cuttack, No. 217, 26 October 1865; *RCF*, Vol. II, p. 18.
50. *BRP*, November 1865, Commissioner of Orissa to Board of Revenue, No. 249, 30 October 1865.
51. Balasore's Report, 26 October 1865; *RCF*, Vol. II, p. 18.
52. *Ibid.*
53. *RCF*, Vol. II, Balasore, 30 October 1865, p. 18.
54. N.N. Banerjee, Report on the Agriculture of the District of Cuttack (Calcutta, 1898), p. 180.
55. T.E. Ravenshaw to Offg. Secretary, Government of Bengal, No. 407, 27 October 1865.
56. *Ibid.*

people could easily be visualised. W.J. Money, the then Collector, Cuttack reported that large portion of the crops had failed and the people petitioned for enquiry to grant remissions.[57] Cuttack district suffered less in comparison to Puri and Balasore due to employment created by Irrigation Company. In spite of this, famine seemed imminent. It proved that the people were suffering from acute starvation.[58] Due to the lack of far sight of the Commissioner, Orissa suffered a lot.

The Progress

The Collector of Puri, Barlow continuously reported about the acute distress in Puri. He also submitted a scheme for the construction of roads by which he would create employment for the famine stricken people. He also suggested to pay wages through food and the storage of food grains by imports.[59] The Bengal Government sanctioned Rs. 69,000/- for the construction of roads but rejected it on the proposal of payment of wages in rice.[60] At this critical situation, Ravenshaw left for the Tributary Mahals towards the end of November 1865 to assess the intensity of the famine in the hilly region and was absent for more than two months. Absence of Ravenshaw delayed the correspondence by many days. The absence of the Head of the State at such a critical time, was a sad reflection of a sorry state of affairs, particularly when there was no urgent political engagements requiring his presence in the Tributary Mahals.[61]

Towards January 1866, rice was not available in Puri. The public works, was the only means for the relief of distress.

The construction of road was undertaken in lieu of relief to the sufferings of the entire population; if the Government had not made the mistake of insisting on payment in cash and wages rather than the supply of food to the labourers.[62]

At the end of January 1866, a critical situation arose. On 31st January Ravenshaw returned to Cuttack from his tour and immediately informed the Board about the scarcity of rice in Puri and recommended for the importation of rice to Puri. The Government declined to import rice to Puri and allowed to leave on charity.[63] Too much reliance was placed upon private charity by which Orissa suffered a lot. "The price varied on

57. W.J. Money, Collector, Cuttack to Commissioner, No. 201, November 11, 1865; RCF, Vol. II, p. 27.
58. N.N. Banerjee, *op.cit.*
59. RCF, Vol. II, p. 51; P.C. Das, *op.cit.*, pp. 90-91.
60. RCF, Vol. I, Part-I, Pr. 151, p. 46.
61. *Ibid.*, p. 37.
62. RCF, Vol. I, Part-I, Pr. 151, p. 41.
63. P.C. Das, *op.cit.*, p. 91.

an average in the districts of Orissa, of 12 seers per rupee at the end of October 1865, 13 $^{2}/_{3}$ seers on 1st January 1866, $4^{5}/_{8}$ on 13th August and 14¼ on 5th November. In the interior of the districts food was generally not to be procured for money, and when sold, ranged up to about 35 times the ordinary price".[64]

Middle of February 1866, Sir Cecil Beadon, the Lt. Governor of Bengal reached Cuttack on an official visit with his public works secretary, Colonel Nicolls and G.F. Cockburn, Member of the Board of Revenue to investigate the distress in Orissa.[65] The darbar held at Cuttack at Lalbagh on 17 February was attended by twenty Rajas of Tributary Mahals, 80 Zamindars and many officers of the districts. He left Orissa without consulting the local officials or non-officials or without having any clear idea about the extremity of the distress.[66] In his darbar statement he openly said that the duty of relieving individual distress lay with the zamindars and finally said that exployment had been given to many famine stricken under the Irrigation Company's work and on the construction of public roads.[67] On his return of Calcutta he discussed the subject with the Governor-General. In a personal interview he said that the circumstances in Orissa arising out of famine did never require the importation of grain.[68]

"In June 1866 all Orissa plunged into one universal famine of extreme severity".[69] For miles round, one heard the yell for food. Cholera brokeout in Puri and Balasore causing many casualities among the pilgrims.[70] Scarcity of rice was so high that it was not available and starvation became inevitable in Orissa.[71]

Till May 1866 the administration did nothing to control prices. Mass starvation, crime, disease and deaths occurred in the province.[72] The official knowledge regarding local conditions was exposed and the province faced disastrous problem due to the doctrine of laissez-faire.[73] The European newspapers were eager to know the actual condition of Orissa. The Editorial in Englishman said: "It is a question whether we shall pay now to save the living or hereafter bury the dead".[74]

64. *The Star of Utkal*, 8 September 1908, p. 278.
65. RCF, Vol. I, Part-I, p. 55.
66. *Hindu Patriot*, March 5, 1866.
67. RCF, Vol. I, Part-I, p. 57.
68. Despatch of the Government of India to Secretary of State, No. 71, 22 April 1867.
69. *The Star of Utkal*, *op.cit.*, p. 278.
70. RCF, Vol. II, pp. 151 and 179; Extract of D.S.P., Puri, February 27, 1866.
71. Mahtab, *op.cit.*, pp. 441-448.
72. *Calcutta Review*, Vol. XLIV, 1867.
73. Thomson & Garret, Rise and Fulfilment of British Rule in India, (London, 1934), p. 430.
74. *The Englishman* (Editorial), 28 April 1866.

By the end of May rice was not procurable in Orissa at 4½ seers per rupee in any part of the province. Ravenshaw on May 28 telegraphically informed the Government about the alarming situation prevailing in Orissa. On the next day the Lt. Governor telegraphed to his Secretary in Calcutta, requested the Board to send rice down immediately to False Point and Balasore (Dhamara) send the Aracon or any other available steamer letting no time to be lost.[75] Rice were then immediately imported to Balasore, Dhamara and False Point as proposed by Ravenshaw.

There was no information about the scarcity in Tributary states. These have suffered less from famine and were not subjected to loss by flood. Here the crops were abundant and such type of harvest had not been reaped for years.[76]

The Ganjam district which suffered from terrible famine of 1866 had remained at that time under the Madras Presidency. The number of deaths reported was 10,898[77] but it had not suffered like that of any part of the Orissa province.

By January matters were so acute that, the Collector applied for special relief but his application was rejected.[78] In March it was clear that famine was in the province, but the Government was sanctioning a very small work but did not sanction the proposed work like Chilka canal. The Collector reported about 200 deaths from starvation and 1,543 deaths were reported from small-pox and cholera and many others due to want of food. Realising the urgency of the situation the Government immediately arranged for relief. By the end of June the Government diverted Rs. 20,000 from the North-West Famine Fund. The excavation of Chilka canal was started with the request of the Collector. The Board of Revenue supplied seed paddy in the month of August. In the month of October another phase of rice was granted by Government to the Relief Fund.[79] The Relief operations were intensified at a time when people had died in large numbers. Heavy rains and floods in Orissa added fuel to the miseries of the people and many were killed by the effect. The natural calamities played havoc in Orissa due to the absence of effective measures by the Government.[80] "Three million people died and almost a third of the population was wiped out"[81] and it may be called from all quarters as a man-made tragedy.

---

75. *RCF*, Vol. I, Pr. 283, p. 89.
76. *RCF*, Vol. II, p. 413.
77. T.J. Maltby, *The Ganjam District Manual* (Madras, 1918), p. 157.
78. *Ibid.*, p. 199.
79. T.J. Maltby, *op.cit.*, p. 199.
80. OFC, Vol. I, Part-I, pp. 93-94.
81. John Boulton (translated), *op.cit.*, p. 27.

Relief Committees

With the instruction of the Governor, the District Relief Committees were formed and subscriptions raised for the relief of the distressed in all the districts of Cuttack division.[82] In July some centres for the distribution of cooked food were established; some in August and in September. There were about 88 centre in the three districts; all were in operation. Among these centres, there were 43 in Cuttack, 22 in Balasore and 23 in Puri district.[83] The Government expressed its concern over the issue towards the end of May when the intensity of distress was at its height and consequent upon this the Board in about the middle of June threw themselves into sincere work.[84] And the rate of mortality gradually increased. According to Phakir Mohan Senapati:

> "As soon as the news of relief centres, reached the rural areas, starving wretches came racing to the towns. For a fortnight to three weeks they had not seen food. They kept alive on tender leaves and inedible roots and fruits. They were in no condition to cover such distances: over two-thirds of them died on the way. The remainder reached the relief centres only to gorge themselves and die, some of dysentery and some of cholera. Their stomachs had shrunk. When they saw rice, they gobbled as much as they could but their digestive systems had gone: they could no longer cope with so much"[85]

The feeding centres became the temporary homes of houseless crowds. The recipients of relief (food) were debarred from the society.[86] The caste feeling was so strict that even some people died without seeking food at all.

The number of mortality became highest in August as a result of heavy storm and rains. The people died being exposed to cold and wet during this period.[87] The flood in August washed away the nearing ripe crop and aggravated the misery of the people.[88] The total population in 1865 in Cuttack division was 3,015,826 out of which 814,469 have perished and 115,028 have either emigrated or disappeared making a total loss of 929,427 persons and leaving 2,086,329 surviving

---

82. *RCF*, Vol. I, Pr. 269, p. 85.
83. *Ibid.*
84. *RCF*, Vol. I, Pr. 317, p. 98.
85. John Boulton (translated), *op.cit.*, p. 30.
86. *Ibid.*, Pr. 311, p. 97.
87. *BRP*, September 1866, T.E. Ravenshaw to Board of Revenue No. 604, August 30, 1866.
88. *BRP*, Minutes of V.H. Schalach, Junior Member, Board of Revenue, No. 37, January 1867.

inhabitants. The general percentage of loss of population during the famine was 30.81.[89]

Role of Zamindars

It may be stated that the Government forced the zamindars to help their ryots when they were also suffering from famine. It was fallacious on the part of Government to rely upon he landlords to fulfil their obligation vested on them. They were required to help the distressed people with charities. But as the majority of the landlords were nonresident Bengalis and the minority of them were the Oriyas, the reliance of Government on them could not be proved successful. There was some exception to this. Two zamindars like Chaudhury Reghunath Das and Babu Radhashyama Narendra were appreciated by the people for their benevolent work for the famine destitutes of their areas.[90] The Raja of Parikud also stood pre-eminent in the matter of charities.[91] Another zamindar of Sugada pargana of Mahanga Mauza, Babu Jagu Sing was famous for his helping hand for the famine stricken people.[92] Durga Narain Bose, Zamindar of Luckinarainpore and Anterjami Misser (Mishra) Zamindar of Narda also advanced large quantities of grain among their tenantry.[93] Raja Bhagirathi Mahendra Bahadoor of Dhenkanal was fully engaged in extending charity not only to his own subjects but also to the famished crowd coming from the coastal areas.[94] The total number of zamindars *i.e.*, 9 in Cuttack, 3 in Puri and 15 in Balasore extended their helping hands to their destitute people.[95] The death rate gradually increased in the area where the zamindars forgot their responsibilities.

Intensity of Famine

In the district of Cuttack, Kendrapara received maximum injury in the famine. Jagatsinghpur, Pattamundai, Jajpur, Salepur were slightly affected by the intensity of the famine.[96] It was the labouring and artisan classes

89. Board document, T.B. Lane Secretary to the Board of Revenue, L.P. to the Secretary, to the Government of Bengal, No. 1801M, Fort William, 8 November 1867.
90. *U.D.*, 25 August 1866.
91. *BRP*, December 1865, G.N. Barlow's telegram to Secretary, Board of Revenue, December 1865.
92. *U.D.*, 25 August 1866.
93. T.E. Ravenshaw, Offg. Commissioner, Cuttack Division to the Secretary to the Board of Revenue, L.P., No. 501, Cuttack, 24 July 1867.
94. *RCF*, Vol. I, Pr. 330, p. 101.
95. *BRP*, February 1866, R.B. Chapman, Secretary, Board of Revenue to Commissioner, Orissa, No. 16A, January 26, 1866.
96. *RCF*, Vol. I, Evidence No. 1 by Doorjadhan Das, Deputy Magistrate.

that died in greater number by starvation than other classes of people. In Cuttack district, the number of deaths among agriculturists, including pahi labouring classes was 10,262 or $4^1/_3$ %, number of deaths among the bonafide labouring classes (Panas, Kandaras, Bhois, Bisrees and Sowars etc.) was 11,262 or 4¾ % and among the artisan classes was 13,681 or 5¾ %.[97]

Almost all the places of Puri district were ravaged by the saverity of the famine. The first group comprises Malud and Parikud. The harvests in 1864 and in 1866 were scanty, so that the people were in a state of chronic distress. The pargana of Chaubiskud, and the third group, the police division of Gop, were areas in which the pressure of the famine was very severe and manifested itself very early. The central tract, comprising Kotedesh and the portion of the district through which the Cuttack road passes were less affected compared to the other parts. The greater part of the Khurda estate suffered less than the rest of the district, but the adjoining Kuhuri and Banpur areas suffered severely in the famine.[98] Relief came too late and the people were so reduced by starvation that they died in numbers. The number of cultivators, in the general sense, includes the bult of the rural population, and undoubtedly a large number of small farmers did perish in the famine. The labouring classes were the earliest and most numerous victims of the famine.[99]

According to Assistant Collector, Manson, the great mortality occurred in the pargana of Kismut Napu, Kimut Katsahi, Shahabunder and Syari which were situated on the banks of Subarnarekha. The extreme depopulation of Kismut Napu was because most of the population consisting of fisherman is miserably poor and has suffered intensely. The Chakla Soro includes a large number of parganas which have suffered severely from famine. Ankurah and Berah also were scenes of intense suffering. The last group of the Bhadrak subdivision, were Soso, Adda Rupiya, Balkhund, and Randia Urgurah. These tracts have suffered less on the whole than any other portion of the district, the average number of dead and missing being only 26½ per cent.[100] It was reported that a famine stricken famished woman at Mahanga was in the habit of eating human flesh from the dead bodies.[101] It was also reported that canibalism took place in Kendrapara in the northern division of the town. A Hindu of low

97. T.E. Ravenshaw, *op.cit.*
98. H.C.B.C. RaBan, Offg. Collector to the Commissioner of Cuttack, No. 297, 15 June 1867.
99. *Ibid.*
100. T.F. Bignold, Offg. Collector, Balasore to the Commissioner of Revenue Cuttack, No. 393½, 16 July 1867.
101. *OHRJ*, Vol. IX., October and January 1961, Nos. 3 & 4, p. 72.

caste had seized the corpse of the child which was floating in the Gobari river, cooked and devoured it.[102] From the table given below can be understood the population of the Orissa province after and before the famine.[103]

TABLE 5.5
COMPARATIVE STATEMENT SHOWING THE AREA AND POPULATION AND POPULATION PER SQUARE MILE OF CUTTACK, PURI AND BALASORE AND THE PROVINCE OF ORISSA AS STANDING AT THE TIME OF SURVEY AND BEFORE FAMINE

District	*Computation referring to what period*	*Are in square miles*	*Population*	*Population per square mile*
Cuttack	By the Survey	3,370	12,71,865	378
	Before Famine	3,370	15,03,829	446
	After Famine	3,370	10,72,463	318
Puri	By the Survey	2,083	5,87,915	282
	Before Famine	2,083	7,79,718	374
	After Famine	2,083	5,28,712	253
Balasore	By the Famine	3,065	6,51,033	212
	Before Famine	3,065	7,32,279	239
	After Famine	3,065	4,85,113	158
Total	By the Survey	8,518	25,10,813	294
	Before Famine	8,518	30,15,826	354
	After Famine	8,518	20,86,288	244

Relief Operations

From the above study it can easily be understood that the people of Orissa were poor and poverty-stricken during the period under study. The poverty of the people and famine problems aggravated the famine 1866 to a drastic situation. According to George Campbell:

> "The circumstances of the province of Orissa are in some respects exceptional. The ryots are in general poorer and more ignorant than those of Bengal and Behar."[104]

According to Boothby, Agent and Manager for the East India Irrigation and Canal Company, the famine had fallen heaviest on

102. *RCF*, Vol. I, Evidence No. 1 by Doorjadhan Das, Deputy Magistrate.
103. T.B. Lane, Secretary to the Board of Revenue, L.P., *op.cit.*
104. *RAB*, 1874-75, p. 13.
105. T.E. Ravenshaw, Offg. Commissioner of the Cuttack Division, to the Secretary to the Board of Revenue, L.P., No. 958, 1 November 1866.

labouring classes, artisans and small cultivators capital.[105] The Government measures were inadequate in the beginning to save human lives. The British Government in India faced a new problem during the famine of 1866 which did not exist in the past. Low income of the people of Orissa increased the responsibility of Government.[106] The then officers of British Orissa Government had not any special experience in dealing with the famine. They allowed the system of poor laws which was experienced in Britain. The British poor laws of 1834 and the views of J.S. Mill and Turgot provided the framework for the poor relief system which was adopted in India.[107] The same was adopted in Orissa as a famine relief policy. The system which was suited to an advanced country like Britain, how could it possible to a poor state like Orissa? The Government no doubt started relief and poor houses and also carried relief and poor houses and also carried relief to the doors of people those who were unable to come. To secure higher economy, Government imposed restrictions on people entering into relief camps. The relief operation started in Orissa was discriminatory in form when it was demanded for all. The test of admission posed a big problem. The Government failed to take specific measures to save human life.[108]

Relief works were undertaken under two heads *i.e.*, (*a*) public works, (*b*) private works. The first works (public works) were taken over by P.W.D. and Collectors or respective districts and the second work was private works undertaken by the local zamindars and Rajas of estates.

The public works were started through pojects, construction of roads and renovation of tanks or ponds to give immediate employment to the destitutes. But the list of works which were undertaken at the time of famine was embodied in the famine code drawn after 1876-78.[109] But these were not undertaken at the time of Orissa famine of 1866 and which claimed lives of many.

Under such circumstances the Government was forced to import rice to Orissa towards the end of May 1866. The Rs. 6,00,000 from North-West Province Famine Fund was placed at the disposal of the Bengal Government. The additional grant of Rs. 20,00,000 was sanctioned on 25th June 1866 for Orissa Famine.[110] The table shows the relief operations which were undertaken by the P.W.D. in 1867.

---

106. *U.D.*, 11 August 1866 and 29 June 1867.
107. B.M. Bhatia, *op.cit.*, pp. 111-112.
108. *IFC*, 1880, Pr. 61, p. 17.
109. Resolution of Government of India, Letter No. 44F, 9 June 1883, *BRP*, July 1883.
110. *BRP*, August 1866, Extracts from the Proceedings of the Government of India, No. 2217, 25 June 1866.

TABLE 5.6
RELIEF MADE BY P.W.D. IN 1867

Month		*No. of Persons*
January	..	12,443
February	..	17,102
March	..	23,489
April	..	13,056
May	..	16,662

Source : *IFC*, 1880, Part-I, pp.44-46.

From the table can easily be understood about the gradual increase of labourers. During the first instance of 6 months of 1866, 1260 people were employed in the Government estate of Khurda. At that time people demanded wages in kind not in cash. The Irrigation Company realising this gave wages partly in cash and partly in kind and attracted many for works. Under the Irrigation Company near about 9,000 people worked daily.[111] The Irrigation Company's work was stopped due to non-availability of rice and funds and people became victims of starvation. The average number of people employed by Irrigation works in Cuttack from January to June 1866 was as follows:

TABLE 5.7
NUMBER OF EMPLOYMENT IN IRRIGATION WORKS

Month		*Average number employed daily*
January	..	14,666
February	..	10,763
March	..	7,803
April	..	9,146
May	..	8,120
June	..	5,238

Source : N.N. Banerjee, *op.cit.*, p. 181.

From this it could easily be understood about insufficiency of relief works.

The Government also sanctioned Rs. 69,000 for carrying out the earth work in the Cuttack and Ganjam road and the Cuttack and Puri road, which helpful to the area of distress, the parganas of Malud, Parikud and Sathparah situated in Puri district. Due to the increase of distress,

111. *IFC*, 1880, Part I, pp. 45-46.

Government also placed at the disposal of the Superintending Engineer and Commissioner of Orissa Rs. 30,000 for the development of the following works.[112]

Works taken over		*Rupees allotted*
Taladanda and Pattamundai Roads	..	14,415
Tanks at Bhadrak	..	5,000
Branch road through Soro	..	2,000
Roads and Tanks at Balasore	..	2,655
Roads running through Khasmahal of Nuanund	..	1,400
Agarparah Road	..	3,000
Petty Works	..	1,500

Source : Office note on the measures that have been taken in the P.W.D. of the Government of Bengal in connection with present famine and scarcity, Fort William, 20 August 1866.

To give employment to the most distress tracts of Puri district *i.e.*, Malud and Parikud, the Satparath Tank work was undertaken. Narendra Tank in the town of Puri was restored to supply drinking water and to help the destitutes of the town.[113]

The Relief Committees were orginally formed in the district of Balasore and Cuttack in December 1865, and in the Puri district in January 1866. They carried on their operations till May 1866; with the money raised by private subscriptions when the Government assigned the balance from North-West Famine Fund. Towards October 1866 the fund was exhausted and the Calcutta Relief Committee supplied the Orissa Relief Funds. The total receipts and disbursements for 1866 amounted rupees 5,49,514 and rupees 5,17,141 shown in the Table 5.8.[114]

Three special General Relief Managers were appointed to the three districts of Orissa. Toynbee at Puri, Kirkwood at Cuttack and Rampini in Bhadrak (instead of Balasore) to supervise the relief works.[115] Till the month of June 1866, relief operations had not been conducted on any extensive scale.

During July their expansion was much retarded by the great dealy in the inland transport of the imported rice from False Point.[116] All that

112. Supplement to Calcutta Gazettee, 20 June 1866.
113. *RCF*, 1866, Pr. 57, p. 230.
114. T.B. Lane, Secretary to the Board of Revenue, L.P. to the Offg. Secretary to the Government of Bengal, No. 1965M, Fort William, 5 December 1867.
115. *Bd.Doc.* From Hobhouse to E.C. Molony, Cuttack, 10 March 1867.
116. *Bd.Doc.*, Abstract of Assistant Collector, Kirkwood's Report, 10 October 1866.

TABLE 5.8
STATEMENT OF RECEIPTS AND DISBURSEMENTS OF THE ORISSA RELIEF FUNDS FOR 1866

District	Receipt					Disbursements				
	From Government	From Calcutta Committee	From private subscription	Miscellaneous	Total	In purchase of food	In cash	Miscellaneous	Total	Balance
Cuttack	1,39,000	30,000	11,673	2,921	1,83,594 22,000* 2,05,594	1,66,299	2,393	27,017	1,95,709	9,885
Balasore	1,71,000	41,000	21,763	8,538	2,42,301	1,80,583	38,552	7,428	2,26,563	15,738
Puri	70,000	15,000	14,632	1,987	1,01,619	63,126	2,038	29,705	94,869	61,750
Total	3,80,000	86,000	48,068	13,446	5,49,514	4,10,008	42,983	64,150	5,17,141	32,373

*Amount borrowed from Importation Fund.

time there was no other good harbour in the Orissa coast except False Point. Importation of rice fetched difficulty due to the outburse of the monsoon and the False Point was situated faraway from Cuttack. There was also greatest difficulty in carrying the cargoes to the interior due to the lack of communication facilities. Taking all these situations into account, the Government could have done something by spending lavishly on importation by engaging small steamers to carry the grains near the boats.[117] The rice which was imported in large quantities but it was not sold at less than the market price. The amount of food grains imported to Orissa till November 1866, was 10,000 tons.[118] There can be no doubt that all these causes exercised a very deterrent effect. Due to inadequate relief operations, the loss of life was severe.[119]

In Cuttack there were 44 Relief Centres, at which two distributions of cooked rice took place daily. The daily average of the people given relief varied from 1,301 in June to 23,482 on 31st December 1866, and was greatest in October and November, when 38,541 and 34,968 persons, respectively received food. The number of Relief Centres in Puri was 23, of which 9 were in the subdivision of Khurda. The daily average of the people relieved was 7,547, the highest number having been 11,330 in the week ending the 27th October.

The number of paupers in Balasore was augmented by crowds of famished persons who came from the hill states of Nilagiri and Mayurbhanj. There were 22 Relief Centres. The daily average of the number fed was 6,579 in the middle of June and 8,250 at close of December, with this period the numbers fluctuated, exceeding 40,000 at the end of September and culminated in 81,477 on the 17 October.[120] In the month of August a great increase of distress and of mortality occurred in consequence of heavy floods and the inhabitants of many villages were cut off from the relief centres by the inundation, and great numbers died, both from starvation and disease in Cuttack district.[121] The Table 5.9, showing relief operation from June to November 1866.[122] The distress continued till November and the general famine came to a stand still when the new crop began to come into the market.

---

117. *RCF*, Vol. I, Part-I, Pr. 293.
118. *RIF*, 1880, Vol. I, Part-I, Pr. 53.
119. R.C. Dutt, *The Economic History of India in the Victorian Age*, Vol. II, London, p. 246.
120. T.B. Lane, Secretary to the Board of Revenue, L.P. to the Offg. Secretary to the Government of Bengal, No. 1965M Fort William, 5 December 1867.
121. *Bd.Doc.*, Kirkwood's Report, 10 October 1866.
122. *RCF*, Vol. 7, p. 101.

TABLE 5.9

STATEMENT SHOWING RELIEF OPERATION FROM JUNE TO NOVEMBER 1866

District	Quantity received in local stores and Relief Committee	Quantity issued for consumption						
		To Government Department	To Public	For sale at cheap rate	Starving	Total consumed	Without labour	Light labour
Cuttack	148,767	3282	49,754	31,520	52,565	137,121	12,381	7,177
Puri	47,383	1028	18,973	1,940	16,626	42,567	3,205	3,426
Balasore	75,427	4473	10,526	11,643	46,816	74,458	21,945	4,552
Total	271,577	8783	79,253	49,103	116,007	253,146	37,531	15,155

Role of Missionaries

The Christian Missionaries were the first to draw the Government's attention for alleviating the distressed condition of the people. The destitute children were taken by the missionaries which nourished them like sons and educated them and made them economically purposeful.[123] They were made outcast by the Hindu society because, they ate at the relief centres.[124] The roles of Christian missionaries during the time of famine was praise-worthy.

The friend of India, a missionary newpaper, published from Serampore, highlighted about the critical situation of Orissa. J. Buckley and J. Philips, missionaries of Cuttack and Jaleswar informed about the scarcity situation. The newspaper appealed on 12, 1866 for public contribution to a relief fund. Similar narratives also were published in paper of J. Forbes the Collector of Ganjam. Buckley described the situation:

> "The meagre forms of starvating man and women and the plaintative cries of helpless children that come around to beg for food I have no words to describe"[125]

The Calcutta missionaries raised funds by appeal to the public and distributed among the people in the form of cash. The missionaries roused social awareness among the public by which Government was forced to extend his helping hand to the destitute.[126] W.A. Miller, a missionary of Puri visiting several places of district informed the Collector and relief committee about the condition of the distressed. The Baorees, Tantees and low class men were the worst sufferers at the time of scarcity.[127]

The English and American ladies, Roman Catholic and Baptist Missionaries, Mohamedan and Hindu gentlemen came forward to take charge of orphans and deserted children.[128] The missionaries took active interest to feed the poverty stricken and save many from death who must have otherwise perished.[129]

On the whole the activities of Christian Missionaries biased the Government to take up some measures for orphans and destitutes. The

123. John Boulton, (Translated), *op.cit.*, p. 31.
124. *Ibid.*
125. *OHRJ*, Vol. II, January 1981, "The Role of Christian Missionaries in the famine of 1866" by D. Swaro, p. 25.
126. *OHRJ*, Vol II, *op.cit.*, pp. 25-26.
127. *RCF*, Vol. I, *op.cit.*, Statement of W. Miller, No. 87 examined at Cuttack on 26.12.1866.
128. *RCF*, Vol. I, Pr. 86, p. 253.
129. David B. Smith, Report on Pilgrimage to Jaggernanuth in 1868 (with a narrative of a tour through Orissa), p. 41.

orphan poors were allowed to get allowance by the Government (three rupees each per mensem and twenty or thirty rupees cash to start in life with) under the guidance of the missionaries.[130] The famine orphans were estimated at 1,553 and allowances were given till the 17 for boys and 16 years of girl's age. The Famine Committee decided to grant marriage allowance to girls and bonus to boys to start life.[131] Measures were taken to uphold or rescue a number of female children sheltered by prostitutes in the town of Cuttack during the period under study. They were still under age. And eleven children were in this way removed and handed over to the mission orphanage in Cuttack on the same terms as other famine orphans Compensation was also given to the prostitutes for the girls taken away from them.[132] The missionaries played an important role in the famine of 1866 and their services were invaluable and was acknowleged by Government in no uncertain terms.[133]

Relief to the Peasants

Relief was made to the peasants in the form of a suspension and remission of land revenue and grants loans to them. The relief expenditure per head per month in Orissa was less than the north-west provinces famine of 1860. The following table given the average per capita cost of relief per month in different famines during the period under study.[134]

TABLE 5.10
RELIEF EXPENDITURE PER HEAD OF THE POPULATION ON GOVERNMENT RELIEF DURING FAMINES

Year	*Province*	*Cost*		
		Rs.	*As.*	*Ps.*
1860	NWP	3	10	0
1866	Bengal & Bihar	2	1	8
1867	Orissa	2	8	0
1869	NWP	3	3	8
1874	Bengal & Bihar	2	15	10
1874	NWP	1	11	9
1877	Bombay	3	1	7
1877	Hyderabad	3	9	6
1878	NWP	2	6	3½

130. *Ibid.*
131. *RAB*, 1867-68, pp. 216-217.
132. *Ibid.*, 1869-70, p. 137.
133. *RCF*, Vol. I, Pr. 423, p. 133.
134. Quoted in B.M. Bhatia, *op.cit.*, p. 117.

In NWP and the Punjab in 1860 grants were given to the cultivators for the purchase of seeds and cattle. There is no record of any advance found having been made except some what extraordinary experiment of establishing in Khurda in the great Orissa Famine of 1866.[135] The rigidity in revenue collection on the part of British made the peasantry in Orissa more dependent on money-lenders for payment of land revenue. Rigidity in and revenue collection at the time of distress made the people more prone to sufferings.[136] The entire instalments of revenue due in November 1866 were remitted on the condition that the local instalments of rent from the ryots and tenants should also be remitted by the zamindars.[137] To induce the ryots to cultivate their lands, advances of seed rice were made to all who were unable to secure a supply for themselves.[138] The Orissa famine of 1866 forced the Government to adopt a famine policy to avoid in future such type of calamity. The total importation of rice to Orissa up to the end of 1867 was 1,116,810 maunds and the gross expenditure up to the end of 1867 was approximately Rs. 46,57,172.[139] The Orissa Famine was the most intense in India under the British reign. "Money was spurned as worthless" and prices of rice "were far higher than those known in any recorded famine in the century".[140] It was quite impossible on the part of anybody to distinguish between the mortality directly or indirectly caused by starvation. No recorded history will suffice to draw an accurate line about the death from scarcity.[141]

Consequences

The Orissa Famine of 1866 revealed the defects of the administrative system of Bengal Government. The Famine Commission of 1866 pointed out that the people suffered most from the defects of the information available and the reluctance of Government to take direct action. T.E. Ravenshaw, the then Commissioner of Orissa and Sir Cecil Beadon, Lieutenant Governor of Bengal and Groutes, the President of the Board of Revenue were responsible to a great extent for the outbreak of famine in May 1866.[142] Ravenshaw at the time of distress did not grapple with the situation because he was newly appointed as the Commissioner of Orissa. His mistake he realised and after the famine he took keen interest

135. B.M. Bhatia, *op.cit.*, p. 19.
136. *U.D.*, 15 September 1866.
137. *RAB*, 1867-68, pp. 216-17.
138. *Ibid.*, p. 218.
139. *Ibid.*, p. 219.
140. C.E. Buckland, *Bengal Under the Lieutenant Governor*, Vol. I, p. 333.
141. *Ibid.*
142. *OHRJ*, Vol XII, No. 1, 1974, p. 22.

for the improvement of the province through the promotion of Vernacular education and established a number of Vernacular schools in moffusil areas. He also established a medical school at Cuttack in January 1876 with the help of Dr. W.T. Stewart, a Civil Surgeon. Ravenshaw's weakness towards the Oriya people was quoted in *Utkal Dipika* "Mr. Ravenshaw has a strong desire to see Orissa once more. He offered to go out to India in connection with the present famine, but the Government of India said that they were not in need of any outside help. They would have saved money, saved many lives and saves many blunders, if they had availed themselves of the services of such a valuable old officer, especially at the services were gratuitous".[143] In spite of the heavy expenditure, its severity was felt very acutely in every nook and corner of Orissa. It exacted a heavy toll of human lives. The population before the famine was calculated by the Famine commission of 1880, to be 37 lakhs and the mortality to a milliant.[144] *Utkal Dipika* depicts about the population of Orissa before and after the famine of 1866 and it is given below:[145]

TABLE 5.11
POPULATION OF ORISSA BEFORE AND AFTER FAMINE OF 1866

Population of Orissa	*Cuttack*	*Puri*	*Balasore*	*Total Population*
Before Famine	15,03,829	7,79,718	7,32,269	30,15,826
Death from Famine	3,78,009	2,18,852	2,17,608	8,14,469
Migration due to Famine	53,357	32,113	29,558	1,15,028
Total animal loss	4,31,366	2,50,965	2,47,166	9,29,497
Present population	10,72,460	5,28,753	4,85,113	20,86,329

From the table it may be sagely concluded that one-third of population died during the famine of 1866. Total loss of life, cattle property and crops was incalculable. George Campbell remarks about the famine:

> "We were shocked by the human remains we saw all around. From an Indian point of view the area of very intense famine was rather small, being confined to as few millions of people, and the period of intensity was short, being no more than a single half year. But within these limits, it was, I think, by far the most acute famine experienced in any part of India in the present (19th) century".[146]

The Famine Commission of 1878 remarked: "It is a melancholy

143. *U.D.*, 7 August 1897.
144. *IFC*, 1880, Part-I, Prs. 45 & 52.
145. *U.D.*, 18 January 1868, Vol. 3, Part-III.
146. R.C. Majumdar (ed.), *British Paramountcy and Indian Renaissance*, Part-I, p. 830.

reflection that while a larger sum of money was spent on this famine than had ever been spent before, it should be associated in history only with the memory of a greater mortality than had even been recorded".[147]

Much has been done by the British after the famine of 1866 to prevent the recurrence of such calamity. The canals, harbours, and regular system of communications were improved with Calcutta to break the isolation of Orissa, which was the main cause of the great famine.[148]

After the famine, the Bengal Government inaugurated a more active system on the problem. The famine Commission presided over by Sir George Campbell made certain recommendations regarding the prevention of future famine and it was also welcomed by the Bengal Government. Taking this into account irrigation facilities were provided for the well being of the farmers of Orissa. Before the devastating famine of 1866, there was neither a good metalled road nor railway system in Orissa. It was quoted in Famine Commission Report, "Orissa was at that time isolated from the rest of India, the only road leading to Calcutta across the country interested by large rivers and liable to inundation was metalled and unbridged, and there was little communication by sea".[149] This was the main cause for the famine of 1866. The horror of the famine forced the authorities about the necessity of improving the False Point, which was surveyed, deepend and the channels were buoyed. The Kendrapara canal work was undertaken to reach the tidal waters in direct communication with False Point. After the improvement of the port, it remained open throughout the year.[150] Communication with Orissa also was developed by the provision of access by sea at the False Point and the Dhamra river. Both those roads leading to and those within the province were ordered to be completed as rapidly as possible.[151] The modern system of development was the result of the famine (1866). The then socio-political and economic consciousness was developed among the people of Orissa only after the famine.

The Orissa famine also had indirect influence upon the relief operation during the Bengal-Bihar Famine of 1873-74. "The reaction after the failure on the occasion of the Orissa Famine had caused a tendency towards too much rather too little alarm".

The terrible famine of 1866 was the most intense one in the Indian subcontinent under the British Raj. This was the instance where the

147. C.E. Buckland, *op.cit.*, Vol. I, p. 391.

148. W.W. Hunter, *Statistical Accounts of Bengal*, Vol. XVIII, p. 148; *The Star of Utkal*, 8 September 1908.

149. C.E. Buckland, *op.cit.*, Vol. I, p. 330.

150. *U.D.*, Part-IV, 3 July 1869, No. 27.

151. C.E. Buckland, *op.cit.*, p. 394.

British authority frankly admitted their mistakes. The then Secretary of State for India, Sir Stafford North Cote, in the House of Commons declared "the catastrophe is a monument of our failure, a humiliation to the people of this country, to the Government of this country and to those of our Indian officials of whom we had perhaps been a little too proud. At the same time we must hope that we might derive from its lessons which might be of real value to ourselves, and that out of this deplorable evil good of no insignificant kind might untimely arise".[152]

The apathy of the Government towards economic conditions of the people ceased and non-interference policy of laissez-faire was rejected with a suitable policy decision.[153] This drought (1865) felt in greater intensity on Orissa in Lower Province of Bengal because it was dealt by group of officers completely ignorant of the signs of its approach, unprepared to face it and inexperienced in the field of relief administration and on the other hand the native inhabitants of Orissa were not, in any respect, more aware of what was coming on them than the British officers.[154] At the time of great Orissa Famine, there was no newspaper except *Utkal Dipika* which was the only Oriya newspaper that highlighted the wretched condition of people and exposed the Government policy, helped in saving many lives and urged the Government for taking immediate measures for the speedy recovery of the province.

---

152. C.E. Buckland, *op.cit.*, p. 386.
153. G.C. Patnaik, *op.cit.*, pp. 327 & 379.
154. C.E. Buckland, *op.cit.*, p. 329.

6

Famines and Scarcities After 1866

Years of misrule of the British Government and its negligence to the traditional irrigation facilities in Orissa, resulted in the occurrence of the great famine of 1866 in the province. It became severe due to the callous attitude of the government which had taken no care to develop irrigation facilities and communication system in Orissa since its occupation in 1803. Truly speaking, the British Government in India had no interest in the welfare of the people. As Orissa was included in the Bengal Presidency and the high officials of the British authority were residing in Bengal away from Orissa, she passed neglected in the sphere of administration. She was the only province in British India which fell victim to natural calamities every year. Frequent occurrence of floods, droughts and famines hit the economic condition of the people. During the British administration Orissa suffered more from famines than during the Mughal and Maratha rule. Out of 31 famines in India in the 19th century, 18 occurred after 1850.[1] Along with Oudh, Bihar, Bombay, Madras and North-Western provinces, Orissa suffered extensively from the natural calamities.[2] As such, India experienced the severity of widespread famines in the later part of the 19th century.[3]

The occurrence of the famines in several years impoverished the people of Orissa and their economic condition became precarious. The severity of the famines left impact of grave concern on the common people. This can clearly be established in the following graph by comparing the price level of normal period with that of distressed period.

Though the people of Orissa were sincere and hard-working, yet they had never been able to improve their condition. the natural calamities had crippled the very core of their existence in the absence of any suitable remedial measures by the Government. The famines and scarcities occurred in 1870, 1874, 1877, 1888-89, 1889-90, 1896-97, 1899-1900.

1. H.K. Mahtab, *History of Orissa*, Vol. II, (Cuttack, 1960), pp. 445-447.
2. B.M. Bhatia, *Famines in Orissa*, (London, 1963). p. 58.
3. A. Loveday, *History and Economics of Famines in India*, (London 1914), p. 25.

Graph Showing Fluctuations in the price of RICE from 1836 to 95

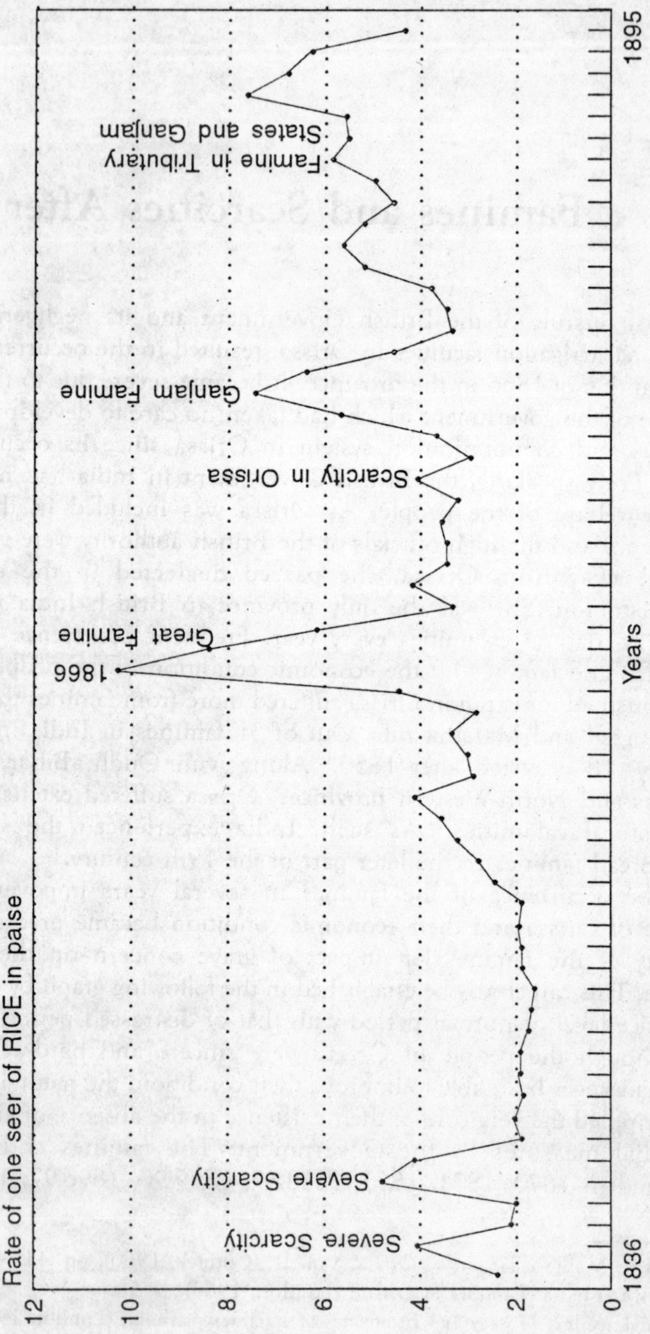

Source — Maddox Report, Vol. I, p. 118

Fig. 12

Frequent visit of famines to Orissa brought untold miseries to here people, Lack of proper administration by the Britishers to alleviate the distress of the people destroyed the socio-economic condition of the people.[4]

There were many factors to stimulate the famine, such as scanty rainfall, shortage of food supply and lack of transport and communication. The speedy rise of food prices also aggravated the situation.[5] The suffering of the people due to price hike, was clear sign of man-made sufferings during the 19th century. Human and institutional factors contributed more than natural factors to the sufferings in Orissa. Under the modernizing influence of railways and the growing grain trade, the famine problem was transformed from one of intense local sufferings limited to the area of severe drought to that of high prices of food over a wide area accompanied by the inability due to poverty of a large mass of the agricultural population to feed themselves. Famines before the coming of railways were sporadic, infrequent and local in their incidence and a major famine occurred one in every 50 years. The last phase of the 19th century never saw a countrywide famine.[6]

The second half of the 19th century witnessed less but routined natural calamities in Orissa. The severity of famines was not high like that of 1866 owing to the application of some remedial measures. These famines and scarcities where like a recurrent feature to the British administration in rural India.[7] Millions of people perished in Orissa due to lack of transport, communication, irrigation and relief measures during the time of famines., Frequent occurrence of famines and scarcities made the condition of people deplorable.

In this chapter an attempt is being made to summarise briefly the famine from 1866 to 1900 and to trace the cumulative impact of continuous impoverishment of the people and how the Government managed the other famines after 1866.

Famines and Scarcities

Famines and scarcities were recurrent features of Orissa during the 19th century.[8] Frequent occurrence of droughts, untime rainfall, food export and lack of communication were the immediate causes of scarcities in the

---

4. B.M. Bhatia, *op.cit.*, pp. 58-63.
5. Vaughan Nash, *The great famine and its causes*, (Bombay, 1900), pp. I-II.
6. W.W. Hunter, *Annals of Rural Bengal*, (London, 1868), p. 50. H.S. Srivastav, *The History of Indian Famines, 1858-1918.* (Agra, 1968), pp. 23-25.
7. Debidas Roy, *Food Administration in East India, 1839-1954*, (Calcutta, 1958), p. v.
8. *Orissa Prasanga O Anyanya*, Vol. 16, Gandhi Rachanabali, (Cuttack, 1980), pp. 5-7.

latter part of the 19th century. The good year for the crop production is marked when there is an average rainfall in June, a copious rainfall in July, August and September and a more than average rainfall in the first half of October. Any diversification to these causes leads to scarcities in Orissa. The following table produces the same.

TABLE 6.1
RAINFALL AND CROP PRODUCTION

Year	*Rainfall*	*Crop production*	*Consequences*
1865-66	Heavy and Untimely	Less production due to drought	Severe famine
1884-85	Heavy and timely	Bumper crops	Prosperity
1885-86	Less and timely	Good crops	Prosperity

Sources : P. Mukherjee, *Irrigation, Inland Navigation and flood problems in north Orissa during the British Rule*, H.K. Mishra, Famines and Poverty in India, p. 206.

Scarcity of 1869 to 1871

In the year 1869 the *biali* and *sarada* crops were seriously affected due to want of rain in the Orissa division. But the heavy rains in July saved the situation. The local distress was felt around the Chilka lake. It was saved because of manufacture of salt which gave employment to the distressed People.[9]

In 1870 the crop position became bleak owing to want of rain in August. Towards the month of September and October the position became hard. The local officers in Puri and Cuttack informed the Commissioner about the general failure of crops. They also suggested to take measures to relieve the distressed people of the tract suffering from drought.[10] When the Government was alert to face another famine, a copious rain in September 1870 saved the situation.[11] It was not found necessary to adopt relief measures anywhere except in some parts of Puri and Khurda, where relief works were sanctioned in order to provide labour for those whose crops had suffered.[12]

Taking these circumstances into account Sir W. Grey addressed the Supreme Government urging "the extreme importance of carrying on irrigation works to completion without delay, and at the same time expressing his opinion that this province would never be thoroughly safe

9. *BAR*, 1869-70, pp. 136-137.
10. *Ibid.*, 1870-71, p. 48.
11. *Ibid.*
12. *Ibid.*

from one of two calamities either drought or inundation, till those works were completed".[13]

In the Orissa division an amount of Rs.41,381 were remitted, *viz.*, in Puri Rs. 34,139, in Balasore Rs. 6,808 and in Cuttack Rs. 434 on account of loss of crops resulting from drought and inundation and for the lands left uncultivated in consequence of death, desertion or indigence or ryots.[14]

In 1871 symptoms of famine were felt in Ganjam and Issakpattan (Vizagpattam) areas of the southern part of Orissa due to scanty rainfall. At Issakpattan, rice was selling at 10 Balasore seers for one rupee. Still it was not easily procurable and the prices were rising day by day. So the Government in apprehension of the occurrence of a famine had warned the Collectors of these areas of their duties by which they should try their best not to make the event a great disaster just like that of 1866. The Collectors had made arrangements for the importation of rice from other areas of the province. The Government bore the cost of water supplied to the poor people in wanting areas. But it was a matter of great astonishment that there was no rain in the districts but the river Godavari was overflowing with flood waters during the prevailing scarcity period. But the people as well as the areas got no benefit out of this overflowing as they depended much on the rainfall, the want of which caused failure of crops in those places. The people doubted about the coming of a great famine just like that of 1866.[15] The prices of rice were increasing highly at some places like Parlakhemundi where rice was sold at 18 seers per rupee. At Ganjam, rice was selling at 24 seers per rupee.[16]

Paddy and rice were exported to those areas from Puri and Cuttack through the water route of Chilka and by bullock carts through land routes. It was estimated that paddy imported to those areas in January 1872 was 40,000 maunds and rice up to 7,300 maunds. The need of the water was felt more. So the existing water tanks were purified which provided employment to labourers. In spite of these measures some starving people emigrated from Parlakhemundi, Huma and other Telugs and others had made a preparation to start the migration. At some places people suffered from fever and small-pox. The animals were also affected at Putasarapur of Ganjam, and the Government officials continued their works on an emergency basis. But the people were haunted by the fear of a great famine.[17]

---

13. *BAR*, 1870-71, p. 48.
14. *Ibid.*
15. *U.D.*, 16 December 1871.
16. *Ibid.*, 3 February 1872.
17. *Ibid.*

In 1871 scarcity in rice prevailed in spite of land laying between Chilka lake and the sea, comprising Sathpara and estates of Raja of Parikud and of the Talukdar of Malud of Puri district whose crops were entirely lost due to scanty rainfall in September and the repeated failure of crops exhausted stored food and finance in hand. To alleviate the distress of the people of the two estates Commissioner of Orissa was authorised to grant Rs. 3,000 to ryots, who had land in possession, relief in the shape of loans on the best security. And those who had nothing, relief was given in the shape of charity.[18] Relief works in lieu of repairs of bunds, embankments and tanks were started to afford employment to the destitutes of the two estates. The Commissioner was also authorized to spend further Rs. 2,000 if the fund proved insufficient to meet the purpose. Added to this, charitable subscription was opened in Orissa for giving help to the disabled, old, and sick who were unable to earn their living.[19]

Scarcity of 1873-74

In 1873 people felt alarmed due to the famine in Bengal.[20] To their bad luck, scarcity conditions also prevailed in Soso of Balasore district. A total area of 100 square mile was hard hit by drought. The Commissioner had estimated that about 37,000 people were affected. Heavy export of rice in 1873 out of Balasore left little for 1874. The price increased in 1874 when symptoms of drought appeared in Soso. The people of Soso failed in procure rice at such a high rate and sufferings of people continued.[21]

G. Stevenson, Assistant Collector of Bhadrak called a meeting on the 30th December 1873 of the zamindars and others in the subdivision who had landed property. A considerable number of them attended the meeting and a relief fund was opened for relief to the sufferers. Importance was given to the supply of water to the people of distressed areas. The supply was not satisfactory. The native gentlemen were empowered to appoint members of committee to administer the relief funds. They submitted the list to the Collector on 3rd January and that was approved. Wells were sunk throughout the pargana where the scarcity of water was most severely felt. A Munshi Abdul Janni agreed to dig a large tank at Namee. For this purpose he was aided by a supply of some 30 kodalahs for the use of the workmen. The offer of Government to advance money to local zamindars for the improvement of their estates was denied by Soso landowners.[22]

---

18. *BAR*, 1871-72. Part-II, p. 4.
19. *Ibid.*
20. *U.D.*, 27 December 1873.
21. *Utkal Putra*, No. I, Vol. 4., 4 January 1874.
22. From G. Stevenson, Assistant Collector of Bhadrak to the Collector of Balasore, No. 146, 20 September 1874.

Meetings were held in Cuttack and Balasore with the view of opening subscription list for the relief of the inhabitants of the distressed districts. W. Fiddian, in his memo annexed, estimated the aggregate of subscriptions at Rs. 5,000/-. The Deputy Collector fixed 36 places for the immediate sinking of wells and list of 64 other localities was also selected in the drought areas for the sinking of wells. The average cost of sinking a well came to Rs. 11-14-5.[23]

With reference to the Commissioner's 2nd para the roads in and about Soso; on which money from the District Funds had been expended were[24]—

(*a*) Agarapara Road - completed in June last at a total cost of Rs. 200/-.

(*b*) Aranji to Cowpar finished in the same month at a cost of Rs. 20/-.

(*c*) Agarapara to Kupari completed during August last at a cost of Rs. 100/-.

(*d*) Barapada to Maraigaon road worked out at a cost of Rs. 215-4-0.

A sum of rupees 2989-8 annas was collected towards Soso Relief Fund out of which Rs. 500 and Rs. 250 was donated by T.E. Ravenshaw the Commissioner of Orissa and W. Fiddian respectively. Rs.165-1-1½ was spend towards sinking of 10 wells in different places to supply drinking water.

At that time the price of rice had increased due to heavy export of rice to Calcutta. The zamindars were also not in a mood to help their subjects through some contributions. So the people apparently felt the necessity of help of the Government authority as famine was knocking at their doors.[25]

Scarcity of 1877

At the beginning of September 1877, the condition of the crops in the tract between the Chilka and the sea was worse than before. As the later rain did not come in abundance there was great distress among the small population of Andhari, Parikud, Malud and Bajrakot.[26] By the early October sufficient rainfall was not received in any part of the district. The *sarada* rice plants on high lands were reported to be suffering much

---

23. From G. Stevenson, Assistant Collector to Bhadrak to the Collector of Balasore, No. 146, 20 September 1874.
24. *Ibid.*
25. *U.D.*, 27 December 1873.
26. Supplement to Calcutta Gazette, September to December 1877, p. 1010.

and in some places they were destroyed. The want of sufficient rain was generally felt.[27] Towards October 12, the *sarada* rice plants on high lands were affected severely in many places. The same was the condition of crops in low lands. The crops had almost entirely failed in the tract between the Chilka and the sea.[28]

The outturn from low lands was expected to be fair; but on high lands hope of production was disastrous. Not more than 1/16th of the paddy crop on the tract between the Chilka and the sea could be saved.[29] The rice crops on high lands and on some low lands in some places in the Khurda subdivision had been reported to be suffering seriously. The state of the crops in the Puri subdivision was more gloomy than the reported last.[30] There was also a considerable loss of crops in Banches, Athais, Matkatpatna and parts of Oldhar.[31]

As the cultivated lands of those areas were not productive enough, the people depended much on salt manufacture and trade for their livelihood. But faulty policies of the Government on salt trade compelled the people to depend on cultivation. So a bad harvest in 1876 was sufficient to make the people starve. The zamindars of the locality were reluctant to help the distressed people. The people had nothing to eat. The police authorities reported to the District Collector of Puri that the people were living on *saga*.[32] It was also reported that the ryots of Parikud were selling their cattle to buyers who were despatching them to Ganjam.[33]

In the tracts situated between the Chilka and the sea the condition of the people was worse than before. Relief was being given mainly from funds contributed by private individuals.[34] On 24th September 1877 a meeting was held at Puri in order to collect public funds, charity and contribution from the rich persons to help the famine stricken population of the Chilka region. By the initiative of Armstrong the Collector of Puri, a Relief Committee was formed and he was requested by the people to suggest the Collectors of Balasore and Cuttack to collect charity funds. The Secretary of Relief Committee wrote a letter to the Collector of Balasore and Puri in order to make collection by request. The people also became nervous because of the increased prices of rice. In order to

27. *Ibid.*, p. 1086.
28. Supplement to Calcutta Gazette, *op.cit.*, p. 1122.
29. *Ibid.*, p. 1170.
30. *Ibid.*, p. 1210.
31. *BAR*, 1877-78, p. 128.
32. *U.D.*, 6 October 1877.
33. From I.S. Armstrong, Collector of Puri to the Commissioner of Orissa division, Cuttack, No. 92T, Tanghi, 15 December 1877.
34. Supplement to Calcutta Gazette, *op.cit.*, 1877, p. 1269.

meet the situation and help the people some philanthrophists contributed a large amount not only in cash but also in kind.

Also the condition of the people of Khurda and Mahanga was precarious because of the symptoms of a secret famine. The poor people were eating once in a day. The starved people of Mahanga had looted rice stores of the Mahajans. Now the Government felt the necessity of imparting relief to those areas.[35]

The Collector of Puri had sent the Sub-Deputy Collector (Baboo Kumudnath Mukherjee) to those affected regions of the Chilka in order to impart relief and distribute charity. The condition of the people was precarious as there was no stock of paddy in their house and had no money in their hand. The Government started relief operations by beginning works on 6 tanks and on embankment. The destroyed dirty tanks were enlarged, made deep and their water supplied to near by cultivable lands. About 800 labourers were employed. Large number of labourers were returning to their homes without employment due to shortage of money. Only Rs. 100 was to be spent in a day as per the rule. The unemployed labourers had preferred to die with their children and wives in their houses than to go to other places for employment. They were living only on 'saga' and other grass plants.

The Calcutta Committee contributed an amount of Rs. 3,000 in order to help the people of the famine stricken area. The cause of this great scarcity was the exportation of large amount of rice to Madras Presidency due to famine.[36]

The Lt. Governor sanctioned the suspension of the levy of the District Road Cess and the Public Works Cess in the parganas Parikud, Malud and Bajrakot in Puri districts due to total failure of crops.[37] The Lt. Governor had also sanctioned an advance of Rs. 5,000 for the purchase of seed grain to be lent to the most destitute cultivators in Malud and Bajrakot and the loan was to be recovered by instalments from the next years crop.[38]

Recommendations of Famine Commissions

The famine Commission of 1880 besides other things recommended to

---

35. *U.D.*, 6 October 1877.
36. *Ibid.*, 10 November 1877.
37. Revenue Department Local Taxation No. 386, Babu Rajendra Mitra Assistant Secretary to the Government of Bengal to the Secretary to the Board of Revenue, Land Revenue Department, Calcutta, 6 February 1878.
38. Financial Department Famine, No. 1213, H.H. Risley Esq. Under Secretary to the Government of Bengal to the Commissioner of Orissa, Calcutta, 30 March 1878.

grant relief to ryots through remission, by suspending revenue and rent payment in the event of bad harvests and drought.[39] It was accepted by the Government to maintain statistics of harvests of classified agricultural land periodically and inform the ryots about rent and revenue remissions. This policy was also adopted for Orissa to protect tenantry from scarcity and famine. But in practice little was done to improve the condition of tenants.

After the all India famine of 1876-78 a Commission was established in 1878-80 which recommended a 'famine code', a set of rules which was the basis of famine relief works for the able bodied people and free relief to the rest of people under the domain of destitution. For the supply of food no interference with private agencies was suggested. For efficient distribution of food, increase in the production of food by scientific programmes of irrigation was given paramount importance. Various types of incentives to land owners were given to start farm works. Land owners would get relief through suspension of land revenue and would get loan to start efficient farm work.[40]

On 9th June 1883 the Famine Commission announced the code. The Commission highlighted not to undertake any isolated case of distress, but it could undertake and solve only the scarcity, afflicting a group of people. Relief works, and other employment opportunities for needy agricultural labourers were recommended.[41]

Gratuitous relief, distribution of doles in the villages and feeding of destitutes in free kitchens were meant for physically disables, infirm and old people. Following recommendations of the commision, Government of India issued circulars to all provinces to follow the Code.[42]

Then the "Famine Code" became a guide to administration, for dealing with famines which was not there before. For this Government committed to undertake the followings:

(*a*) Continuous system of collecting information and statistics from every local areas to provincial Government.

(*b*) The type and nature of relief works to be taken up in times of famines.

(*c*) classification of labourers to provide different sorts of relief and wages to be paid.

(*d*) organization of gratuitious relief.

---

39. *RAB*, 1882-83, (Calcutta, 1883), p. 27.
40. Famine Relief Codes and Other matters pertaining to administration of 9 June 1883, Department of Revenue/Agriculture, Simla, 1892, pp. 2-9.
41. *Ibid.*, Prs. 1-10.
42. *Ibid.*, Pr. 7.

(*e*) a system of village inspection.

(*f*) suspension of revenue.

(*g*) grant of taccavi loans.

(*h*) relaxation of forest laws during famines.

(*i*) protection of cattle to avert fodder famines etc.

District administrations were assigned to take up these works with intimation to provincial Government.

The deviations from these accepted principles caused famine in the tributary states of Orissa in 1888-89 and Ganjam in 1888-89.

"For seventy years our whole Government of Orissa has been a tale of woe according to the confessious on an English officials."[43]

Famine in 1878

There was great distress among the landless labourer classes in Daruthung and Andharua of Khurda subdivision. They lived on roots and leaves for about four months, only taking small quantity of rice occasionally. The people noted that five persons* among labouring class died from starvation within two months. The people of labourer classes were suffering on account of high price of rice and there was very littly demand for their labour.

The condition of the labourer classes of Andharua was worse than that of Daruthung. The people of Andharua were unfit to do any work. They must have died from starvation if they would not have provided with some relief.[44] The Commission had ordered the Collector to sanction a small sum for village roads and also sanctioned sum of gratuitous relief out of the Calcutta Relief Fund. The rate of rice had fallen from 9 seers to 10 and 11 seers owing to the arrival of boats loaded with rice from Calcutta and other places. The Commissioner also ordered to look after the villages and inform about their progress.[45]

Scarcities in Tributary States 1887-88

The Superintendent of Tributary Mahals of Orissa submitted a report in 1888 to the Lt. Governor of partial failure of crops in most of the states.

---

43. H. Ricketts, "Our Mis, Government in Orissa", Friend of India, 3 October 1874.

* Their names were (1) Padi Mazi, (2) Chandro Mazhi, (3) Operti Baoori of Noagaon, (4) Bhagbat Naik of Barman, (5) daughter of Baisnab Jena of Daruthung.

44. No. A Camp Bhubaneswar 2 August 1878, Baboo Srinath Bhadro, Deputy Collector incharge to the Commissioner of Orissa.

45. No. 1100, A. Smith Esquire Off. Commissioner, Orissa Division to the Deputy Collector, Khurda, Cuttack, 9 August 1878.

Rainfall was recorded in Angul, Khondmals, Keonjhar, Mayurbhanj, Talcher, Dhenkanal, Daspalla, Narsinghpur, and Ranpur, and the statement shows the quantity of rain in each of those places during each month of the year.[46]

TABLE 6.2
AVERAGE RAINFALL IN EACH STATION OF THE TRIBUTARY MAHALS DURING THE YEAR 1887-88

Name of Killa	*Total rainfall in inches and tenths*	
	1886-87	*1887-88*
Angul	57.5	36.6
Khondmals	59.1	46.3
Daspalla	59.7	49.8
Talcher	48.6	48.7
Dhenkanal	77.8	48.7
Mayurbhanj	61.3	49.9
Ranpur	63.5	35.8
Keonjhar	31.5	30.1
Narsinghpur		32.4

The table shows that rainfall during the year under report was everywhere deficient than that of the preceding year.

Dhenkanal, Pal-Lehara, Keonjhar, Talcher, Angul, Athmalik, Khandapara and Daspalla suffered most. So it can be concluded that rice must have been considerably below the average, Narsingpur, Ranpur, Nayagarh and Khondmals suffered less, while in Mayurbhanj, Nilgiri, Hindole, and Baramba little loss was sustained. In Tigiria and Athgarh the crops were average and in Boad the harvest wad bad.[47]

The people of Angul felt alarmed in 1887 about their future livelihood as the crops failed due to scanty rainfall. Both kharif and Winter crops failed badly.

There were a few famines in Angul from 1883 to 1887. These made the condition of people precarious. They had spent everything to live and at the end of 1887 they were expecting death out of starvation. The price of rice was high and became scarce in market. The great difference in price between different states, *viz.*, from 13 seers of rice per rupee in Angul to 26 seers in the Khondmals were due to the lack of better communication.[48] Most of the people were living on wild fruits and other

46. No. 47 of 1888, Supplement to the Calcutta Gazettee, November 21, 1888, p. 2308.
47. No. 47. of 1888, Supplement to the Calcutta Gazette, *op.cit.*
48. *BAR*, 1887-88, p. 6.

cattle edibles. Many of them migrated to other districts. Robbery and theft increased day by day. The Government servants also suffered due to little procurement of rice. It was considered that death on a large scale would surely occur if an immediate operation would not come in time. The people also dreamt of the happenings of the great famine of 1866. The people necessitated Government's help not in cash but in kind.[49]

A large number of bullocks and buffalos died of small-pox. The selling and buying of paddy and rice had already stopped. Importation from nearby Garjat areas had come to a stand still. The people made queues to those places where rice was sold. Some got rice with high prices and some did not. Some of the people with their children cried loudly because of hunger. The condition of the poverty sticken people had reached such a precariously indescribable point. The lower class untouchables even ate the dead bodies. The river, the tanks and all other water resources got dried. The people had rememberd the late Madras famine. The local Tahasildar along with the police inspector had enquired the moffusil areas in order to know the extent of devastation. Uparbisi, Tinidesa, Kendhara, Tansee, Padibdea and Paranagagada were enquired. The subjects carried due to starvation. Many of them fled to other Garjat areas due to Government initiative to collect revenue. Many hunger sticken people had applied to the Commissioner of Orissa to get Government's help through paddy and ricc. At some places death occurred due to starvation. The Government authorities yet paid no heed towards this condition of the people of Angul.[50]

The people of Dhankanal, Baramba, Narsinghpur, and Ranpur were affected by the cholera. In Dhenkanal medicines were distributed to the people in the affected tracts.[51]

The partial failure of crops in tributary states in 1886-87 and recurrence of short harvests in 1887-88 had caused some privation among the poorer classes. They were saved from severe distress by an excellent mango crop and making use of jungle roots, fruits and leaves. The aboriginal tribes were living on these jungle fruits for six months every year.

Famine of 1888-89

In the year 1888-89 distress occurred at some palces including all the three districts of Orissa. The places were Khurda in the district of Puri, Banki in the district of Cuttack and Bhograi, Baliapal, Chandbali and Basudebpur in the district of Balasore.[52]

---

49. *U.D.*, 22 October 1887.
50. *U.D.*, 19 November 1887.
51. *BAR*, 1887-88, p. 6.
52. *GAROD*, 1888-89.

Towards the end of July and beginning of August, 1888 starvation was felt in Khurda. The people reaped no good harvest during previous two years. Their entrance to jungal areas were restricted; they got ruined due to firm settlement also. The Collector of Puri, on coming to know the starved condition, sent the Deputy Gagan Chandra Das and Sub-Deputy Darpanarain Das with Rs. 25,000 to Khurda. The acting Director of the Agriculture Department also made certain arrangements to help the people. An embankment work had started in order to employ the people.[53] Towards the latter half of August number of persons employed on Estates Improvements works was 944 (687 men, 54 women and 203 children) at a cost of Rs. 2,839. The daily average number of persons receiving gratuitous relief was 1,505 (315 men, 366 women and 824 children). Taccavi advances, amounting to Rs. 59,853-8, were made to 20,734 cultivators during the month of August, the amount advanced during the fortnight under review having been Rs. 18,944-8.

The stock of food grains in the subdivision was reported to be sufficient and mahajans in some places had begun to resume their business of lending grain. The price of food grains such as rice ranging from 15 to 21 seers, and moong and kulthi selling as mch as the same rates.[54] The Collector issued instructions to the subdivisional officer regarding restriction of advances and to all circle officers for confining gratutitous relief strictly to those who could not work for their living. From the latest sources available 8 persons had died due to starvation. It was not peculiar to Khurda, but was common in most years to all thickly populated countries and districts. It was also reported that all reasonable precautions had been taken for the saving of life.[55]

The Lt. Governor sanctioned all the grants applied fr Khurda, *i.e.*, Rs. 15,000 for gratuitous relief, and an additional sum of Rs. 25,000 for loans under the Agriculturists Loans Act.

Two deaths occurred in Ghatikia from starvation. "The distress was greatest in Zilla Rameswar", said the officer-in-charge of the circle, "two children died at Talpara, although relief had been given to them and more was promised".

According to the report of H.J.S. Cotton, the officiating Secretary to the Government of Bengal :

---

53. *U.D.*, 11 August 1888.
54. C.F. Worsley Commissioner of the Orissa Division to the Secretary to the Government of Bengal, Revenue Department, No. 1843 R, Cuttack, 20 September 1888.
55. C.F. Worsley Commissioner of the Orissa Division, to the Secretary to the Government of Bengal, Revenue Department, No. 1843, Cuttack, 20 September 1888.

"The suffering is greatest amongst the savars and the weavers. Many of the people have been reduced so much in flesh that there is nothing but skin and bone left. One such women died the day before yesterday (14th) in my present, and near by bungalow, when coming to ask for relief. She came from Zillah Khordha and was going to Chandpore to her fathers house, the husband having failed to maintain her. She dropped on the way at night, and heavy showers of rain passed over her head, and in the morning when she was discovered by me, life was all but extinct. No efforts could bring back life to her. There is no doubt that she died of the effects of cold and hunger. Her home was not in my circle. She was about 40 years old".

"An women of Damon Bhoi died in the woods while collecting tunga (diosoorea) roots before I came to Jankia".

According to Taylor, the subdivisional officer, no pressure was being put on ryots to pay up arrears due and the collection was practically at a standstill. The staff were now being employed chiefly in connection with relief works.[56]

Sir Steuart Bayley had instructed the forest department to relax the Forest Rules and the adoption of useful works within the forest in the Orissa Division. The Superintending Engineer of the Orissa Circle was conveyed through the Public Works Department for the commencement of thorough repairs of the Cuttack-Ganjam and the Cuttack-Puri roads. The Lt. Governor was also satisfied that everything within the power of the officials had been done for the relief of distress.[57]

In the Government estate of Banki there was a temporary scarcity in September and October when relief works where started on a moderate scale. The total expenditure amounted to Rs. 7,500/- and was spent on following heads:

On relief works	Rs. 2,500
Taccavi Advances	Rs 5,000
Total	Rs. 7,500

Of the Rs. 2,500 expended in relief works, Rs. 500 was contributed by the district board.

56. H.J.S. Cotton Offg. Secretary to the Government of Bengal to the Secretary to the Government of India, Revenue and Agricultural Department, N. 3066-199 Fam. 10 December 1888.
57. W.C. Taylor, Subdivisional officer, Khurda to the Collector of Puri, No. 481, 18 August 1888.

The condition of a portion of the tenantry in the Kanika wards estate was also very poor and it was necessary to remit the arrears of rent due from them.[58]

In Balasore there was some unmistakable signs of distress in thana Chandbali and Basudebpur on account of the inundation in September.[59] The people had begun to sell their cattle and household goods in order to buy cereals. The well-to-do families had also sold their gold and silver ornaments in the bazar. Very coarse rice was selling at one anna a seer or Rs. 2-8-0, a maund and in the Chandbali Bazar at the rate of 1½ anna and sometimes even 2 annas a seer Rs. 2-8-0 a maund was not a famine price, but it was too high a price for a man who earned only 1½ anna a day and had perhaps 4 or 5 persons to feed.[60]

Private subscriptions were raised at both Balasore and Bhadrak in these thanas and also in thana of Baliapal. Relief Funds were also formed in above thanas. The tract which suffered most from failure of crops was Bhograi, where quite 13/16th of the rice crop was destroyed in an area of 50 square miles with a population of 32,000. Besides the employment provided by the Public Works Department in repair of embankment and in excavating a large tank in the Bhograi Block, the local board spent money in cold weather and had granted Rs. 450 in order to provide the destitute labour. The Collector also granted advances amounting to Rs. 4,620 from the subscriptions raised to supply food to a number of women and children. Distress in Bhograi had still continued and about 300 persons received relief and the Collector had been authorised to spend the grant of Rs. 1,500 sanctioned by the Government if any emergency arises.[61]

Famine in the Tributary States (1888-89)

The deficiency of the crops of 1888 in many of the Tributary states of Orissa was the cause of some anxiety, to the Government of Bengal, and the necessity for special vigilance in Angul-once a tributary state but confiscated in 1847 by the British, was impressed on the Commissioner of Orissa.[62] The people of Angul suffered a lot towards the end of 1888. The people ate wild fruits and leaves and were reduced to mere skeletons. There was no rainfall in the year 1888 also. In Angul the worst affected areas were Purunagarh, Gandibeda, Tinidesa, Taynsee, Kandara,

58. *GAROD*, 1888-89.
59. *Ibid.*
60. Baboo Atal Behari Motia, Subdivisional Officer to Collector of Balasore, No. 22J, 26 September, 1888.
61. *GAROD*, 1888-89.
62. *RIF*, 1898, p. 14.

Teekarpara, Uparbis, Khemba, Kalings and Talamul, because the crops failed there both in the year 1887 and 1888. The number of deaths occurred due to starvation in those areas was twenty four. The people lived in so deteriorating condition that it was though hundred would die unless the Government would protect them. Nothing was done for the middle and higher class prople who starved in moffusil areas.

At some places an item of relief had started towards the end of August 1888. Everyday a help of one pie, 3 pie and one rupee were given to every child, woman and man respectively from Angul Famine Relief Committee. Apart from providing any substantial help and relief, the Government officials tried to extract revenue arrears from the cultivators, who were reduced to the condition of hewers of wood and drawers of water and they lived only hand to mouth.[63]

The Angul Famine Relief Committee had imparted relief to the lower middle and higher class people. It gave help to the diseased, distressed, weak, helpless and the disable labourers to make them alive. The members of the committee had made enquiries about the condition of the people before and after providing relief, the committee also gave salt as an item of relief.

The number of the people increased day by day before the helping committee because of little help by the Government authorities. But the condition of the people had grown worse day by day as the funds were becoming less both in cash and in kind.[64]

According to the records available, the Government had adopted some charitable relief, *viz.*, the remission by Government of Rs. 4,917 arrears of rent, the relaxation of Forest Rules, the opening of Estates Improvement works, and the judicious distribution of small sums.[65] The Assistant Superintendent of the Tributary Mahals visited Angul and made a special enquiry and reported regarding the condition of the people, the state of the crops and the sufficiency of the measures taken to relieve local distress. In Angul a remission of rents for the year 1895 amounting to Rs. 4,917 had been sanctioned by the Government.[66]

The population of Khandapara was 66,296 with an area of 244 square miles in 1889. The Assistant Superintendent described the condition of

---

63. *U.D.* 1 September 1888.
64. *Ibid.*, 6 October 1888.
65. C.F. Worsley, Commissioner of the Orissa division to the Secretary to the Government of Bengal, Revenue Department 1843R, Cuttack, 20 September 1888.
66. H.J.S. Cotton, Offg. Secretary to the Government of Bengal to the Secretary to the Government of India, Revenue and Agricultural Department, No.3066-119 Fam., December 1888.

people as being perhaps in greater distress than that of any of the neighbouring states. It was found that considerable advances of paddy had been made by the Raja to the cultivators; but in many cases such advances were refused to the landless classes. The arrangements for the supply of gratuitous relief were most inadequate and the Assistant Superintendent urged the Raja to take proper relief measures. At Kantilo in Khandapara the Raja had opened an annachhatra, about eight mile off, which was said to be attended by 2,000 people belonging to the lower castes. The Assistant Superintendent was not satisfied with the Raja's helping hand towards the destitutes.[67] Except few measures like this, the Raja appeared to have made no real attempt to provide suitable relief for the landless classes and aboriginal tribes,[68] for which they migrated to other places.[69]

The king of Baramba provided relief to the distressed people through *annachhatras*. Some employments were also created by digging of tanks and construction of roads. The jungle restrictions were also withdrawn. In spite of all these measures people migrated to other places in search of livelihood.[70] Relief proceedings were first commenced in this state in August 1888 and the total amount spent up to the 31st July was Rs. 17,780 of which Rs. 9,654 had been spent during 1889. The measures taken seemed sufficient to relieve the existing distress. The Manager who carefully handled throughout the distress, hoped all difficulties would be over by the end of October.[71]

Nayagarh with an area of 588 square miles and a population of 144,622 and Ranpur with an area of 203 square miles and a population of 36,539 greately suffered from the scarcity. The young and inexperienced Raja of Nayagarh had done little to relieve the distress of his people. A sum of Rs. 15,000 was granted to him for relief operation. Frascr, S.D.O., of Khurda was deputed there to inspect and submit a first hand report of the situation. He reported that the sum granted for relief was totally inadequate to meet the demand.

He also supposed that distress would prevail among the aborigines and semi-Hinduised tribes whose number was about 17,000 in the state. The Manager reported that since rice had been imported from Cuttack,

67. John Edgar C.S.I. to the Secretary to the Government of Bengal Revenue Department, No. 2744, Calcutta, 19 August 1889.
68. Scarcity in the Government estate of Angul, Revenue Department Famine, Darjelling, 21 September 1889.
69. *U.D.*, 25 May 1889.
70. *Ibid.*, 1 June 1889.
71. John Edgar to the Secretary to the Government of Bengal, Revenue Department No. 2744, Calcutta, 19 August 1889.

prices have gone down and rice was sold at 11 seers a rupee instead of 10 seers. In lieu of relief works a sum of Rs. 290-2-0 was spent on the road works. Two *annachhatras* were opened, one at headquarters and the other at Itamati for distribution of cooked rice among weak and infirm persons. Four additional *annachhatras* were also opened at Mahipur, Sunamuhin, Sarankul and Godipara. The average attendance in *annachhatra* held at headquarters was 600 and about 200 in other centres of relief.

The distress among the people of Ranpur had been reduced due to the advances of paddy made from the state granaries and by private holders of stocks. The number of the distressed people fed at the *annachhatra* was 252 and the cost of feeding them during the fortnight was Rs. 115-3-3, of which Rs. 95-3-3 was paid from a fund locally raised for relief. The total expenditure incurred by the state on account of relief during the fortnight was Rs.618-7-3 and the total expenditure since the commencement of operations to the end of July amounted to Rs. 5,697-6-2, as shown below:[72]

TABLE 6.3
TOTAL AMOUNT BORNE BY THE GOVERNMENT ON ACCOUNT OF RELIEF

	Rs.	*A.P.*
Expenditure incurred from State Funds	2,736	-14-0
Expenditure incurred out of Government loan of Rs. 5,000	2,960	-8-2
Total	5,697-	6-2

Hindol was also attacked by starvation and drought due to scanty rainfall.[73] The Raja of Hindol in order to help his subjects through employment, ordered for digging of 4 wells, 2 small tanks and 3 big tanks. He also laid down the construction of a big canal embankment. He also provided paddy and crops seed to the cultivators and granted them remission of revenue.[74] The superintendent also deputed Patten, the Superintendent of Police to inspect the distress tracks of Hindol.[75]

Athamallick was most sparsely populated among the Tributary States. She also suffered as severely as those of any other state by the failure of

72. John Edgar to the Secretary to the Government of Bengal, Revenue Department, No. 2744, Calcutta, 19 August 1889.
73. *U.D.*, 1 June 1889.
74. *Ibid.*, 20 July 1889.
75. John Edgar, *op.cit.*, No. 2744, Calcutta, 19 August 1889.

crops in recent years. The Raja was a benevolent personnel who had devoted fully to the work of relieving distress during the past two years. The scarcity had been felt less in this state than in any other of those affected.

The assistant Superintendent after inspecting Athamallick told that since April last cholera had appeared which carried away 83 persons. Death due to starvation was 20, of whom six were the residents of the Killa, and the rest were immigrants from other states.

"The Raja informed me that on the first appearance of distress the village headmen were directed to send to him at the state expense all starving persons they found within their respective villages. This, however they failed to do regularly and during his tour he found in one village that two children had died from starvation, On further enquiry a few more deaths from starvation appeared to have occurred in some other villages. The defaulting sarbarakars were punished, and since June 1st every sarbarakar had been bound down under recogniance to send down such persons without fail. Twenty destitute persons were now kept in a poor house at the headquarters, but there were besides, other beggars in the interior who were supported by private charity and did not therefore, wish to come to the poor house".

The state had suffered from two successive bad seasons, by which the partial failure of the last harvest alone would have caused much anxiety. Before the commencement of the calendar year relief was given to the following extent:

	Rs.
Grain advances	3,824
Cash advances	742
Gratuitous relief	290
Relief Works	471
Advance for cutting timbers	700
Total	6,027

Since the beginning of January relief had up to date been given to the following extent:

	Rs
Grain advances	6,752
Cash advances	4,723
Gratuitous relief	2,240
Relief Works	3,895
Advance to weavers	267
Total	17,877

In the last year Rs. 5,000 worth of rice was purchased and kept in store and in the present year further purchases were made for Rs. 3,167. From this stock rice was soled at market rates and those who had no present means to pay in lieu of credit Rs. 989 worth of rice was given to them. The timely advances made by the Raja helped a lot to the people but in time of calamity, it was the landless classes, the daily labourers, weavers and other handicraftsmen who suffered most.[76]

In the year 1889, Angul was affected by the severe famine, which occurred due to the accumulated effects of the starvations which had happened previous to the famine year. (The starvations has been previously discussed in this chapter). The enquiry made by Kalipada Mukherjee, P.A. to Commissioner revealed that death due to starvation was 147 and due to cholera etc. 1910.[77]

The whole estate was said to have suffered from a partial failure of crops for some years and some tracts were more distressed than others. The average price for the principal food-grains was estimated as follows:

TABLE 6.4
AVERAGE PRICE OF PRINCIPAL FOOD-GRAINS

Kinds of rice	*Price (in annas) per year*	
	1887-88	*1888-89*
Biali	2	6
Sarada	6	6

The mahua, mango and palm crops also totally failed in Angul. The high prices of grain in the estate and in the adjoining states had contributed more to the distress, caused by the loss of crops.[78] A sum of Rs. 12,000/- was placed by the Government of Bengal at the disposal of the Commissioner of the division for advances to the cultivators. Out of that only Rs. 3,000/- had been disbursed. The monthly reports from the native Superintendent of Angul territory at length indicated such serious distress that in July Sir John Edgar, the Chief Secretary to the Government of Bengal was deputed to Orissa. He found the situation more critical than had been realised by the local authorities.

Relief centres gave employment to only 493 persons and gratuitous relief to 1998 persons, and both the amount of wage on the wroks and

76. John Edgar to the Secretary to the Government of Bengal, Revenue Department, No. 2744, Calcutta, 19 August 1889.
77. Scarcity in the Government estate of Angul, Revenue Department Famine, Darjeeling, 21 September 1889.
78. Scarcity in Angul, Revenue Department, Famine, Calcutta, 16 August 1889.

the ration given on gratuitous relief were unquestionably insufficient. Measures were at once taken to make relief effective. The estate was divided into 3 circles, each under the charge of a European Officer and assisted by a medical subordinate. Their duties were to visit each village to superintendent the distribution of gratuitous relief to those who could not work, to give light work such as basket wroking and husking rice, to those capable of light work, to distribute seed and subsistence advances to cultivators, and to other for spinning and weaving and to provide for the able bodied such work on roads and embankments near their villages as it was found practicable to carry out in the rainy season. The cost of these measures was estimated at Rs. 41,000/- and to prevent any risk of food supplies in the territory running shot, Rs. 15,000/- was also spent on purchasing forwarding unhusked rice from Cuttack. With these measures and favourable rains the distress was brought under control.[79]

The hopes of the people were revived, the landless classes obtained agricultural loans, the able bodied labourers found work and helpless of both sexes received gratuitous relief etc. To save the people Government granted the following sums for their relief.

TABLE 6.5
ADVANCE SANCTIONED BY THE LT. GOVERNOR FOR THE RELIEF IN FAMINE OF 1889

Items	*Amount in Rs.*
For works	7,000
For loans	12,000
For gratuitous relief	16,000
For medical relief, miscellaneous and rice	4,895

Sources: "Scarcity in Angul", Revenue Department-Finance Resolution of Government of Bengal 16 August 1889 (Calcutta, 1889).

The relief works, loans, gratuitous relief and advances granted to the peasants, helped in averting a serious famine.

In the Khondmals, the distress was less severe than in the Angul subdivison. The failure of crops in the Khondmals was as great as in other parts of Orissa. There was the want of rain in the early part of 1888, and there was also failure of the mango and mohul crops.[80] The supply of the jungle products upon which the mass of the people had mainly to depend also began to fail and it was apprehended that, if the rains did not soon break, there would be serious famine. Fortunately, however, before the end of May there was some rain, which though

79. *IFC*, 1898, p. 14.
80. John Edgar, *op.cit.*, No. 2744, Calcutta, 19 August 1889.

small and insufficient for agricultural purposes, revived the jungle plants and trees. In June there was a rainfall which averaged 5 inches allover the Khondmals and the pressure was relieved. In spite of this, it was found necessary to start relief works, such as the building of rest houses and dharmasalas and cutting of jungles. There was however, less pressure than in the Angul subdivision and the condition of the people was much better. The state of things was attributed to the fact that the forests in the Khondmals were not reserved or protected and the people were able to fail back on the supplies of grain, edible roots, wild fruits and other products of the jungle which contributed largely to the means of subsistance of aboriginal tribes. The greatest famine within the memory of the present inhabitants since the great Orissa famine of 1866, was partly due to the short harvest of 1887 and 1888, partly to the failure of the mango and mahua crops in 1889 and partly to the effects of a long drought which prevailed from October 1888 to the end of May 1889, on account of which all grain was tightly hoarded for some months and the labourers were deprived of employment.[81]

The suggestions made by Sir John Edgar for the amelioration of the aboriginal tribes of Orissa and the protection of the people from the results of scarcity was the early construction of the proposed railway from Panchpara to Puri. It was a measure of security against the consequences of failure of crops by which the contact between Orissa and the outer world could be made. The second remedial measure suggested by John Edgar was the reorganization of forest administration because vast numbers of landless paupers were dependant upon the forest products for their very subsistence.[82]

Ganjam Famine 1888-89

Failure of administration and absence of immediate relief measures gave rise to a serious famine in Ganjam in Madras Presidency in 1888-89.* From the administrative report it was found the season on 1884-85 was described as a bad one for rice lands and the prices of the principal food grains rose during the latter half of the year. The year 1885-86 was described as worse than its predecessor as regards the wet crops and the prices of all food grains, except wheat, were stated to have gone up, in consequence. The Chilka canal works were opened in that year to furnish work to the people living in the tract of country to the north of the Rushikulya river, because they were in a distressed condition owing to

81. L.S.S. O'Malley, *BDG, Angul*, p. 102.
82. Scarcity in the Government Estate of Angul, Revenue Department, Famine, Darjeeling, 21 September 1889.

* Ganjam is now a district in Orissa.

the failure of their crops.[83] A comparison of rainfall of the last four years with that of the 1888-89, up to the end of October, shows (Table 6.6) that in that year the rains had been fairly scantier than any of the others.

The prices of rice and ragi, the grains consumed mostly in the district, were far higher during the month of October 1888. The price-rise was evident due to the failure of north-east monsoon.[84]

TABLE 6.6
MONTHLY RAINFALL IN ORISSA FROM 1884-85 TO 1888-89

Month	*1884-85*	*1885-86*	*1886-87*	*1887-88*	*1888-89*	*Remarks*
April	0.8	0.7	0.12	0.50	0.24	The figures here given are taken from the Collector's office. They differ slightly from those compiled in the office of the Board of Revenue.
May	1.3	2.7	3.38	1.81	0.37	
June	5.2	2.5	4.64	5.98	2.37	
July	6.2	6.7	8.47	8.19	3.28	
August	5.2	6.2	10.15	9.45	7.42	
September	11.8	4.4	11.12	5.19	4.47	
October	4.9	4.9	15.71	7.12	1.95	
	36.1	28.1	53.59	38.24	20.10	
November	0.07	7.2	5.88	1.87	-	
December	0.3	3.3	4.52		-	
January	0.4	0.1	0.44	0.29	-	
February	1.8	-	-	0.67	-	
March	0.8	1.7	0.89	0.11	-	
Total	39.47	40.4	64.92	41.18	20.10	

Month	*First week ending October 6th*		*Second week ending October 13th*		*Third week ending October 20th*		*Fourth week ending October 27th*	
	Rice seers per rupee	*Rice seers per rupee*	*Rice seers per rupee*	*Rice seers per rupee*	*Rice seers per rupee*	*Rice seers per rupee*	*Rice seers per rupee*	*Rice seers per rupee*
October	12.20	23.84	10.29	20.23	9.97	21.58	10.12	21.62

83. Madras Presidency loose records Revenue, 1888 G.O., 12 December 1888, No. 860, State of Ganjam District, p. 2.
84. Madras Presidency loose records, *op.cit.*, p. 3.

There was no rainfall in 1888 between 1st October and 31st December and only one cyclonic storm occurred which gave 7.7 inches of rain between the 29th October to the 9th November. The crops which consisted chiefly of unirrigated rice and ragi had failed seriously by the 15th October over large areas. Water and pasturage became very scarce, grain-dealers in panic, refused to sell grain; prices rose rapidly and grain riots and robberies occurred. Madras Government deputed Gartsin, Member of the Board of Revenue to proceed to Ganjam at once and report on the condition of affairs. He arrived in the district on the 4th November 1888. He considered it beyond doubt that the high prices of food grains would affect the prospects of the people especially thc poorer classes and the weavers. He recommended for the opening of large works to be carrried out as ordinary public works by professional agency. And under the powers vested in him by Government at once opened the Rushikulya canal project on the ordinary price work system through contractors. He recommended advances to the weavers and in reteard to gratuitous relief to the helpless and those unable to work.[85] The Rushikulay project was important as a famine-relief work. The scheme had two objects the diversion of the water of two rivers – the Mahanadi and the Rushikulay into a canal which was to be navigable, and also to supply water for irrigating about 120,000 acres of land in the Ghumsur and Berhampur taluks. It involved the construction of two large reservoirs, four anicuts and seventythree miles of canal, besides a large number of subsidiary works, such as bridges, under tunnels and irrigation sluices etc.[86]

The Revenue Board mentioned scarcity rates for Ganjam as per the following:

TABLE 6.7
GANJAM SCARCITY RATES

		Seers per rupee
Rice	..	11.2
Cholam	..	14.7
Ragi	..	16.6
Cumbu	..	15.4

It was found that five people had died of starvation that year in the village of Koratoli about four miles from Chatrapur.

The inhabitants of the village also prayed for relief works, gratuitous

85. *IFC*, 1898, p. 15.
86. Madras presidency loose records 1888, *op.cit.*, p. 8.

relief and grants of money and food.[87] The statistics of Garstin noted that the current season in Ganjam had proved exceptionally unfavourable owing to the failure of the south-west monson. There was a very large decrease in breadth of cultivation and exports of grain suddenly ceased. He also recommended the Ganjam Gopalpur canal be put in hand at once as an ordinary P.W.D. work. It would give employment to about 4,000 coolies for five months and an allotment of Rs. 60,000 would, in Garstin's opinion, suffice for this work. The Governor in Council also approved the immediate execution of this project.[88] The summary of the seasons reports for the week ending 30 March 1889 noted that due to the absent of rainfall the dry crops injured severely in Ganjam. Among the cereal prices as compared with the previous week, rice was higher. Number of coolies employed on the last day of the week on the Rushikulya work was 11,097, on Gopalpur canal 8,149 and on Taptapani ghat road 338. Their number for the week on Rushikulya work was 70,316, on Gopalpur canal 56.781 and Taptapani ghat road 2,157. Total number of gratuitous relief week ending on 23rd March was 2,868.[89]

It was found from the weekly report of the 6th April 1889, that the paddy crops had suffered to an enormous extent, especially in Ghumsur taluk owing to the failure of rains, the average out turn being only between 3 and 4 annas. There was total loss in some villages. The ryots demanded for loans under the Agricultural Loans Act, to purchase seed grain for the ensuing cultivation season. The villagers were in a great distress owing to the failure of crops and the consequent high prices of food-grains, the scarcity of water, the prevalence of epidemic and the occurrence of accidental fires, frequently resulting in loss of considerable property. The labouring classes, those able to work, resorted to reservoir works to earn their livelihood, but the wages earned by each man were not sufficient to maintain the whole of his family. The agricultural classes were mostly in a distressed condition because many of them were denied to resort to reservoir works owing to caste prejudices. Many of them borrowed money form *sahukars* on interest. They paid the loans by selling rice bringing from Sambalpur, Puri, Rambha and other places by carts and kept the rest for their consumption.

Minor irrigation works, at an aggregate amount of Rs. 10,512 had been executed in 88 villages in Ghumsur taluk and sanctions also had been received to repair drinking water tanks and to sink wells in some villages in Ghumsur taluk. The number of deaths from cholera during

---

87. Madras Presidency loose records, 1888, *op.cit.*, p. 17.
88. *Ibid.*, p. 20.
89. Fort St. George Gazette, Supplement From January to June 1889 (April 9, 1889).

the week was 51 and the number reported since January last was 299, *viz.*, 249 in Ghumsur taluk and 50 in Aska.

Persons who were actually suffering from starvation were paid batta under the famine code up to the sanctioned scale. The number of persons who were receiving such help was 170 in Ghumsur and 139 in Aska. It was difficult to find out the correct stocks of food grains in this division,[90] for the week ending on 13th April shows that there were large falling of number of labourers both in Rushikulya and Gopalpur canal works owing to an outbreak of cholera. Carr (Additional Special Assistant Collector, Ganjam) reported about the death of a person from starvation from a village in Dharakot estate.[91] The Government sent two additional medical subordinates to Ganjam.[92]

Towards the end of April 1889, the average rainfall was 11 inches. Among the cereal prices, as compared with the previous week, rice was lower and rest were higher. Cholera was prevalent which took 1,070 souls. Number of coolies employed on the last day of the week on the Rishikulya works was 6,991, on Gopalpur canal 4,862, and on Taptapani ghat road 536.[93]

Towards the end of May, the average rainfall was 0.70 inches. Scarcity of water was still prevalent. Prices in the last week of the month, as compared with the previous week, was higher and second sort rice was selling at scarcity rates. The number of coolies employed on the last day of the week on Rushikulya works was 5,731, on Gopalpur canal 5,180, on Taptapani and four other ghat roads 1,461. The number of distressed relieved on last day of the week ending 18 May was 2,728.[94]

Great distress was reported from all quarters of the district, except Balluguda. Due to prevalence of cholera, coolies were afraid to remain on works and stayed in their villages without any means of subsistence. In Purushottampur and Berhampur they were becoming emaciated. In Ghumsur and Surada they were unwilling to accept the famine rates of hire and rather "preferred to die of starvation".

The mortality from cholera during the end of fortnight had reached of 2,500. It had spread everywhere but the Berhampur taluk suffered the most. Gratuitous relief was taken on a larger scale.[95]

---

90. Letter from J.G. Horsfall, Collector of Ganjam to the Secretary to Government, Revenue Department Chatrapur, April 1889, No. 2389 Enclosure No. 3.
91. Resolution by Board of Revenue, 18 April 1889, No. 191.
92. Miscellaneous, 26 April 1889, No. 317, Revenue.
93. Fort St. George Gazette, *op.cit.*, May 7, 1889.
94. Fort St. George Gazette, *op.cit.*, June 4, 1889.
95. Proceeding of the Board of Revenue (Revenue Settlement Land Records and Agriculture), 25 May 1889, Mis. No. 2062.

The Government was of the opinion that it was not desirable to grant advances for the purchase of seed-grain without security.

The Collector also authorised not to exceed Rs. 10,000 in the purchase of seed-grain for gratuitous distribution in case of undoubted need and further allotment of Rs. 5,000 was also sanctioned for the improvement of the water supply. In accordance with the provisions of the Famine Code the Collector was authorised to commence the road from Digapudi to Govindapur as a relief work and the payment was made early.[96]

The Lt. Governor of Madras visited Ganjam and immediate order was given to start relief to save lives.[97] But the Lt. Governor of Bengal never visited famine stricken tracts of Orissa during the famine of 1866 or later. Numerous kitchens were at once opened for the distribution of cooked food and orders were passed for the formation of relief circles, appointment of circle relief officers and the distribution of doles and grain or money in the villages to the aged, the poor, the sick and the destitute. Seed grain for the cultivators was also imported from the Godavari district. The Madras Government put the Collector instead of the Revenue Board, in direct communication with itself in regard to management of famine. The careful inspection of the villages and opening of the kitchens revealed the existence of severe and wide spread distess. Numerous gratuitous relief to the villagers who were incapable for labour increased rapidly. The numbers on village relief increased form month to month.[98]

The month of August marked the highest point in relief. Messrs. McMurray, Story, Marshall, Sherman, Powell and Brown had joined the district as famine officers and were posted respectively at Purushottampur, Ballipadar, Ichapur, Ganjam, Russelkonda and Berhampur to exercise strict control.[99] The total imports during the week amounted to 16,446 cwts, or 823 tons, of which 7,353 cwtc were by sea, 4,845 from Orissa and 4,268 cwts from the central provinces.[100] With a good harvest on the ground the numbers in gratuitous relief were reduced to 28,000 by the end of September. Relief was discontinued at the end of October and at some places by the end of November.[101]

The expenditure on the famine account amounted to Rs. 3,64,000 on professional works, Rs.2,45,000 on civil agency works and Rs. 3,50,000

---

96. Government of Madras, Revenue Department, Miscellanous, 28 May 1889, No. 431.
97. *IFC*, 1898, Ch. II, Pr. 27, p. 16.
98. *IFC*, Pr. 29, p. 17.
99. Government of Madras, Revenue Department, 17 August 1889, Nos. 711, 711A.
100. *Ibid.*
101. *IFC*, 1898, pr. 29, p. 17.

on gratuitous relief. Rs. 1,70,000 was advanced to weavers and for seed-grain Rs. 2,68,000 was suspended. This heavy expenditure could have been cut short if relief had been moved freely given in the first stage of distress.[102]

Deaths from direct starvation were nearly recorded during famine, but they were usually attributed to the secondary causes of diarrhoea, dysentery, dropsy, anaemia or debility.[103] The average number of recorded deaths per annum in the Ganjam district for the ten years at the end of 30th September 1888 was 19,000 from all causes, and 18,400 excluding cholera. From the 1st October 1888 to the 30th September 1889, the recorded number of deaths was 38,463 from all causes, and 24,422 excluding cholera.[104]

The Collector also mentioned in his weekly report about private charity. The zamindar of Chikiti estate was feeding over 500 people daily with food. Food as also distributed in Parlakhemedi by the zamindars though the number was not exactly known.

As regards the position of the affected area, as to local trade, food-supply and communications, the Government of India was aware that the district was totally destitute of railway communication and was dependent for its supplies in times of scarcity on imports by road and by sea. These means of access during the monsoons, was impracticable. The district was liable, therefore, to be cut off for a time from all external supplies when a failure of the crop occurred simultaneously in the neighbouring districts and provinces.[105]

The Government of Madras Presidency had learnt something from the Ganjam famine of 1888-89 and considered some principles of famine procedure. It also considered the code scarcity rates for all districts. It also considered the code scarcity rates for all districts. It was recognised that the rise of prices to a particular rate should not be taken as criterion for granting relief. "In Ganjam, wages and prices were ordinarily lower than in any other district of the presidency, and any rise in the price of food grains was felt more quickly and acutely by the low paid labourer there then by the better paid one elsewhere".

The Madras Government considered the difficulty of caste scruples relating to the distribution of cooked relief food among people would be removed, when Brahmins remained in charge of preparing food in kitchen,

102. *Ibid.*, Pr. 30.
103. Government of Madras, Revenue Department, 31 October 1889, Nos.888, 888A.
104. *IFC*, 1898, Pr. 31, p. 17.
105. From C.A. Galton, Secretary to the Government of Fort St. George to the Secretary to the Government of India, Revenue and Agriculture Department, Ootacamund, 12 June 1889, No. 486 Rev.

to which none other than the Brahmins had the access. Some discretion must had been given to officers in special cases to substitute grain doles for cooked food.[106]

Some important lessons which were recorded by the Government of India in its Famine Commission report of 1898[107] were realised in the following manner:

(*a*) Precautionary arrangements to be premanently maintained in ordinary times and timely information to the Government by which the approach of famine or scarcity may be detected and to provide for a state of preparedness in respect to measures of relief.

(*b*) When the information received indicates the imminence of famine or scarcity and immediate action to be taken.

The great scarcity occurred in Ganjam due to the negligence of the authority. The Government had not dug any new tanks during the last thirty years, with merely repairing existing tanks, deepening them and cleaning them.[108] After the famine of 1877 and 1878, those Oriyas who had taken relief were put out of caste. They were called in true sense of the term "Chatrokyas".[109]

Famine of 1896-97

In spite of remedial measures adopted by the Government and readiness to meet any famine, there occurred an all India famine in 1896-97 in which, it was reported that, 60 millions of people suffered and about 4 millions died. Heavy flood in 1896 and complete failure of monsoon in October 1896 caused crop failure everywhere. Puri, Balasore and Tributary states of Orissa suffered more from this calamity and Cuttack was less affected. Still affected area in this district was $^{1}/_{3}$rd with a population of 6,24,840.[110] Sudden calamity occurred relating to export of rice and crop failures due to drought and laisses fair attitude of Government. Due to protection afforded by irrigation works etc., mortality was not very high in Orissa like other parts of India. A huge amount was spent on relief

106. *IFC*, 1898, Pr. 32, p. 18.
107. *Ibid.*, Ch.III, Pr. 76, p. 45.
108. *IFC*, 1898, Appendix, Vol.II, p. 119.
109. *Ibid.*, p. 96.
110. P.N. Chopra, B.N. Puri, M.N. Das, *Social Cultural and Economic*, History of India, Vol.III (Delhi, 1974), pp. 190-195.
R.N. Rath (ed.), "Cuttack Natural Calamities, Famine of 1865-66", *The Samaj*, 7 October 1982.
C. Ramsay, *Feudatory States of Orissa*, (Calcutta, 1910), p. 78.

measures throughout India, still the mortality reached the highest in the history of famines.[111]

Since 1866 no famine occurred in the district of Cuttack due to the protection afforded by the Government through irrigation work. But there was some scarcity in 1897 in consequence of unprecedented high flood followed by short rain in September and an almost complete failure of the monsoon in October 1896. All the great rivers overflowed their banks simultaneously and thereby, breached embankments. The submerged the low lands, which remained water logged for more than a month owing to the long duration of the rise in the rivers, and not only was the crop ruined, but also much land was thrown out of cultivation by the deposit of sand. On the subsidence of the flood the cultivators replanted as soon as possible, but the next sowings were sacrificed to drought as the old ones had been to flood. The drought was also of long duration, the rains ceased at the end of September, in some places the winter rice crop which was the main agricultural product of the district failed entirely and in others the harvest was very poor.

The affected area was 1,360 square miles or more than one-third of the district with a population of 6,24,840 souls but distress existed more or less throughout the whole district. Relief was given in all the subdivisions from the middle of March to the end of September 1897, from the Indian Charitable Relief Fund and from the Court of wards fund in Kanika and Kujang. It was given gratuitously in the shape of grain and money doles except in the Kuhunda-Jajpur Circle, where arrangments were made to take from the able bodied recipients of relief such light work as paddy husking, rope making, cotton spinning and cotton weaving. Though there was considerable local distress, very little relief was found necessary and the total distress needed little relief and the expenditure amounted to only Rs. 18,718.[112]

An area of 231 square miles lying along the Chilka lake was flooded in July and August 1896 and was subsequently exposed to drought which ultimately converted into a famine in 1897. The chief cause was the shortness and unseasonal distribution of the rains of 1896. The rainfall was deficient during the month of July and August when the sowing and transplanting of rice were in progress and from the 19th September, rain ceased altogether till the close of the year, thus depriving the young crops at the critical time of the moisture necessary to bring them to maturity.[113]

---

111. P.N. Chopra, *op.cit.*, pp. 190-195.
112. L.S.S.O' Malley, *Bihar and Orissa District Gazetteer*, (Patna, 1933), pp. 125-126.
113. Report in the Administration of the Indian Famine Charitable Relief Fund in Bengal 1898, p. 5.

According to the official statistics and the opinions of all persons of experience, native and European official and non-official the out-turn of flood grains was worse than the previous year.[114]

The total area affected in the district of Puri* was 274 square miles with a population of 89,000. The general condition of the distressed tracts remained unchanged.[115]

The above table shows the number of the Government relief works undertaken whether by civil agency or under the supervision of the public works department in the affected areas.[116]

It was noted in a letter from the Collector or Puri to the Commissioner of the Orissa division dated 26th May 1897, that through the distressed tracts on the Chilka, the district board opened a large road work and an equally large embankment work was opened as a famine relief measure for the first time. These gave employment to a large number of men who were so much in need of it in these tracts.[117] The following table shows the proportions of men, women and children to the total number gratuitously relieved.[118]

TABLE 6.8
PERCENTAGE OF PEOPLE GRATUITOUSLY RELIEVED IN PURI DISTRICT

Analysis of the descriptions of persons gratuitous relieved	*Men*	*Women*	*Children*
Orissa Division, Puri	15.4	25.8	58.7

The district of Puri ordinarily exported largely and imported practically

114. Minute by his honour the Lt. Governor on the Services of Government officers and private gentlemen in connection with the Famine of 1897 and 1898 and final resolution of the Governments of Bengal upon the Famine 1898, p.51.

*

	Square miles	Population
Puri Sadar Subdivision	231	74,000
Khurda Subdivision	43	15,000
Total	274	89,000

115. M.Finucane, Secretary to the Government of Bengal to the Secretary to the Government of India, Revenue and Agriculture Department, Agri. No. 1449 (Fam), Calcutta, 22 July 1897.
116. Minute by his Honour the Lt. Governor on the Service of Government officers and private gentlemen in connection with the Famine of 1897 and 1898 and final resolution of the Government of Bengal upon the famine 1898, p. 51.
117. Selection of papers relating to the famine of 1896-97 in Bengal, Vol.XI, p. 529.
118. Minute by his Honour the Lt. Governor, *op.cit.*

nothing in the way of food grains but the export by sea and rail during the famine period amounted to 1,08,000 maunds only as against 361.642 maunds during 1895-96. In out-of-the-way parts of the distressed area round the Chilka lake, it was found necessary to stimulate the import of grain, and Rs. 3,100 was advanced on loans to traders for the purpose. At Satpara also Rs. 860 was spent in importing grain at Government expenses for sale at cost price.[119]

The death rate for the affected area in Puri was 0.25 against 2.36, the death rate for the whole district.[120]

There was some distress in 1897 due to the partial failure of crops in the Angul subdivision. In 1896 the rainfall was favourable until the middle of September but after that it ceased till November. The injury done to the winter rice crop by this sudden cessation of rain at the time when it was most needed, was aggravated by the visitation of an insect pest locally known as Mohua. The out-turn of this crop was thus not more than 8 to 12 annas in the average. The distress caused by the partial failure of the rice crop was, however, not great and it was found sufficient to open a few relief works and to advance Rs. 20,000 in loans.[121]

In 1897 when other parts of the country suffered from one of the worst famines of the 19th century, Sambalpur was scarcely affected. The out-turn of the rice crop was fair, being 70 per cent of an average crop and good prices obtained from it. Famine was declared only in a small area of 228 square miles with a population of 62,000 comprising the Chandarpur and Kalkharoda zamindaries which were later transferred to then central provinces. In this area famine relief measures had to be undertaken and in Barasambar, where there had been a partial failure of crops owing to the premature cessation of the monsoon, some relief work on roads was started by the estates. Elsewhere it was found sufficient to provide some work on tanks with the help of loans and private subscription. The report of Chaddocks notes that "In Sambalpur with a very fair rice crop, large exports and high prices, money poured into the district and private charity amply sufficient to support to poor whom the high prices affected. A single road work was opened in April and continued till October but this was chiefly intended to meet the needs of a corner of the district where the local crops had been poor and

119. Minute by his Honour the Lt. Governor, *op.cit.*, p. 65.
120. M. Finucane, Secretary to the Government of Bengal to the Commissioner of the Orissa Division, Revenue Department, Agri. No. 661, T.R. Darjeeling, 23 June 1897.
121. L.S.S. O' Malley, *BDG, Angul*, pp. 101-102.

immigrants from Bilaspur were numerous. The numbers on this work only reached 2,200 and rapidly fell as the rains advanced".[122]

This famine gave rise to the appointment of 1898 commission. The commission recommended the programme of irrigation works as a means to avert famines in India.[123] This created avenues for the irrigation commission of 1901-3 to devise ways and means to avert famines.

Famine of 1899-1900

Another famine still terrible in its appearance occurred 1899-1900. To Lord Curzon this was the severest of all throughout the 19th century. But Orissa suffered less in comparison to other parts of India. Scarcity of food grains and high prices of food were the immediate causes of this famine. A commission was appointed for this which submitted its report in 1901.[124]

In 1899 scarcity prevailed in Khurda and its surrounding areas. Relief operation started in those areas under the organised efforts of four appointed relief officials. Road works started in the areas of Khandagiri, Kaipadar, Kuradinall, Tulasipur and Banapur in order to provide employment to the people of those areas.[125]

In 1899 starvation was felt in Parikud tract near the Chilka lake in the district of Puri. Some people became beggars and some left for Assam to work there. Raja Bahadur in order to help the people provided employment to them since October 1899. Also the Raja caused for the supply of little amount of rice to the poor but gentle families. He reported the matter to the Government authorities who provided relief after making an enquiry of the tract.[126]

After 1897, the people of Angul had felt a series of bad years owing to short crops which exhausted their resources and culminated in general scarcity in 1900-01. This was most felt in the Khondmals, specially by those who depended for their sustenance on Jungle produce, such as yams and edible bulbs, the supply of which grew scanty in July. Famine conditions prevailed, loans were given to cultivators, relief works had to be opened and gratuitous relief was given to the old and infirm and to those who were physically unfit to do any work. In the following year their condition generally improved, but in the next year there was a slight falling off. In the third year all signs of distress appeared and there was a marked improvement in their condition. They had mostly paid off

122. *Ibid., Sambalpur, Patna*, 1932, pp. 143-144.
123. Famine Commission 1898. Quoted in R.C. Dutt, *op.cit.*, pp. 197-199.
124. B.M. Bhatia, *op.cit.*, p. 238.
125. *U.D.*, 18 November 1899.
126. *U.D.*, 18 November, 1899.

their debts, their condition and standard of living had improved and the higher classes of agriculturists now spent larger sums on sumuries, special ceremonies and wearing apparel.[127]

As described above famines occurred in different parts of India during the time of Lord Lytton. Since then Rs. 15 lakhs was kept for relief and prevention of famines. Lord Curzon appointed a commission under the chairmanship of Sir Anthony Macdonals to find out ways and means to deal with famines in India. The "Famine Code" of Lord Lytton's time was amended to make it more workable and helpful at different times.[128]

Provision for prompt famine relief, when it occurred and measures to prevent famines were given paramount importance, because it was thought to be difficult to face a famine (due to its huge expenditure and mortality) than to prevent it by timely action.[129]

But Orissa never gained anything from the provisions of 'Famine Code'. The code made a distinction between Famine and Scarcity. When there had been a crop failure compelling people to live upon wild shrubs, it was declared by the Government as scarcity and not famine. In case of a famine elaborate relief operations had to be undertaken. In 1920 Pt. Gopabandhu Das agitated that the Government should declare famine in Puri and grant relief according to 'Famine Code' when people were starving in large numbers. All his labours remained fruitless because the Government never declared it to be a famine.[130] In 1943 when hundreds of people were dying on the streets of Ganjam and Balasore and thousands in Bengal, the Famine Code was not brought into operation.[131]

However the recommendation of the Famine Commission of 1898 and 1901 and Irrigation Commission of 1903 brought amendment of the Famine Code of 1883 and paved the way for progressive irrigation policy. The famine policy and prevention of famines underwent changes after 1903. Agrarian reforms and improving the condition of the people were given importance with the march of events and time. The post famine measures laid a strong foundation for the future economic growth of Orissa from 1866 to 1897. The period was comparatively one of rising economic activities without severe famines. Still conditions of people were no better in 1900 as compared to 1869, because more scarcities occurred after 1866 and starvation and poverty were general.[132] The free trade

---

127. L.S.S. O' Malley, *BDG*, *Angul*, p. 102.
128. H.K. Mahtab, *op.cit.*, pp. 445-446.
129. Quoted in letter from India to Bengal No. AIII-F/9-13, 31 October 1884, Pr. 5.
130. H.K. Mahtab, *op.cit.*, p.447. M.K. Gandhi, *Young India*, 12 May 1920.
131. H.K. Mahtab, *Gandhiji and Orissa*, (Oriya), pp. 251-253.
132. B.M. Bhatia, *op.cit.*, pp. 271-308, R.C. Dutt, *op.cit.*, pp. 445-51.

policy up to the end of 1900 was the cause of starvation in Orissa. Since the famine of 1866 Orissa got a better attention and the Government thought not to neglect the people. The apathy of the Government ceased and recommendations of the commissions were considered seriously for implementation in practice. The recurring famines brought a general awakening in Orissa.[133] The policy of passive observation was replaced by a policy of active initiative and participation. Forest however is right when he says,

> "Famines however will not again be able to claim its victims owing to a blind following of laissez-faire school".[134]

The severity of famines in a laissez-faire situation was the outcome of mass poverty in Orissa, because it is proved that every scarcity or famines left the affected population much poorer than before when survival is in question. People were compelled to sell their possessions. They tried to get back things again in normal years. As a matter of fact they spent more to procure for what they sold in a distress period.[135] Thus they gradually became poorer. The inaction of the Government too worked to the detriment of the standard of living of the people and they were rather pushed to poverty and indebtedness. This apart, as the people very often had no reserve for scarcity period and got no employment, the purchasing power came down and they faced difficulty while purchasing their basic commodities.[136]

Again unrestricted export of rice was the cause of famines, scarcity and poverty in Orissa. The cumulative impact of a number of scarcities and famines in Orissa impoverished people more and more.[137] High prices of food made it more difficult to purchase and death was inevitable unless the Government devoted adequate resources to save lives. Adhoc measures were taken to relieve distress and a better food policy was not adopted throughout the 19th century.[138] Thus more deaths due to starvation were seen. The Government also adopted a lenient policy on production and distribution of grains.[139] According to Shlomo Reutlinger,

---

133. B.Mohanty (ed.), *Atharasa Chhasathi* (1866), *U.D.* (Oriya), Preface, p. 10; *IFC* report, 1880, p. 1.
134. George Forest, *The Famine in India*, (London, 1900), p. 16.
135. *EPW.IX*, Bombay, 1974, p. 1861, also see *EPW*, Vol. X, Bombay, 1975, pp. 1609-23.
136. Drought in Orissa during 1954-55 (Final Report), Government of Orissa, Revenue (Special Relief) Department, Bhubaneswar, pp. 7-8.
137. Bipin Chandra, *Rise and Growth of Economic Nationalism in India*, New Delhi, 1969, p. 163.
138. Debidas Roy, *op.cit.*, p. VI.
139. B.M. Bhatia, *op.cit.*, p. 25.

a senior world bank expert, "People suffer from food security mainly caused by lack of purchasing power".[140]

All these man-made factors as discussed above gathered together and caused havoc in Orissa during the period under study. The ultimate solution to famine in Orissa *i.e.*, economic development through increase in agricultural production, improvement of transport, communication, irrigation etc., were neglected in comparison to the neighbouring states. The people of Orissa died in large numbers whenever the Government neglected or failed to take proper preventive efforts. The frequent famines in Orissa became the stumbling block to the economic prosperity of the people of Orissa.

140. *The Statesman*, 29 December 1985.

7

British Policy Towards Famines and Scarcities

Under the native rule frequent occurrence of famine was an evil which was unmanageable. As the Government during that period lacked the resources and administrative efficiency, it could not face the terrible consequences of the famines. After the advant of the British, initially there too continued the old system, as far as famine was concerned. There was no well-defined policy regarding the administration of famine relief in the first half of the 19th century. So Orissa suffered a lot from frequent occurrence of natural calamities. Only on the adhoc basis relief measures had been taken. The matter still worsened because the remissions of revenue were hardly given.[1] After all, "no attempt was made in those early years of our dominion to grapple with the famine question or to construct any system of famine relief, when a famine occurred, the efforts made to relieve distress were usually on a small scale, disconnected and spasmodic".[2]

Hence the frequent occurrence of famines led to Government to adopt in the second half of the 19th century, a Famine Commission which was to be put into operation at the time of a famine and to derive its causes and courses and to suggest remedial measures for its eradication in future. Recommendations of Commission to prevent recurrences of famines and scarcities are examined below:

Famine Commission of 1866

To know the causes and damaging effects of the famine of 1866 and to recommend measures for preventing further recurrence, the secretary of state ordered an enquiry[3] and a Commission, consisting of George Campbell (afterwards Sir G. Campbell, Lt. Governor of Bengal) then a

1. G. Kaushal, *Economic History of India, 1757-1966*, New Delhi, 1979, p. 153.
2. *RIF*, 1901, p. 1.
3. The Despatch of Secretary of States No. 85, 9 October 1866, BRP, December 1866.

judge of the High Court as President, Colonel W.E. Morton, R.E. and H. L. Dampier as members, was appointed in December 1866 by the Government of India. The Commission was asked not only to find out the causes but also to suggest remedial measures to guard against recurrence of similar calamities. The Commission submitted its report on 6th April 1867 after they had visited Orissa.[4]

The Famine Commission after a detailed inquiry blamed the local officials and the entire system of administration of Bengal, *i.e.*, the Commissioner of Orissa, the Board of Revenue and the Lt. Governor. The Lt. Governor having been misled by the Board misled the Government of India. The executive knew a little about the material condition of people of Orissa and administered as judicial officers. The Famine Commission observed, "Bengal thus was administered judicially and not by executive power. The executive reigns but does not govern. It has litle executive machinery and it may be said that in principle it avoids interference with the mass of the people".[5] The Commission however recommended the following measures against the recurrence of any future famines.

The Commission highlighted the evils associated with land and salt policies and recommended some remedies for them. Irrigation work was recommended for drought-prone areas of Orissa and improvement of communication and transport both by land and sea to bring the province in connection with the outer world was highlighted.[6]

The faulty process of land and zamindari system which was in vogue was the greatest obstacle in Orissa, basically an agricultural state. The settlement of the Government revenue was made only with the zamindars and the actual cultivator remained as ever subject to uncertainty and extortions. The Commission warned the Government that so long as the condition of the tenants had not improved any attempt to promote agricultural improvement was bound to fail. Expenses for cultivation were not borne by them and their middle men was involved in litigation cases and the zamindars, in effect, did nothing for the improvement of land.

The Famine Commission was in favour of middle men, *i.e.*, zamindars, sarvarakars etc., and introduction of ryotwari system in the country.[7] The permanently settled estates, the killas were mismanaged as reported and mortality was high during the famine in these estates.

---

4. Report of *RCF*, 1866, Vol. I, Part-III, p. 40;
   C.E. Buckland, *Bengal under the Lieutenant Governors*, Vol. I, p. 331.
5. Report of *RCF*, 1866, Part-I, Pr. 410.
6. Sir George Campbell, *Memories of my Indian Career*, Vol. II, London, 1893, pp. 159-164.
7. Report of *RCF*, *op.cit.*, Part - III, Prs. 32-35.

In temporarily settled estates, ryots were found to be broken and impoverished. The Commission wanted the Government to take charge of the estates temporarily in the same course as was followed for the permanently settled estates.[8]

The Commission did not champion the cause of permanent settlement in Orissa. It recommended for a long term settlement of 30 years which may be treated, as effective as a permanent one and recommended for a liberal revenue assessment in Orissa.

People in general were dependent upon agriculture and half of the revenue was drawn from it. And the climatic disturbances of food crop were mainly a matter of conjecture. Agricultural statistics were not available in Orissa due to absence of approximate statistical information, as it was found in other part of India. The Commission recommended liberal treatment of zamindars in matters of suspension and remission of revenue. It warned the Government that it was not possible on the part of zamindars to treat the ryots liberally when they themselves were not spared. It commended for the revenue authority to maintain agricultural statistics and to pursue suspension and remission of revenue reaching the ryots.

In apprehension of being assessed more in the coming settlement (1866-67), many put lands out of cultivation. They were almost in an uncertain state on the eve of the famine.[9] People feared an increased assessment on account of irrigation at the next settlement and hence did not use canal water. In defence, Commission suggested the continuance of existing settlement for 30 more years.

On the eve of famine there was mass unemployment among salt manufacturers; due to the cessation of the Government manufacture. The famine first spread in Puri and the mortality among them was very high.[10] However the Commission did not recommend anything for improvement of this class. To avoid that in future the Commission paid special attention to irrigation works. It recommended for the establishment of district irrigation departments. The Commission was satisfied with the progress of the East India Irrigation Company and asked the Government for speedy prosecution of the irrigation works. The head works on several branches of Mahanadi would provide adequate protection to the province against inundation and the Commission insisted on the speedy completion of Kendrapara canal then in progress. It would give not only irrigation to a large tract of country but a much needed communication between Cuttack and the sea. It also desired that the canal from the Kathjori

8. *Ibid.*, Part-II, Pr.19.
9. *RCF*, *op.cit.*, Part-I, p. 45, Part-II, pp. 15-17 and Part-III, prs. 28-29.
10. *Ibid.*, Part-II, pr. 49 and Part-II, Prs. 15-17.

should be undertaken to provide irrigation to Prui district, which would establish an easy inland water communication system up to the Chilka lake and through the lake to the Ganjam district of the Madras Presidency. The canals would permeate the delta and supply a link of communication between different parts of the province, so wanting in such a time. The East India Irrigation Company should be treated liberally to complete these works.[11] Lord Lawrence during the famine of Orissa in 1866 laid down some principles to meet the calamity. He asked the officials to first avert death by starvation. He created a department of irrigation under Colonel Stratchey.

The severity of the Famine of 1866 necessitated the Government to create a network of irrigation canals. These public utility works were financed by loans raised from open markets. This construction of canals, made a headway in Orissa.[12] The Commission noticed that the embankments in Orissa were maintained partly by the zamindars and partly by the Government. But invariably the maintenance lacked suitable and efficient plans, and so the embankments were incapable of meeting great floods. It was recommended that the Government should maintain river embankments through proper and efficient plans to check floods. The subject concerning the complete protection of the country against floods was, however, left to a special committee on inundations to work out the details.

The Commission put emphasis on the development of communications in the province. It recommended for speedy construction of a Trunk Road from Calcutta to Cuttack and road connections among different parts of the province. Improvements of roads from Cuttack to Puri, Cuttack to Kendrapara and Pattamundai, Cuttack to Sambalpur and of several other local roads were planned.[13] The Commission also recommended for providing communication between Calcutta and Cuttack on waters and thus the proposals were laid down that the betterment of the canals connecting the two should carefully be undertaken to facilitate the process of navigation.

The Commission also put emphasis on the improvement of ports and considered False Point to be the best harbour on the whole coast of India between Hooghly and Bombay.[14] This harbour as recommended, might be sufficient for a very large class of steamers to work. The defects like means of disembarking cargo and movement of passengers at the

11. H.L. Dampier, Secretary to Government of Bengal to Secretary to Government of India, No. 3345, 22 October 1868, *BRP*, November 1868.
12. V.R. Bhattacharya, *New face of rural India*, New Delhi-1984, pp. 14-16.
13. *RCF*, 1866, Vol. I, Part-II, Prs.28-32; H.L. Dampier, Secretary to Government of Bengal to Secretary to *op.cit.*
14. *RCF, 1886*, Vol. I, Part-II, Pr. 30.

anchorage from the port to mouth of the canals might be facilitated. It recommended to keep one dismantled ship to receive and a suitable small steamer and cargo boats to run between receiving ships and the mouth the canal. Like this, False Point could be a port of call and other communications would spring up and uninhabited waste lands of False Point would be busy with traffic. The Commission also recommended for the improvement of other ports of Orissa.[15] But recommendations of Famine Commissions served as a guideline for the improvement of the province which was neglected before. But as a matter of fact the recommendations were not fully implemented and Orissa could not prosper much as compared to Bengal, Bombay and Madras provinces.

Indian Famine Commission, 1880

Queen Victoria was proclaimed as the Empress of India on 1st January 1877 and in the same year a famine broke out.[16] Scarcity of rain and a long continuous drought following it, first broke out in the Deccan and gradually extended to the north. As its consequence, a widespread all-India famine became inevitable.[17] This famine was again a red-signal to a devastating catastrophe and the British Government paid all its attention to the solution of the problem. A Famine Commission was appointed in 1880 which recommended among other things a "Famine Code" and the code presented a set of rules to the Government in 1883 which offered the following main suggestions for effectively dealing with famine in the future.[18]

(1) It was the foremost duty of the state to offer relief to the needy in times of famines.

(2) The relief was to be administered in the shape of providing work for the able-bodied men and distributing food and money to the ages and infirm.

(3) The Scheme of relief works should be prepared in advance so that actual operation might begin immediately after the outbreak of famine.

(4) The works should be of permanent utility and on an extensive scale so as to provide employment to the famine stricken people.

(5) The remissions of land revenue and rents were to be made in the affected areas for a fixed period.

---

15. *Ibid.*, Prs. 27-32.
16. R.C Dutt, *op.cit.*, Vol. II, p. 310.
17. *IGI*, Vol. X, pp. 525-526.
18. *RIF*, 1880, Quoted in a Note in the Famines of India by G.C Das, *OHRJ*, Vol. VIII, October 1959 and Jan. 1960, Nos. 3 & 4.

(6) The construction of a network of railways all over the country was highly necessary so that the relief measures could be extended to the affected areas at once.

(7) The local authorities (provincial Governments) should bear the major share of the responsibility in organizing and extending the relief works.

(8) The duty of the Central Government was to supplement to provincial funds.

(9) A sum of Rs. 15 millions should be set apart annually to constitute of the Famine Insurance Fund.

Famine Relief Measures

In 1866 great Orissa famine relief measures were inadequate, as a result of which about a third of the population or nearly a million persons had perished.[19] Such measures were improved and rationalized in 1880. Efforts were also made for the improvement of roads and railways which played important roles in rushing food to famine stricken areas. It also stressed for agricultural education in India. Dr. J.A. Voelkar was invited in 1889 to study India's agricultural problems.[20] Accordingly the first agricultural research institute was started in Pusa in 1903. The recommendation of Indian Famine Commission 1880 improved the relief policy and necessitated the Government to be more active and alert than before. But it is clearly proved that Orissa did not get much benefit from the recommendation of Famine Commission or Famine Code.

Preventive Measures Against Famine

As a mark of prevention of the famine, many efforts were made to check its recurrence. First, some old irrigation works were repaired and new ones were constructed. Protective in nature, these works were undertaken, mainly to protect the farmers against failure of rains. Secondly, in order to aid the speedy disposal of above works. A Famine Insurance Relief Fund was started which was raised to about Rs.300 crores in 1939-40. Thirdly, collecting statistics about people's conditions in various districts, the Government took measures for agricultural improvements by means of development of irrigation, transport and communications.[21]

Afterall no remarkable change was found in the lot and condition of the people, because of high land revenue throughout the period.

---

19. *RIF, 1880*, Part-I, Pr.51, p. 17.
20. B.M. Bhatia, *op.cit.*, pp.200-202.
21. *Ibid.*, pp. 122-127, 196-200.

Indian Famine Commission, 1898

After the all-India famine of 1896-97, the Famine Commission of 1898 was setup, which recommended for the enlarging of irrigation works and as a result Irrigation Commission of 1901-3 was set up later under the chairmanship of Sir Colin Scottman Crieff.[22]

The Famine Code contained in it the following schemes:[23]

(1) It prescribed the preparatory or precautionary arrangements to be permanently maintained in ordinary times which would give way to the maintenance of efficient channels of information and thereby detect the apprehension of a famine in a good time and thus to provide for a state of allertness with respect to relief measures when the emergency arises.

(2) The second chapter deals with suggestions that after getting of the information relating to the imminence of scarcity or famine, the authorities had to submit special reports and to immediately take the preliminary actions.

(3) The other 13 chapters prescribed the duties and responsibilities of the officials concerned at the time of real scarcity or famine and various measures of relief to be undertaken.

The system of relief measures was developed to some extent. But the Famine Code was not helpful for Orissa. The famine of 1888-89 in Angul was also severe due to the negligence of relief work. The Secretary of State for India also admitted that British officers were certainly responsible for the severity of famine.[24]

Other Commissions

In 1901, another commission after the all-India Famine of 1899-1900 was set up and recommended the following:

(1) Boldness should be the motto and relief should be neither wasteful nor too small.

(2) The Commission recommended specially for Fodder Famine of 1899-1900.

(3) Promptness in remission and suspension of land revenue.

(4) Promptness in giving taccavi loans in liberal terms.

(5) It recommended to set up an Irrigation Commission to lay down definite policy regarding selection, financing and maintenance of canal works.

---

22. R.C. Dutt, *op.cit*, p. 104.
23. *RIF, 1898*, Ch. III, p. 45.
24. Remarks of the Secretary of States for India, Quoted in *RIF*, 1898, Ch. II, pp. 13-14.

Whether it be an All India Famine or a Famine in Orissa, the Commissions recommended the same approach to fight against famines and scarcities. Prevention of Famines and Scarcities could only be taken through development of agriculture, irrigation, transport and communication etc.

The recommendations of the Famine Commissions were no doubt valuable and may be regarded as mile stones to ameliorate the millions from distress in Orissa, but practically Orissa got less benefit, if not nil and lot of millions remained ever poor, for their desires were unfulfilled as the commissions never recommended specially to fight poverty, unemployment and illiteracy. Thus the problem of poverty and famine and their cause and effect relationship were never tackled in Orissa during the period under study.

The specific relations of irrigation, embankments, transport communications and ports to fight with famines and scarcities may be examined.

Irrigation

Owing to recurrent floods and droughts there was much scarcity of food in Orissa. The scarcity was due not to flood and drought alone, but also to more export, from the province. Lack of irrigation facilities brought regular crop failures and poor production. In the words of Court of Directors of East India Company.

"The province is subject to seasons of extreme uncertainty liable to most remarkable vicissitudes of drought the inundations" (Quoted in the Commissioner's Administrative Report, 1st June 1847).

As per the statement of Madhusudan Das in the Bengal Council on April 4, 1896 the Government was truly interested in the improvement of the agricultural condition of the country.[25] The Orissa Famine of 1866 forced the immediate execution of the canal projects to afford irrigation facilities to the people of Orissa. By the recommendations of the Famine Commission the Government of Bengal decided to accelerate the irrigation facilities through canal projects to protect the people of Orissa from twin evils of drought and inundation.[26]

Orissa economically lagged far behind as large tract of crop fields were laid frequently waste. There were a lot of correspondences in Government level to execute the canal projects in Orissa. The important proposal to use the waters of Orissa came from Sir Arthur Cotton, who was deputed to visit the province, to advise as for controlling the flood

25. *BRP*, April 1896, Statement of Madhusudan Das (Utkal Gauraba Madhusudan Das), Member of the Bengal Council in the Council Meeting, April 4, 1896.
26. *RCF*, Vol. I, Part-II, Pr. 25.

waters of the river Mahanadi. He recommended the construction of irrigable and navigable canals following the principles then being carried out in the deltas of the Godavari and the Krishna. He estimated that an area of 2¼ million of acres might be irrigated and navigation might be opened up between Orissa, Midnapore and Calcutta.[27] On the advice of Sir Arthur Cotton, the East India Irrigation Company was tempted to take up the work with a view to gaining much profit out of it like the irrigation work in the deltas of the Godavari and the Krishna.

The Secretary of Madras Irrigation Company apprised the Board of Directors of the East India Company of the benefits of the construction of irrigable and navigable canals of Orissa.[28] In 1861 Act of Parliament the East India Irrigation Company and the Secretary of State executed a contract for the construction of works for irrigation, navigation and supply of water and other purposes in the districts conjined to the delta of Mahanadi, Baitarani and Brahmani.[29] It started with a most ambitious scheme aimed at making a link between Calcutta and Puri.[30] The project was partly completed in 1867-68. The Irrigation Company however was not able to complete the work due to inadequate funds even though the Government provided money in advance during famine of 1866 to enable the Company to employ more labourers in order to provide relief to the famine stricken people of the distressed districts.[31]

The Famine Commission gave importance to vigorous prosecution of these irrigation works in Orissa as a means of mitigating such calamity in future. It placed before the Government the urgent necessity of completing the Kendrapara canal (then under construction) for providing irrigation to a large part of the state. It also gave importance to take similar works throughout the delta as a means of providing both irrigation and communication between different portions of the province.[32]

Under these circumstances the Government of India represented to the Secretary of State in 1867 to take over the works of the canals in Orissa.[33] Lord Lawrence, the Governor-General was an advocate for irrigation works in India.[34] He was convinced by his bitter experience of

---

27. Memorandum of R.E. Cotton, May 1858; Report of the Indian Irrigation Commission (1901-3), Part-II, Pr. 382.
28. W.A. Inglis, *The Canals and Flood Banks of Bengal*, (Calcutta, 1909), pp. 1-2.
29. Orissa Project, Contract between the Secretary of States and the East India Irrigation Company, November 28, 1861.
30. *Maddox Report*, Vol. I, p. 22.
31. *BRP*, May 1866.
32. *RCF*, 1866, Vol. I, Part-II, Pr. 25.
33. *BRP*, August 1867, Government of India's Despatch No. 114, July 16, 1867.
34. R.C. Dutt, *op.cit.*, p. 262.

the recent calamity in Orissa that such works only could save a great part of these districts from similar visitations in future.[35] The failure of the Government in Orissa in mitigating the evil consequences of the famine by timely measures had been admitted by him personally and he was interested for the speedy recovery of the province. But it was not possible without effective execution of the irrigation works. He assured the Secretary of State that the amount to be invested was not great compared with the object in view.[36] The representation of Government of India reached the Secretary of State at a time when the horrors of the famine were still vivid in the minds of authorities in England. On this letter it was suggested that the company should be asked to give up the Orissa undertaking to the Government of India on being indemnified for past expenditure. By the terms of the deed signed on 30 November 1868 the company received $990,050 8s. 7d, representing the capital of the Orissa undertaking together with interest at the rate of 5 per cent. A sum of $50,000 was also paid for the object of compensation of the servants of the company.[37] The management added some modifications to the original plan outlay. The work sanctioned thereon included Taldanda, Machgaon canals for the irrigation of lands between Mahanadi and Kathjori, the Kendrapara and Pattamundai canal for the irrigation of the area between Chitrotpala and Birupa and 3 ranges of the high level canal for the irrigation of the country from Cuttack to Bhadrak.[38] These works were undertaken for providing irrigation, navigation and drainage system of protect the state from famines and floods. Thus a beginning for constructive and protective works started with equal importance in Orissa.

The Orissa projects became property of Government on payment of a sum of $1,040,050. The incomplete works were to be completed with an estimated cost of Rs. 2,77,13,978 which could provide irrigation for 1,6000,000 acres of lands and construction of 530 miles of irrigational canals. Total revenue estimated was Rs. 54,00,000 per annum including water rates at Rs. 2-8 annas per acre. Deducting working expenses around Rs. 9,54,000 per annum, the Government expected to get Rs. 44,44,500 about 16 per cent on capital per annum.[39]

Thus fixation of water rates and completion of works remained with the Government. It was decided to charge water rate by volume on 22nd February 1864. These were 8 annas per 1000 cubic yards from 15th June

---

35. Quoted in G.C. Patnaik's The Famine and some aspects of the British Economic Policy in Orissa 1866-1905 (Cuttack, 1980), p. 118.
36. IGI, IV, p. 329.
37. W.A. Inglis, *op.cit.*, p. 14.
38. *Maddox Report*, Vol. I, p. 22.
39. W.A. Inglis, *op.cit.*, pp. 15-20.

to 15th November and 1 rupee from 16th November to 14th June. The rate was equal to a rate per acre of Rs. 1-12 annas. Colonel Rundall, the Chief Engineer of the company, suggested the rates to be charged on both volume and area. But commissioner shore fixed the rate by volume and proposed rates per acre as Rs. 4 per acre for autumn rice, Rs. 5 for two crops land and Rs 6 for sugar and cotton. On 23rd June 1866, the Lt. Governor approved the following rates by volume and area.

Re. 1 per 1000 cubic yards from 15th to 31st October.

Rs. 1-8 per 1000 cubic yards from 1st November to 14th June.

Supply by area –

Rs. 3 per acre for a single crop

Rs. 5 per acre per annum

Rs. 1-8 per acre for single waterings.[40]

Later rates were lowered to popularise irrigation in Orissa.

The fear of enhancement of rent created by the administration ruined the prospects of agriculture in Orissa and lessons for famine were fast forgotten. Irrigation works were very slow in progress and only Kendrapara canal was opened to tidal waters.[41]

"Gradual stoppage of irrigation works in Orissa was a suicidal policy",[42] once commented T.E. Ravenshaw in 1870.

The British Government made a geographical mistake by not sticking to irrigational works by neglecting canals in India. The recommendation of Famine Commission of 1866 was kept in the cold storage. The lopsided policy of Government was vehemently criticised later. After 1870, owing to frequent scarcities Government again adopted some programmes of irrigation works in Orissa. As irrigation was a provincial subject these works in Orissa under Bengal never made a headway in comparison to Punjab, Burma* and Sind.[43] Preservation of ancient works and construction of new works would have changed the face of Orissa within 50 to 60 years by safeguarding agriculture and its population protected from famines. The famine condition panicked the Government and towards 1871 Government sanctioned the following works for Orissa.[44]

---

40. W.A. Inglis, *op.cit.*, pp. 8-9.
41. *U.D.*, 3 July 1869.
42. R. Thompson, Secretary, Government of Bengal to Secretary Government of India (Home), No. 36 of 26 September 1870, *BRP*, 1870.

*Burma was than part of India.

43. J.A. Voelkar, *Improvement of Indian Agriculture, 1993*, (Calcutta, 1897).
44. *U.D.*, 25 March 1871.

TABLE 7.1
MONEY SANCTIONED FOR DIFFERENT TYPE OF WORKS

Works	*Sums granted in rupees*
Mahanadi Weir and Sluice	12,00,000
Dam around Cuttack	47,000
Birupa Weir	3,00,000
Naraj Weir	4,50,000
Kendrapara Canal	24,00,000
Taldanda Canal	6,00,000
Jobra Anicut	75,000
Midnapur Canal	23,00,000
Taidal Canal	8,00,000
Total	86,00,000

The works were nearly completed on 29th May 1873. Only 1257 acres were irrigated out of a capacity of 1,95,000 acres owing to fear of enhancement of rent. But Orissa projects never became profitable like works of Godavari delta. The feeling or insecurity of tenants, high rents and revenue and fear of enhacement of rent etc., made the projects more costly.[45] To make it remunerative the water rate from 1-8 annas increased to 1-12 annas in 1903.

S. L. Maddox, the settlement officer, reported that there was little enhancement of rent owing to irrigation. Rent did not rise owing to irrigation but was due to difference between out-turn of irrigated and unirrigated lands. He estimated the out-turn per acre as follows:

TABLE 7.2
OUT-TURN OF RICE AND STRAW IN ORISSA

Item	*Irrigated*	*Unirrigated*
Rice	1110 1bs (13½ maunds)	986 Ibs (12 maunds)
Straw	28 maunds	22-23 manuds

Source : Maddox Report, Vol. 1,p.84.

The financial expenses of canal construction were more than that of income received. The following statement shows the income and expenditure of canal construction during 1872-1899.

45. Report of Commissioner appointed to enquire into certain matters etc., 1884, appendix-G.

TABLE 7.3
INCOME AND EXPENDITURE OF CANALS (1872-99)

Year	*Income* Rs.	*Expenditure* Rs.	*Deficit* Rs.
1872-73	36,623	3,38,009	2,01,386
1881-82	2,23,149	11,03,834	8,80,685
1882-83	3,19,625	3,54,896	35,271
1887-88	1,79,211	5,01,932	1,22,721
1892-93	4,97,375	5,05,507	8,132
1893-94	3,75,365	5,35,467	1,60,162
1898-99	4,65,492	4,95,213	29,721

Source : Annual Administration Report of Bengal Presidency, Orissa Division of the concerned years.

But in spite of all these plans and estimates the canal system was severe failure in Orissa. The main reason for such failure was an inappropriate estimation of coast needed for the purpose and the high anticipation of earnings from it. The unsystematic planning made canals unremunerative during the period under study. The construction of coast canal to connect Balasore with Calcutta via Hooghly river was a sad example of this imbalanced planning. The construction of the canal was commenced in January 1880 at an sanctioned amount of Rs. 44,74,941.[46] It was estimated to get Rs. 2,50,000 revenue per annum and to provide cheap traffic for trade between Calcutta and Orissa. It was fully opened for traffic in 1887. It connected the river Hooghly at Goenkhali 45 miles from Calcutta with the Matai and Charbatia. It ran along the sea face at a distance varying from 2 to 10 miles from the coast. Its construction of the canal was undertaken because it would be valuable as a protection against famine and remunerative as a trade route.[47] But the income from this canal was not up to the mark of expectation due to the opening of railway line in Orissa in 1896.

Though canal system was a failure in Orissa, it ensured a greater benefit in the field of inland navigation. It also provided a considerable income to the Government though not up to the expectation. The table below shows the amount of revenue realised from the traffic only in the year 1875-76.[48]

46. RCF, 1895-96, p. 36.
47. L.S.S. O' Malley. *BDG. Balasore*, pp. 105-106.
48. GAROD, 1875-76, p. 17.

TABLE 7.4
REVENUE REALISED FROM THE TRAFFIC IN THE YEAR 1875-76

Name of the Canal	*Traffic Boats*		*Value of Cargos*		*Total revenue*
	Govt.	*Private*	*Govt.*	*Private*	
High Level	220	1,806	14,775	3,57,733	3,390
Kendrapara	295	3,857	15,364	33,08,702	11,836
Taldanda	324	729	2,621	1,46,418	886
Total	839	6,392	32,760	38,12,853	16,112

The Government was concerned about the low revenue from the irrigation and navigation through these three main canals. After much consideration the Government of India was of opinion to sanction extra funds for the construction of additional distributaries that would be effected in first instance. Lot of efforts be made to induce the people to make the village channels at their own cost and effort. The Government also decided not to spend much on the construction of many distributaries unless direct promises would be made by the cultivators to use the canal water on lease for 5 years on contract.[49] The cultivators did not pay much interest to utilise the water from canal as they were getting water from different sources during the normal period of rainfall. Taking all these causes into account Government was not very much keen in diverting much fund for the purpose. The total cost for work including all charges up to 1881 amounted to Rs. 2,53,18,197 or Rs. 122-8 annas per acre.[50]

Water Rates

The rates charged for water varied from time to time. The rates were too high when the works were undertaken by the Government. The rates were immediately lowered to Re. 1 with the hope that it might be an effective inducement to bring more area under water lease. However, it failed to produce any effect and the rates were again raised to Rs. 2-8-0. Thereupon the area under water-lease showed a considerable falling off and the rates were again lowered in 1872. This measure was described by the Lt. Governor, Sir George Campbell, as resembling a Dutch auction, the seller coming lower and lower, and the buyer still holding out.[51] The Orissa canals had never paid their charged, the water rate being only Rs. 1-8 annas per acre and the receipts for big navigation and irrigation barely covered the working charges and could not pay anything towards

49. *ROC*, File No. III, 1881, p. 10, Government of Bengal Commissioner of Orissa, No. 20541, July 21, 1879.
50. *Ibid.*, Notes of the probable cost of the Orissa canals by the Lt. Governor of Bengal.
51. *RAB*, 1871-72.

the interest. It became natural that the responsible Government officers should be engaged to cast means to meet the deficit. Col. Gulliver proposed an increase of 8 annas of water rate in early 1874 for the protection of this canal project. A. Smith, Commissioner, Cuttack division, referred to the suggestions of Baboo Jagamohan Ray, a Deputy Collector who was associated with the irrigation works suggested the Government of Bengal to increase the water rate up to the extent of 8 annas for favourably situated tracts.[52] In 1877 a Bill was drafted and introduced in Bengal Council. It was designed to realise a compulsory cess from the occupants of land irrigable and G. Toynbee, I.C.S., was deputed to Orissa to investigate into the feasibility of imposing of this overload on the cultivators of Orissa. In 1881 the officers of the Public Works Department suggested for the enhancement of Pahi rent by Rs. 2-8 annas per acre in the ensuing settlement. The Government of India called on the Bengal Government to impose an owners rate all atonce, when the enhancement of land revenue would not be affected till 1897.[53] From the examination of a number of villages of both classes (within and without ranges of canals) it appeared that in the irrigable villages, the rise in ten years had ranged from 5.8 to 17.4 per cent, while in the non-irrigable villages it had ranged from 12.9 to 17.8 per cent.[54]

In Orissa, the value of the canal irrigation was exceptionally dependent on the character of the season the rainfall being ample. It was of no avail as a means of increasing productiveness of the soil. Those who had quoted the success of the Madras deltas seemed to have forgotten that in that delta rainfall did not exceed 40 inches while in Orissa it exceeded to 60 inches per annum on an average. The Appendix 'D' will give a detailed picture of the rainfall in inches in different places of Orissa.[55]

However the irrigation works were unremunerative on financial grounds but it improved the well-being and standard of living of population which were the direct concern of the Government. If these schemes had been planned in the systematic way they would have provided better standard of living of people, during the period under study.[56] As the people were not in a mood to utilise the canal water the Government could not yield a return on irrigation head more than Rs. 2 per acre. Though immediate financial benefit was very less yet the indirect benefit became enormous both for the Government and the people. It would

52. ROC, File No. III, 1881, p. 10, A. Smith, Commissioner of Cuttack to Secretary, Government of Bengal, No. 3261, November 21, 1881, *BRP*, December 1883.
53. *Maddox Report*, Vol. I, pp. 76-77.
54. *Ibid.*
55. *Ibid.*, p. 80.
56. The Famine Inquiry Commission of Bengal 1945, Ch. I, p. 133.

afford best possible protection to the agriculturists of Orissa from flood, famine and inundation which had caused disastrous impact on the material condition of the people. Taking all these things in view the Secretary of State unwillingly sanctioned funds for the completion of the entire system of distributaries which were completed.[57]

Irrigation and navigation were great measures undertaken against drought and famines during the later part of the 19th century. Prior to 1866 the Government was allowing remission and suspension of revenue on an average of Rs. 89,000 (Rs. 27,000 in Puri and Rs. 62,000 in Cuttack) but since the year of famine there had been none practically due to the protective measures of irrigation through canal water which could provide incentive to the cultivators when they were in dire need of water during the years of unusual rainfall. It was a better security against failure of crops of the tenants and the Government was also relieved from a great burden of the future famine expenditure.[58] The canal system on the whole benefited the Government to collect cess or local funds which were made available for the well being of the agricultural class.

A deep insight into the above description would show that the canal system in Orissa was much successful for the use of inland navigation. Though the system was to provide irrigation it was not successful in that regard. The entire system in Orissa was modelled on the shadow of Madras delta irrigation system. But the fact which was ignored was that Madras delta enjoyed an annual rainfall of 40 inches whereas Orissa enjoyed a rainfall of more than 60 inches per year. Hence, the Orissan cultivators were not necessarily requiring canal water for irrigation. The canals in Orissa were constructed more for the purpose of water in lets than for irrigation. The system would have been successful if the farmer would have been induced for better cultivation system involving irrigation. This would have helped the Goverment in getting adequate revenues for royal exchequer and the conditons of the peasants would have been increased.

Embankments

It may be examined how embankments afforded protection from inundations during the period under study. It offered a means of protection from inundation, where river banks were low, causing irreparable damages to cultivable lands. It also acts as protective barrior in coastal belt which was always prone to inundations that threatened to life, property and standing crops. The Government had no systematic policy for embankments. In Orissa some embankments were constructed since the time of Mohammadan and Maratha Governments and some were

57. *ROC*, (1884), Pr. 90.
58. *RCC*, *op.cit.*, Pr. 59.

constructed by the British Government before the settlement. Local zamindars had constructed some embankments that were taken up by the Government.[59] In 1831 embankments were brought under the charge of Public Works Department. It is evident that there was then no regular system of protective works nor any attempt was made to systematize them or anything was done to repair the embankments already in existence.[60]

The embankments in course of time were abandoned as they were not properly levelled. The levelling, repairing and abandoning of bunds and embankments created breaches. The number of breaches in embankments is recorded below:[61]

TABLE 7.5

NO. OF BREACHES IN ORISSA (1852-1856)

Year	*Breaches*
1852	1,167
1853	942
1854	872
1855	1,365
1856	404

Heavy damages caused by breaches created problem to the Government. By the advice of Captain Harris Stones were removed from Barabati fort to repair the Cuttack revetment.[62]

The Embankment Act, XXXII of 1855 failed to give any system to regulate the embankments. Except major embankments the responsibility of maintenance of these has not been defined.[63] From Sir Arthur Cotton's report it was found that he fully relief mainly on spurs and planned embankments on the river Mahanadi to control flood water.[64]

Under British rule embankments have been systematised and large sums have been expanded on the perfecting of the embankments, especially after disastrous famine of 1866.[65] A committe was appointed to inquire into the effects of the inundations of 1866 and suggested the remedy to it. Towards 1868 Government recommended more protective embankments. Following table notes the amount sanctioned for effective protection of embankments in various districts of Orissa.

59. W.C. Taylor, *Report on the Embankments,* 18 December 1871.
60. L.S.S. O' Malley, *BDG, Balasore,* p. 110.
61. W.A.Inglis, *op.cit.*, p. 205.
62. P. Mukherjee, Irrigation, Inland Navigation and Flood Problems in Northern Orissa during the British Rule, p. 33.
63. *BPP*, July 1894.
64. Thomas Jones, Assistant Secretary to the Government of Bengal, No. 2109, 28 May 1867.
65. P. Mukherjee, *op.cit.*, Pr. 22, p. 13.

TABLE 7.6
SANCTION OF AMOUNT TOWARDS PROTECTIVE EMBANKMENTS IN DIFFERENT PARTS OF ORISSA

District	*Amount in Rs.*
Puri	19,99,890
Cuttack	30,95,770
Balasore	23,38,970
Total	74,34,630

Source : W.A. Inglis, *op. cit.*, p. 219.

The settlement records made no specification as to who, whether the zamindars or the Government would take care of the embankments. To check the evils of heavy flood causing damage to life and property the Government had undertaken the charge of repairing of the embankments by spending a part of the state fund. It was expected that the amount spent on this would be recovered from the Rajas of estates through which the embankments were constructed. After this the embankments were somehow repaired and strengthened without any scientific knowhow. The expenditure however proposed thereon by the Inundation Committee was not sanctioned as the Government was the opinion that the exchequer of Indian Empire should not be expended after the embankment of Orissa.[66]

In 1866 W.C. Taylor, Subdivisional Officer, Khurda was deputed to make an accurate record of all existing Government and zamindari embankments, and to the extent to which Government and zamindars were respectively bound to maintain them. He reported that there were about 510½ miles of Government embankments and 248 miles of the zamindari embankments in Cuttack district. Most of these were insufficient in heights to withstand heavy flood. So Taylor considered that another 498 miles were required to complete the system, even by regulating some of the rivers and closing others entirely. But his proposals never given effect to.[67]

After the high flood of 1872 a proposal was submitted at the cost of Rs. 45,00,000 to construct an embankment on the Mahanadi.[68] Again another proposal in 1882 was submitted to Government to remodel the existing embankments on the rivers Kuakhai, Daya and branches of Mahanadi was also overlooked.

The Government turned down the proposals on the pretext of unpracticable financial resources. But the consequence of this negligence

66. *BPP*, October 1871, Rundal Secretary, Government of India to Government of Bengal, No. 4671, September 9, 1871.
67. *Maddox Report*, Vol. I, Pr. 22, p. 14.
68. L.S.S. O' Malley, *BDG*, *Cuttack*, p. 100.

was grevious. In 1872, 1879, 1881, 1892, 1895 and in 1896 high floods inundated the area causing injury to the life, property and agricultural products of the state.[69]

After the famine of 1896 Government wanted to furnish as much work as possible to provide relief to the poor people. Following lines of the letter from the Secretary to Government of Bengal to the Commissioner on the 15th February 1867 prove the eagerness of the Government regarding relief measures.

> "Whatever may be required for the repairs of zamindari embankments with a view to employing the poor and protecting the country from the effects of another flood must be advanced by Government and the question of its recovery from the zamindars may be considered hereafter".

Ravenshaw, the Commissioner of Orissa ordered that the Aul embankment which was in a bad state of disrepair should be taken over by the Public Works Department. The Raja of Aul was to be informed by the P.W.D. that he would be liable to pay the cost of repairs under the Act XXXII of 1855. They repaired the Aul embankments by spending Rs. 33,000. It was also found that section VI of the Act of 1855 limited the liability of zamindars for maintenance of embankments and absence of positive agreement it would not be possible to recover the costs from the Raja of Aul.[70]

The amount had been spent on embankments since the year of Orissa Famine. The average annual expenditure on embankments in the province at different times alone were as follows:[71]

TABLE 7.7
ANNUAL EXPENDITURE ON EMBANKMENTS IN DIFFERENT PARTS OF ORISSA

Years	*Amount in Rs.*
1803-30	17,308
1831-45	10,794
1846-52	13,700
1853-59	40,807
1860-66	59,247
1867-76	88,357
1877-86	48,813
1887-96	53,900

69. P.C. Das, *The Economic History of Orissa in the 19th century*, p. 123.
70. P. Mukherjee, *op.cit.*, pp. 34-35.
71. *Maddox Report*, Vol. I, p. 15.

The average expenditure for the whole province on agricultural embankments from 1878-79 to 1897-98 was Rs. 1,04,600.[72] The average annual expenditure on agricultural embankments in Cuttack alone was as follows:[73]

TABLE 7.8
ANNUALLY EXPENDITURE ON AGRICULTURAL EMBANKMENTS IN CUTTACK DISTRICT

Period	*Amount in Rs.*
1839-45	10,800
1846-52	13,700
1853-59	40,800
1860-66	59,200
1867-76	88,400
1877-86	48,800
1887-96	53,900

Even though from this expenditure there was no direct income for the Government, the embankments were necessary for insuring against inundations and to protect the agricultural community.

Embankments were necessitated to protect the state from inundation but frequent floods and famines required the Government to have more attention to fight floods and famines. But the efforts of Government to implement the valuable suggestions of A.C. Cotton, Colonel Rundall, Capt. Beadle, Lt. Harris and Prof. P.C. Moholanabis would have led of banish floods and droughts from the province. On the whole the problems remained ever unsolved till the end of British rule. Irrigation provides safety from droughts but embankments affords more security from floods than famines. If these works had been undertaken earlier, the floods and famines would not have caused great hardship and taken away more live. Embankments and irrigation works though less remunerative to a poor province like Orissa, became worthful in future. The recommendations of the Famine Commissions to fight against floods and famines served to some extent, but not up to the desired level. The Inundation Committee of 1866 was set up under the chairmanship of T.E. Ravenshaw. As a result, the general embankment Act was passed in 1873 for successful working of embankments in Orissa. Towards the end of 1900 there were 969 miles of embankments in Cuttack 84 miles in Balasore and 257 miles in Puri district.[74]

72. *Maddox Report*, Vol. I, p. 93.
73. *Ibid.*
74. P. Mukherjee, *op.cit.*, p. 36.

Transport and Communications

Orissa remained undercivilised and underdeveloped for a fairly long period (the period under study) owing to lack of improvement in transport and communication. Orissa was geographically isolated from the outside world. Most part of Orissa regions remained remote and inaccessible and people lived in ignorance, supersession, caste prejudice, irrational customs and traditions. This isolation and inaccessibility many times aggravated the ravages of famines in Orissa. It was also responsible for the decline of trade, commerce and manufactures of traditional items.[75] The Britishers realised the importance of transport and communication. To them an efficient means of transport was a pre-condition, for development of trade and commerce and indirectly they propounded free-market economy for benefit of the mother country. The Famine Commissions gave importance to speedy improvements in canals, ports and roads to provide easy and cheap communications to different regions of Orissa to break isolation from outside world. Lord Lawrence also admitted the urgency of speedy development in the field of transport and communication in Orissa.[76] However, the Orissa Famine of 1866 broke the isolation of Orissa and improved the transport and communication system.

The communication which were developed in Orissa may be analyses under following heads.

Roads

There were few roads in Orissa during the first half of the 19th century. They were confined to the coastal plains and their conditions remained unaltered till 1866.[77] In the modern sense of the term there was not a road when the British occupied the province in 1803. There were mere fair-weather car-tracks without bridges and without proper ferry arrangments for crossing the numerous water-courses.[78]

Jagannath road was the only road in the province which was constructed under the guidance of Captain Sackville (appointed as Superintendent) and was completed in 1825.[79] This was completed without bridges and it was unusable during rainy season due to inundations.[80] There were no other roads in the real sense and if there were, those were ill-maintained and were useless in rainy season. So Orissa was more

75. *IFC*, 1880, Part-I, p.43, also see W.W. Hunter, Statistical Account of Bengal, Vol. XVII and XIX.
76. *RCF*, 1866, Vol.I, Part-II, Prs. 25 and 57.
77. B.N. Sinha, *Geography of Orissa*, (New Delhi, 1971), p. 127.
78. G. Toynbee, *A Sketch of the History of Orissa, (1803 to 1828)*, p. 78.
79. *Ibid.*, pp. 78-80.
80. L.S.S. O'Malley, *BDG*, *Puri*, p. 142.

underdeveloped than other parts of India in transport and communication during 19th century.

Roads were constructed and maintained by different agencies of the Government. The coast for construction of provincial roads was paid from the provincial funds and were kept under the charge of the Public Works Department of the provincial Government. The second category of roads were paid out of the District Road Fund and were under the immediate charge of the District Engineer. Local Board Roads were maintained by the Local Boards purely for local utility. The cost of maintenance of such roads were not out of the District Road Fund.[81]

The First among the provincial roads was Grand Trunk Road, the vital road of Orissa that ran from Midnapore in Bengal Presidency to Ganjam in Madras Presidency. It was completed phase-wise. The length of this grand road was 388 miles and completed by Public Works Department in 1875.[82] It reached Cuttack town where it was divided into two, the Cuttack to Puri road and Cuttack to Ganjam road. Cuttack to Puri road was generally known as Jagannath Road which was constructed between 1811 and 1812.[83] There were two other provincial roads; the first from Cuttack to Sonepur, mostly unmetalled and the second from Cuttack to Sambalpur through Athgarh.[84]

The local roads were improved as suggested by the Famine Commission. Near about 4 roads were repaired at Cuttack, 22 at Balasore. But as the roads were unmetalled, these were washed away by frequent repairs and constant vigilance. That's why Government needed more money for the maintenance of roads in this province. Government collected public works, public funds and road cess from the people to meet the expenditure of road constructed and maintenance. The table below notes the amount of road cess collected from the people of different income groups.

In the end of September 1875 from Cuttack alone collected road cess as Table 7.10.

The collection of road cess and their expenditures for the year 1875 in Balasore district is noted in the Table 7.11.

81. *Maddox Report*, Vol. I, p. 7.
82. W.W. Hunter, *A Statistical Account of Bengal*, Vol. XVIII, (London, 1877), pp. 173-174.
83. *Maddox Report*, Vol. I, p. 7.
84. *Ibid.*

TABLE 7.9

ROAD CESS COLLECTED IN ORISSA

Agriculturists whose annual income in between	*Annual road cess*
Rs. 100 - Rs. 500 to pay	Rs. 0-8-0
Rs. 500 - Rs. 1000 to pay	Rs. 1-8-0
Rs. 1000 - Rs. 2000 to pay	Rs. 2-4-0
For subsequent Rs. 200 to pay	Rs. 1.8.0 or more
Business men whose income ranged from	
Rs. 25 to Rs. 1000 per annum were to pay	Rs. 0-8-0

Source: *U.D.*, 23 August 1873.

TABLE 7.10

ROAD CESS COLLECTED AT CUTTACK AND ITS EXPENDITURE

INCOME			
Road Cess		£ 2799	
Ferry tolls		£ 373	
Grants-in-aid (from provincial reserve fund)		£ 500	Total income
	Total	£ 3672	= £ 3672
EXPENDITURE			
Original road construction		£ 2244	
On repair works		£ 2069	Total expenditure
	Total	£ 4313	= £ 2313

Source: The Calcutta Gazette, 19 April 1876.

TABLE 7.11

ROAD CESS COLLECTED AT BALASORE AND ITS EXPENDITURE IN 1875

INCOME			
Road cess		£ 1208	
Ferry tolls		£ 76	
Grants-in-aid		£ 673	Total income
	Total	£ 1957	= £ 1957
EXPENDITURE			
Original works		£ 120	
On repairs		£ 1127	Total expenditure
	Total	£ 1247	= £ 1247

Source: The Calcutta Gazette, 19 April 1876.

The principal District Board Roads constructed in 19th century in Cuttack district connecting Cuttack town are:

Cuttack to Taldanda : 44 miles length out of which 13½ miles were metalled and it was a fair weather road.

Cuttack to Machhagaon : 32 miles leaving Taldanda Road at 11th mile was metalled up to 14th mile from Cuttack.

Cuttack to Chandbali : 63 miles passed through Pattamundai.

Phulnakhara-Madhab Road : Joined the Puri-Cuttack Road at 16th mile from Cuttack.

Tanqi to Haripur Road : Connected the Garjats with Grand Trunk Road at 10th mile from Cuttack.

Jajpur to Kendrapara : 25 miles of bad road and was not bridged at Kharsua and Brahmani.

Jajpur to Kuakhai : 9 miles length a fair road with two ferries.

Beruan to Kalamatia : 16 miles length road was unaccessible during rains.

Jajpur to Pachikot : 19 miles length road was fairly good partly bridged.

Jajpur to Kyanti : having a 17 miles of length of fair weather road.

Salepur to Chatia : crossed two rivers length of 10 miles. It was met all weather road.

Beruan to Balichandrapur : 14 miles long having four unbridged river.

Pattamundai to Sudipur : 11 miles length with unmetalled good road.

Jagatsinghpur to Jajpur : with a length of 9 miles joining the Taldanda and Machagoan roads.[85]

Puri district possessed many roads maintained by provincial Government; District Boards and Local Boards. These were as follows:

Pipili to Khurda : 15 miles joining the Ganjam and Jagannath roads at Makundaprasad near Khurda.

Khurda to Kalapathar : via Zilla Kuspala and Manikgora-17 miles long joined the provincial roads like Cuttack-Sonepur road near Kantilo. A district branch road leaves the Khurda-Sambalpur road at Baghamari was extended up to Itamati, a trading center of Nayagarh.

Sunakhala a village on the district road between Baghamari and Bolagarh was connected with a road made by the Raja of Ranpur and it was linked with Ganjam truk road near Tangi.

The Chilka lake at Balugaon, a trading place on the Ganjam road stretched to Banapur.

---

85. *Maddox Report*, Vol. I, p. 8.

From Chandaka to Khandagiri and Bhubaneswar a good road was made by the Estate Improvement Fund. This 11 miles road was connected with Sardeipur and Balianta road.

22 miles road from Khurda to Patnaikia was maintained by the District Board and stretched up to Jagannath road.

Sunakhala to Aitpur a district road was constructed with a length of 34 miles.[86]

The Grand Trunk Road runs for a length of 95 miles to the end of Balasore district. If afforts communication facilities with Medinapur and Calcutta in the north and Cuttack and Ganjam on the south. Captain Sackville built it between 1812 and 1820 and the portion of Balasore being opened in the latter year.[87]

The District Board maintained 38 roads with a total length of 309 miles in Balasore district. Except 40 miles; the roads were unmetalled and many of them were fair weather road which were impassable for cart traffic even during the rains. In the north the district were specially subject to high floods of Subarnarekha. In June of 1898 The Kamarda-Baliapal-Basta; Kamarda-Jaleswar and Singla-Nangleswar Road were breached in numerous places due to heavy flood. Taking the bridges into account it was rendered unsafe for traffic. There was another important road named as Panchapara-Haldipada Road that connected Balasore, Mitrapur and Remuna. From Gopinathpur to Soro and Anatapur to Soro roads were opened for cart traffic by the District Board. The Jamjhari market road was stretched to Basudebpur which meet the old salt road, and it was extended up to Bhadrak. The most important trade route in the district was Bhadrak-Chandbali road. The commodities of the district were enrouted to Chandbali port for export either via Ruknadeipur or the Basudebpur.[88]

In addition to it, there were 67 village road with a total length of 200 miles under Balasore sadar and Bhadrak local boards.[89] The income and expenditure on roads reveals the intention of Government for improvement of transport and communication which was neglected before. But road ceases were a real burden on the part of poor peasants and peasants were exploited by the zamindars; who collected more than once from peasants. By 11th January 1873, 443 miles of roads were constructed and repaired by the Government of Orissa. Simultaneously road cess was increased for construction of town and village roads and peasants suffered a lot under the Road Cess Act. Towards the year 1884-85 the

86. Report on the Khurda Settlement of 1897-98, Cuttack, pp. 24-25.
87. *Maddox Report*, Vol. I, p. 27.
88. *Maddox Report*, Vol. I, p. 29.
89. *Ibid.*

amount of roads cess was collected in Orissa was Rs. 1,60,000.[90] In Cuttack alone Rs. 76,747 were collected by 1888-89 and the expenditure was around Rs. 76,847. But the Commissioner of the Orissa commented that road cess was not unpopular in Orissa.[91] The Government also collected voluntary cess from tribals to constructed roads in Khondmals in the year 1879-80. It was a good practice that the Government followed during the 19th century. The Sambalpur Medinapur service track opened in the year 1842, passed through Keonjhar Tributary Mahal. This link allowed mercantile traffic straight from Calcutta to the Garjat states of Orissa.[92] Thus isolation of Orissa was broken and inaccessibility of communication to different parts were made easy. Had these been done earlier, the Orissa famine would not have claimed lakhs of lives. This development facilitated trade and commerce within and outside Orissa.[93]

Towards the end of the period under study Orissa had 10 metalled roads to her credit. The details of metalled road in Orissa during 19th century depicted in the table given below :

TABLE 7.12

NAMES OF METALLED ROADS IN ORISSA TOWARDS THE END OF THE 19TH CENTURY

Sl No.	*Name of the metalled road*
1.	Grand Trunk Road
2.	Sambalpur-Cuttack Road
3.	Ganjam Road
4.	Keonjhar Road
5.	Machagaon Road
6.	Taldanda Road
7.	Chandbali Road
8.	Jajpur Road
9.	Sambalpur-Balangir Road
10.	Sambalpur-Raipur Road

Source : N.N. Banerjee, Report on the Agriculture of the District of Cuttack, p. 143.

Numerous unmetalled road were also constructed to make link with towns and villages of Orissa. In Cuttack alone in the year 1876 the following roads were constructed.

90. *U.D.*, 23 January 1871, II January 1873 and 9 May 1891.
91. W.W. Hunter, *op.cit.*, Vol. XVIII, p. 174; *RAB*, 1888-89 (Cal-1889).
92. Final Report on the Survey and Settlement of Keonjhar State, p. 24.
93. *RAB*, 1879-80 (Calcutta, 1880), p. 34.
L.S.S.O'Malley, *BDG*, *Sambalpur*, (Calcutta 1909), pp. 160-162.

TABLE 7.13
ROADS AT CUTTACK

Class of roads	*Length in miles*
First class roads	72 miles
Second class roads	173 miles
Third class roads	336 miles

Source : W.W. Hunter, *op.cit.*, Vol. CVIII, p.174.

Development was the immediate necessity to protect the country from frequent occurrence of famines and scarcities. Britishers became interested in the development of these roads for the purpose of commercial prosperity of the company. But real attention of the Government to road construction and repair was started after the great famine of 1866.

Waterways

As discussed earlier, the surface transport of Orissa was totally inadequte before the Great Famine of 1866. Not only surface transport was inadequate, but also the water communication was also below the average status.

> "In Orissa the loss of life had been principally due to the great difficulty of getting food into the province, there being at that time few roads and those bad and no safe ports."[94]

By the time the famine broke out, there were no ports of any significance in Orissa. But in the times of emergency or any bad weather, the ports of less importance were utilized. Hence it was generally inaccessible to the ordinary course of trade and was often found to have been cut off from the outside world.[95]

Before 1866, the ports in Orissa never drew the attention of the Government. After the famine, the ports were improved, some new ports were also opened, and an attempt was made to improve the inland communication.

The Mahanadi was the main channel of communication in the period under study. Transportation by boat was common an it was less costly compared to other transport facilities. The river was navigable as far as Sambalpur in the rainy season and for sometime after. The journey from Sambalpur to Cuttack downward took 5 days and upward journey from Cuttack to Sambalpur took about 18 days.[96]

94. John Beames, *Memories of a Bengal Civilian*, (New Delhi, 1979), p. 231.
95. G.C. Patnaik, *The Famine and Some Aspects of the British Economic Policy in Orissa, 1866-1905*, (Cuttack, 1980), p. 176.
96. P. Mukherjee, *op.cit.*, p. 30.

The best water ways were neglected in the first part of the 19th century. The long neglect of Maratha and English rules again destroyed the possibilities of development of best ports at the mouths of many rivers in the coastal area. There was no good port in the practical sense of the term except, Balasore port.[97]

The False Point, at the mouth of river Mahanadi, an important port of Cuttack, was the best harbour on the whole coast of India between Hooghly and Bombay. It was opened to traffic in 1860. But the horrors of the famine of 1866 turned the eyes of the authorities towards the improvement of the harbour because there was no good communication between the port and the hinter land. The harbour was surveyed and deepened and the channels were buoyed. The work of the Kendrapara canal was speeded up to reach the fidal waters in direct communication with False Point and throughout the year the ports remained open for carrying out trade and commerce of Orissa.[98]

There were many ports in the district of Balasore such as Balasore, Dhamra, Churamani, Sartha, Subarnarekha and Lychunpore. All these declared ports in 1858 but were of no use except Balasore and Subarnarekha. After the famine these ports drew the attention of the Government. Chandbali was declared a port and was named after Ravenshaw. This port was opened in 1872.[99] Also the port of Puri drew the attention of the Government after the famine. The ports of Puri were– Puri, Devee, Sahandu, Mettacooah, Futtypore and Nundla. These ports were in better position during the period under study but due to lack of proper supervision and maintenance they were turned to be road-stead. During the north-west monsoon, these ports did not allow vessels.[100] Though Orissa had so many ports, yet these were not properly used in the time of need, in 1866.

After mishap of 1866, all ports received proper attention of Government. But False Point, due to its strategical importance, received greatest care. Table 7.14 showing the sum granted for the improvement of Orissa ports in 1874.

The False Point became the busiest port of Orissa in the latter part of the 19th century. The following statement gives a clear picture about the increase of import and export trade at False Point.

---

97. N.K. Jit, The Agrarian Life and Economy of Orissa; pp.100-101
98. *U.D.*, Part-IV, 3 July 1869, No. 27.
99. *GAROD*, 1881-82, (Calcutta, 1882) pp. 22-24; OFC 1866, Vol. I, Part-II, Pr. 30.
100. J. Beames, Commissioner, Cuttack to Government of Bengal, No. 600, July 18, 1877, *GAROD*, 1877-78.

TABLE 7.14

SUMS GRANTED TO IMPROVE THE PORTS OF ORISSA

Name of Ports	*Sum granted in Rs.*
False Point	2,89,000
Balasore	30,000
Dhamra and Chandbali	1,00,000
Puri	20,000

Source : GAROD 1874-1875 (Calcutta, 1874), pp. 150-151.

TABLE 7.15

THE DETAILED INCREASED OF IMPORT AND EXPORT TRADE AT FALSE POINT

Year	*No. of Vessels*	*Tonnage*	*Value of Import Rs.*	*Value of Export Rs.*	*Total*
1860-61	4	2,830	-	67,590	-
1861-62	10	7,756	-	2,46,570	-
1862-63	6	4,016	-	1,78,020	-
1863-64	16	8,681	3,30,930	1,88,280	5,19,210
1870-71	105	52,744	1,32,355	6,69,757	8,02,112
1871-72	86	72,525	9,00,133	4,75,700	13,75,838
1872-73	75	69,999	8,49,547	8,21,429	16,70,976
1873-74	106	86,597	11,42,893	10,60,432	22,03,325
1874-75	110	1,18,375	9,11,659	18,00,471	27,12,130
1875-76	133	1,57,468	13,80,653	12,71,575	26,52,328
1876-77	166	1,49,515	11,88,073	29,06,105	49,40,178
1877-78	202	1,40,952	36,04,023	36,73,016	72,77,039
1878-79	179	1,38,676	19,28,230	28,28,182	42,66,412

Source : GAROD, 1878-79, p. 20.

So the portal trade in Orissa increased day by day. The number of vessels visiting different ports of Orissa increased which testified its flourishing trades. The following statistics gives clear picture of portal communication in Balasore port.

TABLE 7.16

VESSELS VISITING PORTS OF BALASORE

Year	*No. of Vessels*
1869-70	232
1870-71	277
1871-72	275
1872-73	345
1873-74	405
1874-75	387

Source : BRP, Nov. 1875, RAC, 1874-75.

The tonnage of vessels coming to Puri increased stood as 10,553 in 1874-75 against 1,356 in 1868-69. Towards the second half of the 19th century foreign trade became more active. The British Indian Steam Co. and French ships from Mauritius made Orissan ports as their centre for business activities. These trade had terrible impact on the economic development of the Orissan people. The value of import of foreign goods in 1881-82 was Rs. 66,99,026 and the value of export was Rs. 68,42,784. The value of import and export in the ports of Orissa was Rs. 1,19,73,792 in the year 1884-85 against the last years figure of Rs. 1,14,59,770.[101]

In Orissa the rise in exports was closely followed by the rise in imports. In 1873-74 and 1874-75 the export trade of Orissa received a boost owing to sudden demand for rice on account of famine in Bengal. Consequently there was a rise in the value of exports which was followed by a rise in the value of imports. Throughout the later period also the rise in imports kept pace with the rise in exports. The conclusion from the above statement comes to the point that the export surplus or what was called the drain of wealth to England was not remarkable in Orissa as it was for India in general.[102]

The export trade of the province during the 19th century consisted mainly of food stuffs and other agricultural products; skin and hides, oil seeds, jute, timber, jungle products such as lac wax, tusser, feather, coconuts and dried fish and its imports consisted in manufacturers such as: cotton piece goods, salt, gunny bags, kerosine oil, sugar, glassware, liquors, spices, fancy goods, potatoes, tabacoo and metals like lead, copper, zinc, gold and silver. The export of food grains, on the other hand, put heavy pressure on the purchasing power of the poor people and reduced the internal consumption. William Hunter observed that even in normal years one-fifth of the total population of forty million people of India went through life on insufficient food. And the rise of prices was felt as a great hardship to the large population of shop-keepers and Government employees in Cuttack town also.[103]

The small cultivators received no benefit because they did not have much to sell. They sold their product either to money-lender or rice-traders at a cheap rate during the harvesting season. The province of Orissa received some commercial advantage from the increased export of food grains. The export helped to keep up the total value of mercandise and enabled the province to acquire annual exchange balance to meet her obligations.

101. *GAROD*, 1894-95-96, Pr. 103.
102. R.C. Dutt, *The Economic History of India*, Vol. II, pp. 252-253.
103. *GAROD*, 1877-78.

With the rise of prices the conditions of some classes of agriculturists changed for the better. The substantial cultivators, and the rich land owner, were benefitted greatly. They could easily dispose of their product and thereby reaped the benefit of high prices as the communications developed. The condition of the village labourers improved because they received wages in kind.

The increase of export of food grains led to the automatic extension of cultivation. Owing to rising prices and increasing export of rice land was diverted from other crops to the cultivation of paddy. The rise in prices also directly benefited the cultivation classes who paid their rent in cash.[104]

The extension of railway in Orissa contributed much to the decline of sea-brone trade and communication. Efforts were made to make the rivers navigable. But rocky and narrow river beds made it impossible and unsafe. The riverine trade was there between coastal belt and Garjats through Mahanadi and Brahmani rivers.[105] But it was insignificant in Orissa. Alone Cuttack had 527 miles of rivers which provided means of communication.

Railways

The transport and efficient means of communication were regarded as the best ways for prevention of famines. In Orissa these methods were adopted in haste and hence proved unfruitful. The old means of communication through canals, rivers and muddy roads were given paramount importance in Orissa. The impact of western civilization and fruits of Industrial Revolution such as Railways and modern science did not reach at the people of Orissa compared to other states of India.[106] The Government of Bengal was not in favour to construct railways in Orissa. Appeals by the people for railways in 1878 was turned down by Lt. Governor with the plea of costly ventures (20 lakhs of rupees) and heavy bridge works would involve huge coast, that's why railways was not possible in Orissa.[107] The Utkal Sabha under the leadership of Late M.S. Das and Late G.S, Roy, editor of Utkal Dipika mobilised public opinion in favour of construction of railway lines in Orissa.[108]

The first railway line opened in the World (in Great Britain) carrying out public passengers on September 1825. The earliest proposal to start

---

104. *Madox Report*, Vol. I, p. 138.
105. L.S.S.O'Malley, *BDG, Sambalpur*, pp.161-162.
106. G.C. Mishra, *Orissar Vikashare Patra, Patrikar Prabhava* (Oriya) (Cuttack, 1979), p. 129.
107. *U.D.* Part-XIII, 23 March 1878, No. 12.
108. *U.D.* No. 9, February 28, 1880.

railways in India seems to have been made in 1831-32[109] Joseph Locke in 1841 discussed the prospects of railways from Calcutta to Delhi, on the plea of population, pilgrims, traffic in goods, transmission of troops and overall to overcome the difficulties of communication. The first railway line running from Bombay to Thana was opened to traffic on 16th April 1853, the first part of the East Indian Railway Calcutta to Raniganj was completed in 1858 and the line from Madras to Arkonam in 1856.[110] By 1869 India had 4,255 miles of railway lines worth of Rs. 80 crores.[111] The following table depicts the railway mileage in India.[112]

TABLE 7.17

GROWTH OF RAILWAYS IN INDIA FROM 1853 TO 1901

Year	*Mileage*
1853	20
1863	2550
1873	5694
1883	10828
1893	18510
1900	24760
1901	25373

Though greater expansions of railway was possible in India, the claim of Orissa for it was put in different track. In Cuttack, Puri and Balasore the committees were formed to pressurise the Government for railway lines in Orissa. The proposals were also placed before the Government for the construction of railway lines. The committees also suggested that new railway lines should stretched from Raniganj to Puri when the Government were thinking to stretch if from Sambalpur to Cuttack.[113] The Government decision was criticised by the people for its silence on many occasions.[114] The Government clearly declared that irrigational canals were mostly suited to Orissa than railways.[115] However, with much controversy the Government had finally decided to open railway lines from Howrah to Puri. The construction work was expedited and finally it was ready for traffic by April 1900.[116] In March 31, 1900 the Kuakhai

109. G. Kaushal, *Economic History of India (1757-1966)*, p. 385.
110. R.C. Dutt, *India in the Victorian Age*, p. 132.
111. P.N. Chopra, Puri and Das, *op.cit.*, pp. 196-200.
112. R.C. Dutt, *op.cit.*, p. 401.
113. *U.D.*, No. 33, August, 13, 1881.
114. *U.D.*, No. 9, Feburary 28, 1880.
115. *Ibid.*, No. 12, March 23, 1878.
116. *Ibid.*, No. 18, May 5, 1900; *GAROD*, 1899-1900, p. 31.

bridge was completed which started from December 26, 1876 at a cost of Rs. 14,51,000. A cost of Rs. 26,88,200 was spent for the construction of Mahanadi bridge which was completed within two years. The Kathjori bridge was completed within 3 years at the cost of Rs. 13,55,000. The Birupa bridge at an estimated cost of Rs. 6,18,550 was completed within 2 years.[117] Before the inauguration of this line the East Coast Railway line linked Orissa with Madras in the year 1897.[118] The East-Coast Railways connects Calcutta and Madras via Balasore and Cuttack greatly facilitated rice trade between Orissa and Madras. Thus construction of railway line provided a link between Orissa and other states which was the long awaited claim of the people of Orissa. If it was constructed before 30 years ago, the famine of 1866 and other natural calamities would not have claimed deaths in lakhs owing to lack of transport and communication. By 1904 a railway line was opened connecting Baripada (the principal town of the tributary state of Mayurbhanj) with Rupsa. This was constructed by the Maharaja of Mayurbhanj by the help of Bengal-Nagpur Railway Company.[119] The development of railway towards the last part of 19th century revolutionised the means of transport, trade and commerce. Although it was responsible for the decline of many indigenous industries including salt industry and also responsible for the decline of sea-borne trade. It broke down the static character of the economy and made the people mobile and an era of new awakening in Orissa was dawned.

Irrigation was necessary of Orissa first but it was not a sufficient weapon to fight with famines without an efficient system of communication. Railway accelerated the food supply from one corner to another than any other means of communication. However, irrigation stands first to protect the people from famines and scarcities. The controversy between irrigation and railways created a deep gap in development in Orissa. But both were neglected and Orissa became a backward province in this respect to other states of India.

The British colonial policy was very much negligent to the economic prosperity of the people of Orissa. The Government was no ready to spend anything from the exchequer for the welfare of the people. The Orissa Famine of 1866 alarmed the Government for which it was forced to forget the old age traditional and defective administration. The Government switched over to a benevolent administration trying to provide

---

117. *Ibid.*
118. *GAROD*, 1896-97, 1897-98, p. 2.
119. Quinquinial Administration Report of the Orissa Division from 1900-1901 to 1904-5, p. 26.
Surendra Mohanty, *Satabdir Surya* (Oriya), (Cuttack 1970), p. 579.

all possible facilities to the people. According to the recommendations of the Famine Commission the Government initiated Orissa Canal Projects, paid attention towards the maintenance of embankments, control of flood water and undertook protective measures for preventing drought and inundation.

On the whole the famine taught a good lesson to the Government by which they forced to change their traditional monopolistic attitude towards Orissa. The Famine Code was established as a guideline to insure the life of the people against famine in Orissa.

Development of irrigation facility in Orissa however helped a lot to alleviate the distress condition of agriculture and construction of embankments in Orissa saved the crop fields and human locality from floods and inundations. Frequent occurrence of famine during the period under study compelled the cultivators to maintain a gloomy state of unstable economic life. There was also a remarkable improvement in the sea borne trade due to the repair and development of portal communication in Orissa.

Thus irrigation, embankments, roads, ports, railways and navigable canals which were constructed in the later part of the 19th century provided links to Orissa with outside world. Transport and communication which was suppressed in bottleneck manner was partially improved and famines and other natural calamities were checked by an improved distribution system of food grains.

8

Conclusion

In the 19th century Orissa suffered most from the evils of natural calamities like floods, cyclones and famines. The gravity of the situation increased due to the total negligence of the official machinery or the Government or by improper decisions taken by the administrator, who lacked the knowledge about technical skills.

The following were some of the factors which were responsible for intensifying the damages caused by natural calamities.

(1) Improper maintenance of the existing systems like canals, drains, flood banks, roads etc.
(2) Ignoring design structures to withstand heavy gales in areas which were prone to cyclone.
(3) Not providing green belt along the sea shore to prevent the intensity of heavy gales.
(4) Allowing people to enter and live in flood zones. The areas should be divided into zones of occasional floods and frequent floods. People should not be allowed to enter frequent flood zones. This important aspect was totally overlooked by the British authority.
(5) Lack of good network for forecasting natural calamities.
(6) Due to littoral drift, sand bars from at the river confluence points with the sea. These prevent free flow of river water into sea causing heavy silting. The river beds therefore rise and thus their carrying capacities are reduced. This causes great havoc.

CAUSES OF NATURAL CALAMITIES IN ORISSA

Natural Causes of Orissa Famines

The natural causes of Orissa famines included failure of the monsoon, occurrence of floods, cyclones and the most primary of the causes usually being failure of monsoon. The other factors were less important.

There had been 36 floods in all, 18 between 1803-1866 and 18 between 1867-1928 and of these 14 were floods of considerable magnitude in the rivers of Orissa followed by failure of or damage to crop over a large area of which 8 were in the first series of years and 6 in the second. Something worthy of the name of flood therefore occurred once in every 3½ years and a flood caused serious damage to crop once in every 9 years. The most disastrous type of flood was that in which after the crops had been badly damaged by immersion, the rains ceased prematurely early and drought completed their destruction over wide areas[1]. Droughts in Orissa were much more frequent and much more destructive to crops on the whole than floods. On an averaged it is seen that during the period under study one year in five it was a year of drought.[2] To eradicate such situations, as has already been indicated above, provides were made in the Bengal Famine Code in 1908 to relieve people in times of floods in same way as during famines.[3]

Animal pests such as locusts were not responsible for causing any famine in Orissa during the 19th century. But sometimes they intensified the suffering.

The cyclones did immense damage during the period under study to life and property and caused total destruction of crop over wide areas and as an effect of the salt wave for some years huge areas of land had been put out of action.[4] But it did not lead to mass scale scarcity in the region. Famines due to above cause could be foreseen but sufficient protective measures could not be adopted to protect the people of Orissa from such perils.

Administrative Causes of Orissa Famines

The administration of British-Orissa was totally defective. There was not a go between the Government officials and the people. So it greatly affected the administration of famine relief. Besides, all the relief officers were foreigners. Most of them were ignorant of the language of the people and they had no knowledge of either the material conditions of the people or the economic status of the province. With a few exceptions like T.E. Ravenshaw, the Commissioner and the Lt. Governor of Bengal, Sir Cecil Beadon, all were totally unable or unwilling to read the clear signs of the times and their inability or unwillingness to do so was the prime, causes of the oweful mortality in Orissa famine of 1866. They looked at famine

1. Government of Bihar and Orissa, Deposit, Revenue Department File No. IVF-21/1929, March 1930.
2. *Ibid.*
3. Famine Proceedings No. 5, September 1908, quoted in H.S. Srivastav, *op.cit.*, p. 326.
4. Government of Bihar and Orissa, Deposit, *op.cit.*

matters from the point of the administration and finance and not from the point of saving human lives. It was therefore, inevitable that suffering increased, relief measures were started late, rations lowered, and coercion was used too collect land revenue.[5] The famine of 1865-66 greatly revealed the weakness of the administration and the neglect of officers. The same thing was also repeated in the famine of Tributary States of Orissa in 1889 and in the Ganjam famine of 1888-89. The people suffered much under the alien Government due to their apathy towards the people.

Economic Factors behind Orissan Famines

Frequent occurrence of natural calamities in Orissa left the people in impoverished conditions. Towards the end of 19th century, poverty had grown to its highest extent.

As the people very often go without savings, when crop fail within any one area, they are unable to buy food from neighbouring provinces rich in harvest.[6] Thus famines become inevitable which lead to permanent property of people.

In the 19th century was enough rain and enough food in Orissa, but large exports made people go without resources and savings. Lack of purchasing power and resourcelessness of people led to poverty and thereafter too severe famines. The famine of 1865-66 bears testimony to the above statement. The severe cyclone and storm wave of 1876 in East Bengal could not bring any distress to the people. In the year of distress they bought shiploards of rice out of their own savings. There was no general famine and no large relief operations were needed.[7] But it was reverse in Orissa during the period under study. High rent collection and increasing land revenue demanded from time to time in Orissa made the people resourceless.

Moreover frequent variations in rainfall causing natural calamities broke down the saving capacity of the people and made money-lending an integral part of the agrarian society.[8] The British policy of exploitation of revenue aggravated the inherited bankruptcy of the peasantry. Orissa agriculture suffered from various handicaps like insufficient irrigation facility, funds to invest in agriculture and scientific methods to check the diminishing productiveness of the soil.[9]

Rapid growth of population and relative decrease in cultivable land, frequent natural calamities leading to crop failure and indebtedness,

5. H.S. Srivastav, *op.cit.*, p. 327.
6. R.C. Dutt, *The Economic History of India*, Vol. II, pp. v-vi.
7. *Ibid.*
8. *Maddox Report*, Vol. I, p. 132.
9. N.N. Banerjee, *Report of the Agricultural districts of Cuttack*, p. 36.

maximisation of revenue and large scale unemployment after the decline of village based industries forced the Orissa people to migrate to other places.[10]

The tyranny and oppression of the zamindars could not be overlooked. They charged rent even during famines and imposed much upon the tenants. The Orissa famine of 1866 was aggravated to unprecedented extent due to gross negligence of the Government, selfishness of the zamindars and the greediness of *mahajans*. The sufferings were so great that the *paiks* of Khurda, after a lapse of nearly 40 years, rose again in revolt. Since this insurrection occurred in the 9th regnal year of Divyasinghadev, the king of Puri (1866), it is termed as "Naanka Fituri."[11]

The real causes for Orissa's poverty were alien rule, ruin of Orissan industries, imposition of excess revenue and heavy taxation and the defective administrative system which had given power to the money-lender. The agrarian economy of Orissa was further exploited by the foreign rule with the introduction of salt monopoly. The native people of Orissa were not allowed to collect their own salt from her vast sea coast.[12]

Due to the lack of communication facilities, Orissa suffered most in the famine of 1866, than any other province. Most of the people died due to want of food which was not supplied in time because of handicapped communication system. The Government of India improved communication facilities in Orissa only after the great famine. Roads and railways together revolutionised the methods of transport, since the famine of 1866, much had been done to prevent the recurrence of a similar calamity. Harbours, canals and regular steam communication with Calcutta had broken in upon the isolation of Orissa.[13] The system of canals in coastal Orissa was first projected in 1877 and was opened in 1886. The main argument advanced in its favour was the complete isolation of the province of Orissa, there being no communication with Calcutta either by rail or river. The trade of the province was carried out only by the sea route, attended with much difficulties and expenses. It served a useful purpose, being the only means by which grain could be brought into Orissa in time of scarcity. With the advent of the Bengal-Nagput Railway its usefulness came to an end.[14] All these communication facilities developed as a protective measures against natural calamities to protect

10. N.K. Jit, *The Agrarian Life and Economy of Orissa*, p. 235.
11. Naank Fituri, An article by P.K. Mishra in *Orissa Review*, Ratha Yatra Special, June 1979, Vol. XXXV, No. 11.
12. F.M. Senapati, *Fakir Mohan Granthavali* (Oriya), pp. 642-43.
13. *Statistical Account of Bengal*, Vol. XVIII, Calcutta, p. 148.
14. Report on the Maritime Trade of Orissa for the year 1940-41, Cuttack 1941, p. 25.

the affected people only after end of 19th century which was subsequently benefited in the natural calamities of 20th century.

Social Factors

The most important social factors which increased and intensified the sufferings in times of famines were caste, a false sense of respectability, purda and illiteracy.[15]

At the time of great Orissa famine (1865-66) the recipients of relied (food) were debarred from the society.[16] The caste feeling was so strict that even some people died without seeking food at all. The higher caste people in fear of loosing caste did not attain the poor houses and free kitchens. The people of Orissa suffered most from natural calamities due to their ignorance and lack of awareness among them about Government functioning.

Famine Relief Policy of the British

The period under study is divided into two phases, first from 1803 to 1857 and second from 1858 to 1900. In the first phase there was not any systematic policy adopted by the East India Company, but in the second, there were adopted some systematic policies like formulation of famine codes and the protective measures.

First Phase (1803-1857)

In the first phase near about twenty natural calamities visited Orissa. During the time of natural calamities, the East India Company marked the rejection of active intervention to alleviate the distressed condition. Being influenced by Malthas ideas the Company's Government adopted the policy of non-intervention in the first half of the 19th century in framing any policy to mitigate the sufferings of the million from natural calamities.

Under the East India Company, the Government had granted remission and suspension of revenue several times under the head of natural calamities. But it was not sufficient to mitigate the scarcity condition of the people. According to Henry Rickets there was favoured no sympathetic treatment to the zamindars in time of natural calamities from which Orissa suffered frequently. He also regretted that remissions of revenue much depended on the personal attitude of the collectors and due to the absence of any systematic enquiries the people suffered much at the time of natural calamities. At that time inundations were more common and in general more destructive than droughts but no systematic preventive measures were adopted to prevent the people from such perilous disease.

---

15. H.S. Srivastav, *op.cit.*, p. 335.
16. John Boulton (translated), *op.cit.*, p. 97.

Another major obstacle for which the people of Orissa suffered most was the non-interference policy with trade and the restrucitions on the food grains at the time of famine. The rice dealers also sometimes hoarded the commodity and created artificial scarcity to get more profit. The long neglect policy of the alien rule was exposed at the time of great Orissa famine of 1866 and it was supposed to be the greatest disaster that had ever visited India.

Second Phase (1858-1900)

The Government assumed full responsibility in 1860-61 to provide work to the able bodied and promised to double the private subscriptions raised in India for gratuitous relief. The establishment and organization of poor houses was the most important measure adopted during the period.[17]

In this regard Colonel Barid Smith's (appointed by Lord Canning to enquire into the causes and extent of the famine of 1860) suggestions were not followed by the Government, for which it failed to adopt sympathetic policies towards the famine stricken people of Orissa in 1866 and still worse, the food grains were provided to the people too late when a lot had already died out of hunger.

The famine Commission presided over by Sir George Campbell to enquire into the famine of 1866 made certain recommendation regarding the measures to be adopted for prevention of famine in future. He emphasized upon the development of communication system and for construction of protective embankments and canals for irrigation. On the view of Commission's suggestion, measures were taken in Orissa for preventing the recurrence of such type of calamities. Communication systems for which Orissa lagged behind were improved, by the provision of access to see at the False Point and the Dhamra river.

The report of the Famine Commission of 1880 made it clear that in case of bad harvest caused by drought rent remission to the ryots should be granted.[18] This suggestion was accepted by the Government and it was decided to classify agricultural lands and to maintain statistics of harvest periodically, and to inform the ryots about rent remissions. This was the first step to protect the ryots from illegal evictions from their holdings on the zamindars.[19]

---

17. H.S. Srivastav, *op.cit.*, p. 336.
18. Revenue and Agriculture Department, Revenue Branch, Proceeding No. 53, Extract from the proceeding of the Government of India, Revenue and Agriculture Department, 12 October 1882.
19. *BAR*, 1872-73, p. 27.

The Famine Commission issued a set of rules on June 9, 1883 to administer the famine relief in India. It divided guidelines that the Government should not interfere in any individual case of distress and only keep a vigile eye on adverse conditions. It also instructed to the local officers to help the destitutes and provide work to the agricultural labourers near their village.[20]

On the 17th March 1892, the Government declared some modification in the famine policy. It divided relief works into civil agency and professional agency works. The former was placed under district authority and the latter under public works department. The workers were classified into four classes: (*a*) able-bodied persons accustomed to labour with skill, (*b*) able-bodied persons but not skilled, (*c*) able-bodied persons but to accustomed to hard labour, (*d*) persons not able-bodied but fit for light employment.[21] The (*a*) and (*b*) received full wage. But the authority would give the wage to the (*c*) and (*d*) judging the degree of calamity. Agricultural works were carried out at the time of famine. The famine relief administration (Famine Code) was brought to a crucial test in the famines of 1896-97. The code put emphasis on employment by engaging more people in the railway earth work, by advances of Government in accordance with the Agricultural Loans Act, 1884, through medical aid, agricultural banks and through remission of rents during the years of distress.[22] In accordance with the laws many were engaged in the railway work which was in rapid progress and many were employed in the district board work.[23] During the time of 1896 famine, the people suffered due to the measures taken according to the Famine Code.

The Famine Commission of 1898 was set up after the famine of 1896-97 to bring some latest modifications. At last the Famine Commission of 1901 was set up after the famine of 1899-1900.

Land Revenue and Natural Calamities

According to Colonel Barid Smith an oppressive revenue demand was the direct cause of famines in India.[24] Though the Indian famines were caused by failure of rain, their frequency and intensity was due to the

20. Resolution of the Government of India regarding Famine Code and other matters pertaining to famine administration, Department of Revenue and Agriculture, Simla, 1892, pp. 2-9.
21. Resolution of Government of India regarding the Famine Code and other matters pertaining to the famine administration, Simla 1882, p. 27.
22. *RIF*, 1901, Pr. 8, p. 2.
23. Selection of Papers (Famine), Vol. II, p. 207, Collector of Puri to Secretary Government of Bengal, D.O. letter, Nov. 17, 1896.
24. R.C. Dutt, *op.cit.*, p. 189.

chronic poverty of the cultivators caused by overassessment of the land revenue.[25] Smith also recommended a permanent settlement of the land revenue as a protective measure against the worst effects of future famines which would also increase the general revenue of the country with the general prosperity of the people.[26]

The East India Company promptly introduced temporary settlements from 1804 to 1837 in Orissa because land revenue was a major share of Company's total revenue in Orissa. It brought untold misery and suffering to the people because the concerned officers were interested to get more *jama* for the advantage of the company without the effects of short term settlements. In 1837, the first 30 years settlements became effective but failed to provide protection to poor tenants and cultivators from the oppression of the greedy zamindars. Before the expiry of the 30 years settlement in 1867 many of the land holders had allowed their cultivable lands to fall barren so that their *jama* would not enhance. It came out as one of the primary causes of the famine of 1866. So this settlement was extended for another 30 years by which the settlement could help the people to recover for some extent from the calamity of season.

The peasants suffered most due to the defective land revenue system. The permanently settled estates of Orissa differed from the temporarily settled estates in many respects besides that of fixity of revenue.[27] The landlords in permanently settled estates oppressed the peasants in various ways. In temporarily settled estates, there were revisions of settlements and the revenue demanded was often increased from time to time. The Bengal Tenancy Act of 1885 was introduced in Orissa to improve the condition of tenants and protect the tenants from illegal cesses by the landholders.

Communication and Natural Calamities

In the beginning of the British rule, construction of roads, canals, bridges and embankments was totally neglected, Baird Smith put emphasis on extension and completion of irrigation works and of roads and communications as remedial measures against natural calamities. In this regard orders were despatched by Lord Canning too all the provincial Governments for their careful consideration.[28] But they did not give much importance on it. The great Orissa famine of 1866 put emphasis on the Government not to neglect them any more but to pay greater attention to protect Orissa from such disastrous natural calamity.

The measures to fight against natural calamities were undertaken

25. H.S. Srivastav, *op.cit.*, p. 352.
26. R.C. Dutt, *op.cit.*, p. 190.
27. L.S.S. O' Malley, *BDG*, *Cuttack*, p. 185.
28. R.C Dutt, *op.cit.*, Vol. II, p. 191.

with greater zeal in the real sense of the term only in the latter part of the 19th century.

The Orissa coast canal was opened for traffic partly in 1885 and fully in 1897, connecting the river Hoogly at Goenkhali, 45 miles from Calcutta with the Matai and Charbatia. It helped the development of trade and commerce which passed through navigable water ways. The coast canal which was meant only for navigation to help small traders and businessmen to expand their concerns came to a vain with the opening of railways.

The introduction of railway was one of the important factors for the well being of the country. The railways greatly protected the masses from the scarcity of food material at the time of famines. The Famine Commission of 1880 put emphasis "that measures may be adopted for giving India direct protection from famine arising from drought."[29] So the railways helped a lot at the time of famine to transport commodities to the scarcity places immediately. But Orissa saw the opening of railways towards the latter part of the 19th century. The East Coast Railways to Puri was opened for traffic on 1 February 1897. The Bengal-Nagpur Railway service started in 1899. By 1904 a railway line connecting Baripada with Rupsa station of the Bengal-Nagpur railway was opened. All these developments helped to break the geographical isolation of Orissa and opened traffic with neighbouring provinces.

Lack of good ports on the coastal belt of Orissa was one of the causes of the famine of 1866. The existing ports were out of order in the rainy season. So the steamers could not land cargoes on the surf beaten shore except in such small quantities as sea boats could carry. Due to the non-availability of good ports, in Orissa, the rice could not be imported on a large scale in order to provide relief to the famine stricken people. At the time of great famine of 1866, the ports of Orissa were hopelessly in bad condition. After the famine, they drew the attention of the Government. The horrors of the famine brought home to the authorities the necessity of improving these harbours, which were surveyed and deepended and the channels were buoyed. The work on the Kendrapara canal was undertaken to reach the tidal waters in direct communication with False Point at the shore of Bay of Bengal. Before this work, no vessel could approach the coast due to summer monsoon and after the improvements the port remained open throughout the year.[30] The works of the ports of Balasore and Puri were also taken into hand. But the alien rule did not give adequate attention for them which they truly required. The development of roads, coast canal, ports and railway not only broke Orissa's isolation from the outside world but also facilitated

29. *IFC*, 1880, Part-II, p. 150.
30. *U.D.*, 3 July 1869.

trade and commerce by providing mobility of the people to different places at the time of natural calamities to get employment.

Irrigation and Natural Calamities

Irrigation is one of the potent factors to control floods and droughts. Colonel Baird Smith's first report put emphasis on completion of irrigation works as a protective measure against famines.[31] The Famine Commission of 1866 put emphasis on irrigation facility to the people of Orissa. The suggestion of Famine Commission was given importance by the Bengal Government which decided to take up irrigation facility through canals to protect the people of Orissa from twin evils of drought and inundation.

The crop fields of Orissa were frequently subject to destruction due to natural calamities. At last with the advice of Arthur Cotton, the East India Company was tempted to build a canal in Orissa to deal with the flood waters of the Mahanadi and other rivers and to drive out the evils of drought. Though the project was started earlier in 1863, it failed to complete its objectives. At last the Government took over the work and completed the canal project in 1867-68. This project came out successful in providing irrigation, navigation and drainage system to protect the province from famines and floods.

The Famine Commission of 1880, also put emphasis on irrigation works to protect the country from the evils of famine arising out of drought.[32] The Famine Commission of 1898 also gave increased preference to irrigation works and recommended the active prosecution of new productive irrigation works, as energetically as may be consistent with true economy and ultimate efficiency even though this may involve a higher annual expenditure in the future than in the past.[33] It put emphasis on irrigation as one of the important protective works against famine. The Irrigation Commission of 1901 also put emphasis on large irrigation projects for each province.

Embankments and Natural Calamities

Embankments play an important role by affording a means of protection from inundation. Embankments are built at those places where river banks are low to guard against the spilling of water during flood and to prevent oceanic water from inundating the cultivable land and to control saline water for impregnation of salt in the winter season on the khalary lands. The coastal belt of Orissa which was prone to inundation during the period under study, was watered by a large number of rivers. In the

---

31. R.C. Dutt, *op.cit.*, p. 191.
32. *IFC*, 1880, Part-II, p. 150.
33. *Ibid.*, 1898, Pr. 577.

rainy season, the rivers rising with great intensity during flood caused serious loss to life, property and the crops.

Frequency of inundation forced the Muslim rulers to manage the embankments and for this they handed over the task to the landed proprietors for which remission in the revenue was allowed. Even the Maratha rulers, constructed embankments to protect crop from inundation. The zamindars lost their zeal to protect the embankments due to heavy demands of land revenue by the Maratha Government. With the advent of British in 1803, the Salt Agency was first to undertake the repair works of existing embankments and to construct new embankments and sluice gates for releasing flood waters and to prevent ocean water from causing damage to the coastal belt.[34] Till 1827 no serious attempt was made to keep the existing embankments in good working order. The engineers like Becher, Schultz, and Pennington were appointed by the Bengal Government in the same year to repair the worn out embankments and to supervise the work of new embankments where cement mortar and steel structures were used. After the devastating gale of 1831 in Orissa coast, they gave a proposal to the Bengal Government to construct dyke on the coastal bank from Balasore to Chilka to save the region from frequent inundation.[35] With their recommendation the responsibilities of the management of Orissa embankments were transferred to public works department.[36]

A.J.M. Mills, the then Commissioner of Orissa appealed to the Bengal Government to grant more money to construct more embankments and sluice gates in the Mughalbandi areas for some agrarian development. But adequate attention was not paid to the maintenance of existing embankments. Due to frequency of flood lack of maintenance the existing embankments were either abandoned or damaged.

There were embankments prior to 1867 but on the whole they were for the major portion of the period so small or insignificant that they might be said to have had little or no effect and might be considered as having been non-existant by comparison with those of the present day.[37]

The Bengal Government in 1867 appointed an embankment committee under the chairmanship of Ravenshaw, which submitted its report in 1868, requesting the Government of Bengal to spend huge amount for the protection of embankments in the Orissa province. By 1 April 1878, the Government was in possession of embankments affording

---

34. Balasore Salt Records, Mathew to Packenham, October 1828, pp. 60-62 (OSA).
35. Cuttack Salt Records, Stockwell to Hunter, 9 November 1831 (OSA).
36. L.S.S. O' Malley, *BDG*, *Balasore*, pp. 109-111.
37. Government of Bihar and Orissa, Deposit, Revenue Department, No. 9, March 1930.

protection against flood to 621,400 acres of cultivable land in Orissa.[38] Towards the end of the 19th century there were 804½ miles of protective works either fully or partially under the Government management. But these protective works were undertaken only after the great famine of 1866. Orissa suffered frequently from natural calamities due to lack of protective embankments.

Effects of the Natural Calamities

In the 19th century the Orissan economy was totally ruined by frequent visits of natural calamities. It reflected the failure of the agrarian economy of the province. It was mainly one of the greatest obstacles in the growth of agriculture in Orissa, which basically depended upon agriculture or employment allied to agriculture.

The natural calamities like famine invariably affected our indigenous craftmen, and especially the weavers, extremely and adversely. For example, before the English cotton piece goods came to Orissa, the weavers of Balasore were considered as affluent artisans but after 1833 they were reduced to abject poverty. The weavers like the day labourers were worst suffers with no saving and no means of livelihood of their own. Aftermath of famine was migration of weaving population towards Bengal and many of them became cripled to poor.

There is enough evidence to show that the population was badly affected by the famines which increased death by the spread of diseases in its wake. In the great Orissa famine of 1866 many people died because its intensity was aggravated by the flood of September 1866.

The migration of population increased in the 19th century because of rapid growth of population and comparatively decrease in cultivable land, frequent visits of natural calamities, frequent crop failure and indebtedness of peasants and large scale decline of indigenous industries.

Among the natural calamities the famine of 1866 (*Na anka durbhikya*) came out as a blessing in disguise. The famine became one of the prime factors to expose the defects of the administrative system of Bengal Government. After the famine, the Bengal Government followed lenient policy towards the Orissa province. The recommendations of the Famine Commission were given prime importance by the Bengal Government. Then the alien Government was forced to adopt remedial measures or protective works like construction of the Trunk Road, development of agriculture, railways, anicuts canal system and protective embankments etc. Education was also given importance. The modern system of administration was the result of this great famine. The Socio-economic

38. Report of the Committee appointed to enquire into the management of irrigation work in Madras, Orissa and Midnapore, p. 32.

and political consciousness developed among the people of Orissa only after the famine. This apathy of the Government towards economic condition of the people ceased and non-interference policy or Laissez-faire was replaced by a suitable policy decision.

The horrors of the natural calamities shocked the Orissa people and gave a change to the movement of national awakening. For the second time, the *paiks* of Khurda rose again in revolt after 40 years against evils of long neglected management, excessive taxation and unchecked oppression of the corrupt British officials, exploitations of zamindars and lack of sufficient relief measures. The long sufferings, economic exploitations and the revolutionary political movements were responsible to supply fresh strength and incentive to the Oriyas to demand for a separate province of their own.

Achievements and Failures of the British Policy

The important achievement of the British rule to fight against natural calamities like famines was the adoption of the famine relief policy which was codified in the famines codes. It became comprehensive after the successive famines commissions, with the introduction of communication systems like railways, ports, and roads etc., which became a major strength to help the distressed people at the time of natural calamities. It also checked the severity of famines and controlled the mortality. The recommendation of the Orissa Famine Commission of 1866 headed by George Campbell formed the foundation of definite famine policy by which Orissa was not subject to a famine of such an intensity during the period under study. The foundation of a Famine Insurance Fund and the newly created Indian People's Famine Trust also helped a lot for the relief of distressed people.

Afterall the British Policy cannot be congratulated in this regard. Orissa never gained anything from the provisions of the famine Code because the code made a distinction between 'Famine' and 'Scarcity' and thus whenever there was a failure of crops compelling people to live upon wild shrubs, it had been declared by the Government as a scarcity and not a famine, for in the case of a famine elaborate relief operations had to be undertaken. In the famine of 1943 when many people were dying in the districts of Ganjam and Balasore under acute famine and many people also died in Bengal, the famine code was not brought into operation. The protect the people from perilous disaster of floods and cyclones, no systematic policy was adopted. As regards flod control, nothing concrete was done. Except some minor irrigation works and embankments, the major aspects of flood control were not touched upon. Similarly, as far as cyclone was concerned, the systems set up by the British were not as responsive as warranted by the prevailing situation.

APPENDICES

APPENDIX - A

NATURAL CALAMITIES IN ORISSA IN 19TH CENTURY

Flood and Inundation* Famine or Scarcity** Cyclone***

Year	*Flood and Inundation*	*Famine or Scarcity*	*Cyclone*
1803-04	-	**	-
1804-05	*	-	-
1805-06	-	-	-
1806-07	*	**	-
1807-08	*	**	-
1808-09	*	-	-
1809-10	*	**	-
1810-11	-	-	-
1811-12	-	-	-
1812-13	*	-	-
1813-14	*	-	-
1814-15	*	-	-
1815-16	-	-	-
1816-17	-	**	-
1817-18	*	-	-
1818-19	*	-	-
1819-20	-	**	-
1820-21	*	-	-
1821-22	-	-	-
1822-23	-	-	-
1823-24	*	-	***
1824-25	-	-	-
1825-26	-	-	-
1826-27	*	**	-
1827-28	-	-	-
1828-29	-	**	-
1829-30	-	-	-
1830-31	-	**	-
1831-32	-	-	***

(Contd...)

(Contd...)

Year	Flood and Inundation	Famine or Scarcity	Cyclone
1832-33	-	**	***
1833-34	-	**	***
1834-35	*	**	-
1835-36	*	**	-
1836-37	-	**	-
1837-38	*	-	-
1838-39	*	-	-
1839-40	-	**	-
1840-41	*	**	***
1841-42	*	**	-
1842-43	*	**	***
1843-44	*	-	-
1844-45	*	-	-
1845-46	*	-	-
1846-47	*	-	-
1847-48	*	-	-
1848-49	*	-	***
1849-50	-	-	-
1850-51	*	-	***
1851-52	-	-	***
1852-53	*	-	-
1853-54	*	**	-
1854-55	*	-	-
1855-56	*	-	-
1856-57	*	-	-
1857-58	*	-	-
1858-59	*	-	-
1859-60	-	-	-
1860-61	-	-	-
1861-62	-	-	-
1862-63	*	-	-
1863-64	*	**	-
1864-65	-	-	***
1865-66	-	**	-
1866-67	*	**	***
1867-68	-	-	-
1868-69	*	-	-

(Contd...)

(Contd...)

Year	Flood and Inundation	Famine or Scarcity	Cyclone
1869-70	-	-	-
1870-71	*	**	-
1871-72	*	-	-
1872-73	*	-	***
1873-74	-	-	-
1874-75	*	**	***
1875-76	*	-	-
1876-77	-	-	-
1877-78	*	**	-
1878-79	-	-	-
1879-80	*	-	-
1880-81	*	-	-
1881-82	*	-	-
1882-83	-	-	-
1883-84	*	-	-
1884-85	-	-	-
1885-86	-	-	***
1886-87	*	-	-
1887-88	-	-	***
1888-89	*	**	***
1889-90	*	**	-
1990-91	*	**	***
1891-92	*	-	***
1892-93	*	-	-
1893-94	*	-	***
1894-95	*	-	-
1895-96	-	-	-
1896-97	*	**	-
1897-98	-	**	-
1898-99	-	-	-
1899-1900	-	-	-
1900-01	*	**	-

Sources : Bihar and Orissa Documents; File No. NF-21/1929, Government of Bihar and Orissa Deposit, Revenue Department, March 1930, No.9; L.S.S. O' Malley, Bihar and Orissa District Gazetteer, Cuttack (Patna, 1933), p. 127; L.S.S. O' Malley, Bengal District Gazetteers, Balasore, Calcutta, 1907, pp. 92-103; L.S.S.S. O' Malley, Bihar and Orissa District Gazetteers, Puri, Patna, 1929, pp.179-189.

APPENDIX - B

INCIDENCE OF NATURAL CALAMITIES IN ORISSA FROM 1803 TO 1900

Nature of Calamities	*Years*
Only Flood	1804, 1808, 1812 to 1814, 1817 & 1818, 1820, 1834, 1837 & 1838, 1844 to 1848, 1852, 1854 to 1858, 1862, 1868, 1871, 1875, 1879 to 1881, 1883, 1886, 1892 and 1894.
Only Famine or Scarcity	1803, 1816, 1819, 1828, 1830, 1836, 1839, 1865 and 1897.
Only Cyclone	1831, 1851, 1864, 1885 and 1887.
Flood and Famine without Cyclone	1806 & 1807, 1809, 1826, 1835, 1841, 1853, 1863, 1870, 1877, 1889, 1896 and 1900.
Flood and Cyclone without Famine	1823, 1848, 1850, 1872, 1891 and 1893.
Famine and Cyclone without Flood	1832 & 1833.
Flood, Famine and Cyclone	1840, 1842, 1866, 1877, 1888 and 1890.
No Calamities year	1805, 1810 & 1811, 1815, 1821 & 1822, 1824 & 1825, 1827, 1829, 1843, 1849, 1859 to 1861, 1867, 1869, 1873, 1876, 1878, 1882, 1884, 1898 & 1899.

Source : Compiled from Appendix-A.

APPENDIX - C

FREQUENCY OF NATURAL CALAMITIES IN ORISSA (1803 TO 1900)

Nature of Calamities	Single Year	Continuity: Double Years	Triple Years	More than three years	Total years
Only Flood	13	2	2	2	33
Only Famine and Scarctiy	9	-	-	-	9
Only Cyclone	5	-	-	-	5
Flood and Famine without Cyclone	11	1	-	-	13
Famine and Cyclone without Flood	-	1	-	-	2
Flood and Cyclone without Famine	6	-	-	-	6
Flood, Famine and Cyclone	6	-	-	-	6
No Calamities Year	13	4	1	-	24

Source : Compiled from Appendix-B.

APPENDIX - D

STATEMENT SHOWING THE RAINFALL IN INCHES

Year	CUTTACK			BALASORE			PURI		
	September	October	Total fall of the year	September	October	Total fall of the year	September	October	Total fall of the year
1860	12.50	0.70	46.80	15.20	1.30	50.60	20.00	4.50	74.10
1861	15.68	4.56	76.28	7.40	4.70	76.50	14.10	6.10	73.00
1862	11.98	13.33	62.98	35.40*	29.30*	111.90	16.60	42.20*	136.10
1863	7.10	2.00	69.77	14.95	7.70	86.80	15	7.80	60.90
1864	8.90	2.60	48.70	7.90	6.10	64.80	8.60	6.20	42.20
1865	7.44	...	51.40	9.30	0.30	52.60	5.20	...	36.30
1866	2.60	11.85	60.95	10.50	8.55	68.25	12.10	11.10	77.20
1867	10.11	5.40	50.75	15.22	9.00	67.62	10.60	14.30	70.00
1868	9.80	1.96	52.81	9.60	0.40	77.00	5.05	0.30	50.97
1869	9.23	5.35	48.14	13.19	0.74	40.77	12.48	6.69	44.87
1870	8.80	8.61	49.92	11.46	7.69	54.77	6.58	10.95	43.44
1871	9.67	0.91	50.39	14.82	5.13	63.41	12.39	1:40	56.32
1872	8.76	16.16	71.16	13.97	11.97	71.20	7.04	16.19	75.14
1873	6.27	2.54	38.61	7.61	4.69	48.35	9.21	12.53	52.72
1874	12.13	10.71	86.74	7.60	12.03	55.19	4.87	9.62	61.78
1875	19.26	10.25	91.92	12.69	2.37	59.45	11.37	15.01	64.16
1876	9.83	4.89	41.28	15.95	10.32	82.72	9.61	6.64	43.93
1877	6.25	3.05	41.13	5.51	3.32	67.40	6.70	4.51	35.15
1878	6.40	4.92	54.57	7.90	8.59	61.89	13.56	14.08	54.66
1879	9.44	4.98	60.62	17.09	6.10	49.62	12.11	4.56	53.57
1880	10.29	5.17	67.06	11.63	5.28	74.33	15.14	10.63	87.58
1881	11.27	2.33	59.33.	14.72	8.35	79.71	6.30	4.37	49.83
1882	11.86	7.64	75.96	21.69	10.10	79.02	7.54	7.95	49.93
1883	12.93	0.55	67.24	3.76	1.70	63.21	13.16	4.95	61.18
1884	8.68	2.40	59.42	13.57	4.48	76.24	15.10	17.13	65.01
1885	8.33	2.60	47.74	11.07	1.84	59.83	6.05	5.73	38.16
1886	13.99	11.77	79.70	17.82	5.65	73.96	14.78	6.14	56.55

(Contd...)

(Contd...)

Year	CUTTACK			BALASORE			PURI		
	Septem-ber	October	Total fall of the year	Septem-ber	Octo-ber	Total fall of the year	Septem-ber	Octo-ber	Total fall of the year
1887	7.03	2.26	54.03	4.99	3.09	53.43	6.31	5.68	38.20
1888	8.81	1.34	56.93	12.32	1.64	59.34	7.89	1.66	44.22
1889	5.26	8.24	69.88	6.15	8.52	57.26	6.44	12.43	79.01
1890	17.53	7.89	65.31	18.68	10.16	66.67	14.77	10.61	72.02
1891	23.72	1.68	73.76	16.81	0.76	69.52	16.09	2.83	59.93
1892	10.35	7.39	50.34	11.40	7.93	55.24	8.34	5.87	46.57
1893	15.44	5.03	81.52	19.04	5.65	92.39	17.30	7.96	71.23
1894	6.45	7.76	60.82	6.86	4.70	61.69	7.54	7.50	52.38
1895	8.60	5.89	67.71	6.52	3.73	58.67	12.77	7.31	67.87
1896	9.49	0.03	58.52	10.59	...	62.17	6.83	0.31	53.13
1897	7.89	8.92	63.82	5.90	14.13	65.05	7.45	10.12	55.12
1898	8.56	9.01	59.85	11.33	10.31	59.62	6.57	8.55	58.85
Average	10.22	5.44	60.87	12.20	6.56	66.34	10.52	8.55	58.85

Average of Orissa -			
	Fall in September	... ...	11.00
	Fall in October	... ..	6.85
	Total fall of the year	... ...	62.02

* Cyclone.

GLOSSARY

anicut	-	reservoir of water
anna	-	4 piece (1/16th of a rupee)
chhatak	-	one-sixteenth part of a seer
cutcherry	-	court or an office or a place where any Governmental business is transacted
dalua	-	spring rice
dhan	-	paddy
garjat	-	tributary states of Orissa
jama	-	total amount of rent or revenue payable by a cultivator or a zamindar including all cesses
kahan	-	measure of kauri currency
kanungo	-	subordinate revenue official
kauri	-	a small shell found in Indian ocean used a money
khasmahal	-	Government estate
kangalis	-	The starving people, the starving beggars affected by a famine
killa	-	permanently settled estate
kist	-	instalments of rents
kumuties	-	a mercantile community found in south of Orissa
malangis	-	salt manufacturer
maund	-	weight measure
mauza	-	village
mufassil	-	countryside
mughalbandi	-	the areas lying between hill tracts of sea, revenue assessed lands of Cuttak, Puri and Balasore districts settled by the Mughals
muharir	-	clerk or writer

mahal	-	territory of a tributary king
pahi	-	non-resident
paik	-	the paiks constituted a local militia holding the lands of the military chiefs or Rajas by tenure or military services
pana	-	a sum of 80 kauri shells equal to 20 gandas, 16 panas make a kahan
pargana	-	a tract of the country comprising many villages
parwana	-	a written command from a man in power to a dependant
ryot	-	peasants, agriculturists
sadar	-	principal town
saga	-	edible green plant
sadar jama	-	the sum total of revenue payable to Government exclusive of charges of collection etc.
sahukar	-	indigenous banker and money-lender
sarada	-	a crop
seer	-	weight measure
sicca	-	a stamped coin, especially the name of the silver currency of the Mughal kings adopted by the Indian princes and eventually by the East India Company.
sirastadar	-	record keeper
taluk	-	a portion of zamindari, an estate applied to a tract of proprietory land usually small, a division of a province
taccavi	-	a kind of loan given to the cultivators by the Government for productive purposes
thani	-	resident
telinga	-	whose mother-tongue is Telugu
unnachhatra	-	where cooked rice was served to a large number of famine striken people
zilla	-	district
zamindar	-	landlord, proprietors directly responsible to the state for the revenue of the land.

BIBLIOGRAPHY

I. PRIMARY SOURCES

(A) Manuscripts

Board of Revenue Proceedings, Revenue, 1803-1926, 241 volumes.

Board of Revenue Proceedings, Miscellaneous, 1868, 1 volume.

Board of Revenue Proceedings, Salt, 1817-1863, 15 volumes.

Board Documents (unclassified loose correspondences) 1804-1902, Revenue, Salt, Political, Agriculture, Land Revenue and Miscellaneous.

Board of Revenue Records, Weather Report, 1883-1900, 18 volumes.

Cuttak Revenue, Correspondence (Volume Records), 1803-1870.

Cuttack Judicial Correspondence (Volume Records), 1805-1871.

Balasore Revenue Correspondence (Volume Records), 1815-1890.

Balasore Salt Correspondence (Volume Records), 1821-1872.

Balasore loose Records, Revenue, Irrigation, Land Revenue, etc.

Bengal Revenue Proceedings from 1815-1900 (Volume Records)

- (*i*) Bengal Revenue Proceedings - Land Revenue.
- (*ii*) Bengal Revenue Proceedings - Irrigation.
- (*iii*) Bengal Revenue Proceedings - Miscellaneous.

Bengal Revenue and Agriculture (Famine) Department Proceedings, 1879-1900, 20 volumes.

Proceedings of Bengal Legislative Council (Volume Records) 1850-1880.

Records of the Orissa Canal Projects, File No, 111, 1869, Relevant Papers.

East India Irrigation and Canal Company, Report of Proceedings at the eleventh ordinary general meeting, Friday, November 30, 1866.

Department of Revenue and Agriculture, Government of India (Famine Branch) 1870-1892.

Home Department, Government of India, Revenue Branch 1833, 1840-41, 1860-69.

Famine Branch, 1866-1870, 1873-1885.

Parliamentary Debates, Hansad, Vols. 26, 69, 189.

Board of Revenue, Lower Province, Land Revenue Department, Irrigation Branch, File No. III of 1881, Orissa Canal Project.

Board of Revenue, Lower Province, Land Revenue Department, Irrigation Branch, File No. III of 1887, Flood in Orissa Division.

Public Works Department, Government of India, Civil Works :

(*a*) Communications, 1860-1885.

(*b*) Irrigation, 1864-1885.

(*c*) Railways, 1879-1885.

(*d*) Miscellaneous, 1860-1885.

Board of Revenue form No. 162A, Report on Floods in Orissa, 1868.

Board of Revenue Proceedings, Flood Report (1887-1894).

Proceedings of the Board of Revenue of the 19th Division, Revenue Commisioners office at Cuttack, 1832, 1836, 1840, 1851, 1856-64, 1868, 1891-1895.

Proceedings of Board of Revenue at Fort William, 1835-1856.

Proceeding of Lt. Governor of Bengal, Revenue Department :

(*a*) Scarcity and Relief Branch, 1861-96.

(*b*) Famine Branch, 1861-96.

(*c*) Land Revenue Branch, 1861-95.

Office of the Commissioner, Irrigation Department, Collection No. E/1, File No. 2 of 1905 (Development of system of protective embankments in Orissa and formation of a standing committee for the purpose).

Village Directory of the Presidency of Bengal, Vol. XXXIX, Balasore.

Selections from Official letters and Records relating to the History of Mayurbhanj, Vol. II, 1821-61, Baripada, Mayurbhanj State, 1943.

Government of Bihar and Orissa, Deposit, Revenue Department, File No. IVF-21/1929, March 1930, No. 9.

Frequent occurrence of floods in Orissa (Notes submitted by J.A. Hubback, Commissioner, Orissa Division).

Orissa State Archives, Vol. 183(c), Acc No. 191B (Rect) year 1851.

(B) Printed (Records and Reports)

Administrative Experience Recorded in Former Famines, Extract from official paper containing instructions for dealing with Famine, J.C. Geddes, Calcutta, 1874.

A.J.M. Mill's *Minute on Tributary Mahals*, 1847.

Bay of Bengal Cyclone Memoirs, 1883-1855, Calcutta, 1885.

Collection of Treaties, Engagements and Sanads relating to India and neighbouring countries, C.U. Aitchison (ed.) Vols. II & III, Calcutta, 1892.

Drought in Orissa during 1954-55, Final Report, Government of Orissa, 1956.

East India Report of Famine Commission presented to both the Houses of the Parliament, London, 1881.

Ewer's Report, 13 May 1818.

Final Report on the Survey and Settlement of Balasore District, Kingsford, D.H., Calcutta, 1900.

Final Report on the Survey and Settlement of Orissa, 1890-1900, Vol. I & II, Maddox, S.L., Calcutta, 1900.

Final Report on the Survey and Settlement of Killa, Aul, D. Bose, 1892-1900, Calcutta, 1901.

Final Report on the Survey and Settlement of Killa Darpan, H.K. Mohanty, Calcutta, 1901.

Final Report on the Survey and Settlement of Killa Kanika, S.S. Hussain, 1889-1894, Calcutta, 1900.

Final Report on the Survey and Settlement of Killa Kujang, 1892-1899, Calcutta, 1900.

Final Report on the Survey and Settlement of Khurda Government Estate, Taylor and Maddox, 1897-1898, Calcutta, 1901.

Final Report on the Resettlement of the Cuttack town and Contonment Khasmahals, Cuttack, 1955.

Floods in Orissa rivers during 1955-1956, Final Report, Government of Orissa, Revenue (Special Relief).

General Administration Report, Orissa Division (Annual), 1850-51 to 1900.

History of Mayurbhanj, 1761-1861, Part-I, Rama Prasad Chanda, Calcutta, 1949.

Memorandum of tour through the province of Orissa by the Chief Engineer of Irrigation, 1868.

Minute by his Honour, the Lt. Governor on the services of Government Officers and private gentlemen in connection with the famine of 1897-98 and final resolution of the Government of Bengal upon the Famine, Calcutta, 1898.

Orissa Legislative Assembly Proceedings, Vol. II, 1946.

Orissa Project, Contract between the Secretary of State and the East India Irrigation Company, 1861.

Quinquennial Administration Report, Orissa Division, 1900-1901 to 1904-1905.

Report on the agriculture of the district of Cuttack, N.N. Banerji, Calcutta, 1898.

Report on the Mahanadi River, A. Cotton, Calcutta, 1863.

Report on the Revenue Administration of the Lower Provinces, for the official year 1846-49, Calcutta, 1848.

Report on the Administration of Bengal (Bengal Presidency) 1830-31 to 1900-1901.

Report of the Midnapore and Burdwan cyclone of the 15th and 16th of October 1874, Calcutta, 1875.

Report on the Maritime trade of Orissa for the year 1940-41, Cuttack, 1941.

Report on Orissa Floods, 1926, John Austin Hubback.

Report on the Survey and Settlement on Orissa. A.J.M. Mill's, 1847.

Report of the Commissioners appointed to enquire into the Famine of Bengal and Orissa, 1866, 2 Vols.

Report on Pilgrimage to Jaggernath in 1868 with a narrative of a tour through Orissa, David B. Smith, Calcutta 1868.

Report of the Orissa Famine Commission, 1866, with Appendix.

Report of the Indian Famine Commission, 1880, Parts-I & II, 1880, Part-III, 1885.

Report of the Indian Famine Commission, 1898 with evidence Volume.

Report of the Indian Famine Commission, 1901 with evidence Volume.

Report of the Irrigation Commission, 1901-1903, Part-II.

Report of the Commissioners appointed to enquire into certain matters in connection with the Orissa Canals, 1884-85.

Report on the river Mahanadi and its tributaries 1863, R. Temple.

Report on the Mahanadi river 1881, A Cotton, Calcutta.

Report on the Bay of Bengal, False Point and Jumboo Port, Patna, 1923.

Report on the district of Cuttack, Henry Rickets, Calcutta, 1858.

Report on the District of Midnapore and Cuttack, H. Ricketts, Calcutta, 1858.

Report of the Inundation Committee of Orissa, 1866.

Report on the Embankment of Orissa, 1871.

Report on the Orissa Floods, 1926, John Austin Hubback.

Report of the Committees appointed under the Famine Commission to enquire into the management of Irrigation works in Madras, Orissa and Medinapore, Calcutta, 1879.

Resolution and orders of the Government of India regarding Famine relief code and other matters pertaining to Famine Administration, 1892.

Selection of Papers relating to the Famine of 1896-97 in Bengal, Vols. III to XI, Calcutta, 1898.

Selection from Calcutta Gazette 1824-32, The Days of John Company (ed.), A.C. Dasgupta, Calcutta, 1959.

Tour Diary of G.N. Barlow, Collector of Puri, 1865-66.

(C) Gazetteers and Gazettes

Calcutta Gazette, 1832-1901.

Indian Gazette (Suppement), June 1889.

Cobden Ramsay L.E.B., *Bengal District Gazetteers, Feudatory States of Orissa,* Calcutta, 1910.

Maltby T.J., *The Ganjam District Manual,* Madras, 1918.

Imperial Gazetteer of India, Provincial Series, Bengal, Vols I and II. Calcutta, 1909.

Imperial Gazetteer of India, Vols. III, X and XI, Oxford, 1903 and 1908.

O'Malley L.S.S., *BDG, Cuttack,* Calcutta, 1906.

– *BDG, Balasore,* Calcutta, 1907.

– *BDG, Puri,* Calcutta, 1907.

– *BDG, Sambalpur,* Calcutta, 1909.

– *BDG, Midnapore,* Calcutta, 1911.

– *BDG, Angul,* Calcutta, 1918.

– *Bihar and Orissa District Gazetteer, Puri,* Patna, 1920.

– *Bihar and Orissa District Gazetteer, Cuttack,* Patna, 1933.

Senapati Nilamani, *Orissa District Gazetteers, Dhenkanal,* Cuttack, 1972.

– *Orissa District Gazetteers, Sambalpur,* Patna, 1932.

Senapati Nilamani and Sahu, N.K., *Gazetteer of India, Orissa, Koraput,* Cuttack, 1966.

(D) Encyclopaedia

Encyclopaedia of Social Sciences, Vols. V & VI by Southard, Macmillan.

International Encyclopaedia of the Social Sciences, Vol. V, Macmillan, 1968.

Encyclopaedia of Britannica, Vols. 12 and 22, USA, 1968.

(E) Contemporary News papers and Periodicals used English :

The Hindu Patriot

The Englishman

The Bengal Past and Present

Calcutta Review

Journal of Asiatic Society of Bengal

Orissa Historical Research Jurnal (several volumes)

Orissa Past and Present

The Star of Utkal, 8th September 1908.

The Orissa Past and Present (ed.), P. Parija, Utkal University.

The Statesman

Bharati, Utkal University Journal, Humanities, Vol. VIII, July 1974, No. 14.

Young India, 1920-21.

The Heritage, December 1987.

The Economic and Political Weekly, Vol. IX, No. 44, November 2, 1874; Vol. X, No. 41, October 11, 1975.

Oriya :

Utkal Dipika, 1866-1902.

The Balasore Sambad Bahika, 1870, 1871, 1872.

Sambalpur Hiteisini, 1889-1901.

The Samaja, 7th October 1982.

The Utkal Putra, 1873, 1874.

The Utkal Hitaisani, 1874.

II. SECONDARY SOURCES

Acharya, P.M., *Orissa Itihasa* (Oriya), Cuttack, 1925.

Ambhirajan, S., *Classical Political, Economy and British Policy in India*, New Delhi, 1978.

Badan Powell, B.H., *Land Systems of British India*, 3 Vols. Oxford, 1892.

Banerji, R.D., *History of Orissa* (From earliest time to British period), 2 Vols., Calcutta, 1930.

Basham, A.L., *The Wonder that was India*, London, 1954.

Beames, John, *Notes on the History of Orissa under the Mohammadan, Maratha and English Rule* (ed.), N.K. Sahu, Calcutta, 1956.

—— *Memoirs of the Bengal Civilian*, London, 1961.

Bhatia, B.M., *Famines in India, 1850-1945*, Bombay, 1963.

Bhattacharya, V.R., *New Face of Rural India*, New Delhi, 1984.

Bhola, S.C., *British Economic Policy in Orissa*, New Delhi, 1990.

Boulton, John (translated), *My times and I, Atma-Jivan-Carita of Fakirmohana Senapati*, Cuttack 1985.

Buckland, C.E., *Bengal under the Lt. Governor*, 2 Vols., Calcutta, 1902.

Campbell, Sir G., Memoirs of my Indian Career, Vol. II, London, 1893.

Chandra, Bipan, *The rise and growth of economic nationalism in India*, New Delhi, 1969.

——*Nationalism and Colonialism in Modern India*, New Delhi, 1979.

Chaudhury, S.N., *Economic History of Colonialism*, Delhi, 1979.

Chopra, Puri & Das, *Social, Cultural and Economic History of India*, 3 vols., Delhi, 1974.

Cotton, Sir A., *The Famines in India*, London, 1866.

Das, B., *Social and Economic Life of Southern Orissa*, Calcutta, 1985.

Das, B.S., *Studies in the Economic History of Orissa from ancient time to 1833*, Calcutta, 1878.

——(ed) *Life and Culture in Orissa*, Calcutta, 1984.

——*Glimpses of Orissa*, Calcutta, 1986.

Das, G.C., *A Note on the Famines in India*, Bhubaneswar, 1959-60.

Das, K.B., *Oriya Lokagiti and Kahani* (Oriya), Cuttack, 1958.

Das, M.N., *Economic and Social Development of Modern India*, Calcutta, 1959.

——(ed.), *Sidelights on History and Culture of Orissa*, Cuttack, 1977.

Das, P.C., *The Economic History of Orissa in the 19th Century*, New Delhi, 1989.

Das, Sailabala (ed.) *Madhusudan Das as seen by Many eyes* (Oriya), Cuttack, 1935.

Das, S.N. Pt., *Unabimsa Satabdir Orissa* (Oriya), Part-I, Cuttack, 1969.

De, S.C., *Guide to Orissan Records*, Vols. I to V, Bhubaneswar, 1961-1965.

Desai, A.R., *Social background of Indian Nationalism, Bombay, 1966.*

Desai, T.B., *Economic and History of India under British*, Bombay, 1966.

Dharma, Kumar (ed.), *The Cambridge Economic History of India*, Vol. II, Delhi, 1984.

Dodwell, H.H., *The Cambridge History of India*, Vol. V, British India, 1497-1858, S. Chand & Co., 1968.

——*The Combridge History of India*, Vol. VI, 1858-1918.

——The Indian Empire, S.Chand & Co., 1958.

——*The Cambridge Shorter History of India*, S. Chand & Co., 1958.

Dutt, R.C., *Economic History of India*, 2 vols. Government of India Publication, Delhi, 1963.

Fakirmohan Granthavali (Oriya), Vol. I, Cuttack Students Store, 1963.

Gopal, Lallangi, *The Economic Life of Northern India*, Delhi, 1965.

Griffith, Sir Percival, *The British Impact on India*, London, 1952.

Hamilton, Walter, A *Geographical, Statistical and Historical Description of Hindustan* (compiled by Brajasundar Das, Secretary, Utkal Union Committee), Vols I & II, London, 1820.

Hunter, W.W., *History of Orissa*, 2 vols., London, 1872.

——*Indian Administration, London*, 1882.

——*Land System in Bengal*, Vol. I, London, 1894.

——*The Annals of Rural Bengal*, London, 1868.

——*Statistical Account of Bengal*, Vol. XVIII and Vol XIX, London, 1887.

Inglis, W.A., *The Canals and Flood Banks of Bengal*, Calcutta, 1909.

Jena, K.C., *Land Revenue Administraation in Orissa during Nineteenth Century*, New Delhi, 1968.

——*The Ascendency of the British Raj in Orissa*, Calcutta, 1982.

——*Socio-economic Conditions of Orissa during Nineteenth Century*, Delhi, 1978.

Jit, N.K., *The Agrarian Life and Economy of Orissa : A Survey*, Calcutta, 1984.

Kar, P., *Indian National Congress and Orissa, 1885-1936*, Cuttack, 1987.

Kaushal, G., *Economic History of India, 1757-1966*, New Delhi, 1979.

Loveday, A., *History and Economics of Famines in India*, London, 1914.

Mahtab, H.K., *History of Orissa*, 2 vols., Cuttack, 1956 and 1960.

——*Gandhiji O' Orissa* (Oriya), Cuttack, 1969.

——*History of Orissa* (Published Lucknow University).

Memoria, C.B., *Agricultural Problems of India*, Allahabad, 1976.

Mishra, B., *Orissare Durvikshya* (Oriya), Cuttack, 1925.

Mishra, Godavarish, *Ardha Satabdira Orissa O' Tanhire Mo Sthana* (Oriya), Cuttack, 1908.

Mishra, H.K; *Famines and Poverty in India*, New Delhi, 1991.

Mishra, K., *Utkal Itihasa*, Cuttack, 1933.

Mishra, P.K., *Political Unrest in Orissa in the 19th Century*, Calcutta, 1983.

Mishra, Sadasiv, *Economic Survey of Orissa*, 2 vols., Government of Orissa, Bhubaneswar, 1960.

Mohanty, A.B. (ed.), Madalapanji, Cuttack, 1940.

Mohanty, Balaram, *Introducing Orissa*, Bhubaneswar, 1979.

Mohanty, Surendra, *Satabdir Surya* (Oriya), Cuttack, 1970.

Mohapatra, J.N. (ed.), *Orissa in 1936-37 to 1938-39*, Cuttack, 1941.

Mukherjee, P., *Irrigation, Inland Navigation and Flood Problems in North Orissa during the British Rule*, Bhubaneswar, 1967.

——*History of Orissa in the 19th Century*, Cuttack, 1964.

——*Gajapati Kings of Orissa (reprint)*, Cuttack, 1981.

Naoroji, Dadabhai, *Poverty and Un-British Rule of India*, London, 1901, (reprint), Delhi, 1962.

——*Poverty in India*, Bombay, 1976.

Nash, V., *The Great Famine and its causes*, Bombay, 1900.

O' Malley, L.S.S., *History of Bengal, Bihar and Orissa under British Rule*, Calcutta, 1925.

Patra, Kartikeswar, *The Ports in Orissa*, Bhubaneswar, 1988.

Patra, K.M., *Orissa Under East India Company*, New Delhi, 1971.

Patra, S.C., *Formation of Province of Orissa*, Calcutta, 1979.

Pattnaik, G., *The Famine and Some Aspects of the British Economic Policy in Orissa, 1866-1905*, Cuttack 1980.

Pattnaik, J., *Feudatory States of Orissa*, Vols. I & II, Allahabad 1988.

Pattnaik, Lalmohan, *Resurrected Orissa*, Cuttack, 1941.

Pattnaik, P.K., A *Forgotten Chapter of Orissan History*, Calcutta, 1979.

Pattnaik, S., (ed.) *Sambadapatraru Odissar Katha* (Oriya), Cuttack, 1972.

Ray, B.C., Foundation of British Orissa, Cuttack, 1960.

——*Orissa Under the Marathas*, Allahabad, 1960.

Roy, Debidas, Food Administration in East India, Calcutta, 1958.

Samal, J.K., *Orissa Under the British Crown, 1858-1905*, New Delhi, 1973.

——*Administrative History of Orissa (1866-1912)*, New Delhi, 1986.

——*History of Modern Orissa*, Calcutta, 1989.

Samantray, N., *Odiya Sahityara Itihasa* (Oriya), 1803-1920, Bhubaneswar, 1968.

Satpathy, Binapani, *Land Reforms Administration in Orissa*, Bodhagaya, 1977.

Sen, Amartiya, *Poverty and Famine*, Oxford, 1981.

Sen, S.P. & Ray, N.R., *Modern Bengal : A Socio-economic Survey*, Calcutta, 1973.

Senapati, F.M., *Granthavali*, Vol. I (ed.), Ananta Mishra, Cuttack, 1965.

Sinha, B.N., *Geography of Orissa*, New Delhi, 1971.

Sinha, N.K., *Economic History of Bengal*, 2 vols., Calcutta, 1961-62.

Singh, K. Suresh, *The Indian Famine 1967*, New Delhi, 1975.

Smith, Baird, *Famine of 1860-61*, Vols. I & II, Delhi, 1861.

Srivastav, H.S., *The History of Indian Famines*, Agra, 1968.

Stirling, A., *An Account (Geographical, Statistical and Historical) of Orissa Proper or Cuttack*, Calcutta, 1904.

Sundaram & Dutta, *Indian Economy*, New Delhi, 1989.

Sutton, A., *Orissa and its Evangelization*, London, 1850.

Taylor, William, *Famines in India, their remedy and prevention*, London, 1874.

——*Thirty eight years in India*, Vol. I, London, 1881.

Thumpson, Edward and Garratt, G.J., *Rise and Fulfilment of British Rule in India*, London, 1934.

Toynbee, G., *A Sketch of the History of Orissa, 1803-1828*, Calcutta, 1873.

Tripathy, R., *Crafts and Commerce in Orissa*, Delhi, 1986.

Valdiya, K.S., *Environmental Geology, Indian Context*, New Delhi, 1987.

Venketaramani, M.S., *Bengal Famine of 1943–The American Response*, Vikas Publishing House, 1973.

Wilson, C.R., *The Early Annals of English in Bengal*, 3 vols., London, 1895.

——*English Chiefs at Balasore in the Bay of Bengal, Calcutta*, 1895.

Index